the IT Girl's

GUIDE TO

Becoming an Excel® Diva

by Ani Babaian

WILEY

Wiley Publishing, Inc.

The IT Girl's™ Guide to Becoming an Excel® Diva

Published by
Wiley Publishing, Inc.
111 River Street
Hoboken, NJ 07030-5774

www.wiley.com

For general information on our other products and services, please contact our Customer Care Department within the U.S. at 800-762-2974, outside the U.S. at 317-572-3993, or fax 317-572-4002.

For technical support, please visit www.wiley.com/techsupport.

Wiley also publishes its books in a variety of electronic formats. Some content that appears in print may not be available in electronic books.

Library of Congress Control Number is available from the publisher.

ISBN: 978-0-470-14916-4

Manufactured in the United States of America

10 9 8 7 6 5 4 3 2 1

WILEY

About Ani Babaian

Ani Babaian started earning babysitting money for her first PC in high school, which she built bit by bit as she could afford it. Her love for mathematics and computer science and all things numerical was born from her immigrant struggles to learn several different languages on her journey from Iran to Switzerland, to Germany, and finally to the United States, where she settled in the fifth grade in Denver, Colorado. Her education includes a high school degree from George Washington High School, a college degree in Applied Mathematics from University of Colorado, graduate studies in Statistics from Colorado State, and Master of Business Administration and Information Systems from University of Colorado.

Ani's interests include yoga, snowboarding, hiking, and camping with her boyfriend, and enjoying the view of Puget Sound and a nice soy latte with friends. She enjoys volunteering with Special Olympics when time permits and spends much time with the Armenian community. She lives in Seattle where she hopes to someday have a family and lead a team of women in technology at Microsoft. You can follow Ani on her blog at: www.LiveWithAni.com.

About the Technical Editor

Julie Yack is one of the founding partners of Colorado Technology Consultants, Inc. and currently serves as the company's Chief Operations Officer. Julie is a Microsoft CRM Certified Professional, Microsoft Small Business Specialist, and a Certified Scrum Master. Julie received her Bachelor's of Science from the University of Phoenix in 2004. As an INETA membership mentor and co-founder of SouthColorado.NET, Julie has been named a Community Insider by Microsoft.

Julie is active in the local business arena. She is a member of The Pikes Peak Business and Professional Women's Organization and serves on the membership committee for the National BPW organization. Julie is also a quarterly contributor to the Colorado Business Leaders Confidence Index, providing forecast and economic trend information for Colorado businesses. She has been called upon as an expert by several trade publications to contribute on articles from technology to general business-focused themes.

As a member of the Education Literacy and Information Technology Committee at Challenger Middle School and Pine Creek High School in Colorado Springs, Julie offers insight to help guide the technology education of our future workforce.

Julie has edited several technical books, but this is her first on Excel. Julie uses Excel to get data in and out of Microsoft CRM as well as for more simple things like everyday data tables and charts.

Julie and her family enjoy living and playing in Colorado and traveling together all around the world. You can follow Julie's blog at www.julieyack.com or JulieYack.blogs.com.

I would like to dedicate this book to:

You! We need more of us women in the technology field;

My brother. In every way I love him and would like to dedicate this book to him;

My parents, who tirelessly encouraged and supported me through writing this book. I have only picked up half their persistence and energy to be nothing but the best, but I hope to help many just like they dreamed for me when they came to America and brought us here. My parents always said, "America is the land of opportunity, learn as much as you can, succeed as much as you hope to and don't leave anyone behind. Always extend a hand to help others."

All of my friends, who tirelessly and effortlessly encouraged me to the finish each line of this book and many other challenges in my life. Without great friends and their support I would not have pushed myself as hard and would not have tried as many things. They have kept me honest and on the right path to succeed; friends who volunteered to read the book and stand in line for their own copy.

All my mentors, I know I stand on your shoulders and learn from your mistakes and achievements and that is why I am where I am today.

All those who did not believe in me, gave up, and walked away. To all of you, thank you, you have made me a better person. I always value input and was able to take your input and make myself better.

God, without all the amazing things that came together to make this book possible I could not have found my strength or words anyplace else if not for Him. I changed jobs, moved, survived a pretty harsh accident, and started all over.

Ani would like to thank . . .

I would most like to thank my parents Hilda and Edward Babaian. I know now having them as parents has been a privilege and an honor. They are simple, hard working, try their best and more; they keep looking at every day as a new day to try new things to help my special-needs brother and me. They are an inspiration to me, motivate me, challenge me, and keep me grounded. They are not just my parents, they are my best friends. Mom and Dad, know your efforts were not in vain, you clothed and fed me and kept me warm. You gave me an education and did the best you could and with my efforts I thank you and wish to help others learn what I have about technology and to fall in love with it. Thanks very much for investing time in driving me back and forth from the computer store.

My brother Garni Babaian has made me realize there are people out there that truly can't help others. Garni has helped me realize that for those people who truly can't help others I have to try harder because I can. He's helped me learn how to be grateful for all I have.

My grandparents Abed and Khatoon Gharakhanian for always asking me about my education and pushing me to succeed. I appreciate all your efforts.

All of my friends, thank you so very much for being a great big part of my life. You have been an inspiration, your support has meant the world to me, and your love and kindness is always in my heart. Thank you for always being there for me and allowing me to help you when I can.

My boyfriend Yuri Siradeghyan who always helped and encouraged me, lent a helping hand, supported me with words, actions, and kindness, kept me focused, and loves me even after countless hours in front of my computer while writing this book.

To the few AMAZING teachers who really took their job seriously and made a difference in my life, a great big thank you. I have been blessed to have had many great teachers who saw in me what I couldn't and pushed me until I saw my strengths. They also encouraged me and rewarded me. They were truly an extension of my family. Thank you Dr. Zenas Hartvigson, Mr. Williams, and Mrs. Debra Edell. As well as someone I have always considered a teacher, Gilda Hoghoughi, since she was my first calculus tutor, a great example of a strong Iranian woman, and a great role model.

There were also the few role models and guides along the way who helped me grow, challenged me, were kind with their time, and believed in me. Thank you "handsome" uncle Robert Nabati and Nahid Taheri.

To those who I very much admire and appreciate your investment of effort and time in me, thank you for being great mentors, role models, and guides: Sheila Gulati, Kristy Bride, Linda K. Bolliger, Thom Robbins, Ashwin Karuhatty, and John Fernandes.

I had a dream of helping more women into technological fields and I looked for various ways to help them. I thank Wiley for giving me the opportunity to write this book and to be the first author in the series. I whole-heartedly believe these books will help girls and women take a different look at technology and perhaps utilize it more.

I want to thank my editors Katie Mohr, Ami Sullivan, and my technical editor Julie Yack for a fantastic job motivating, coaching, and pushing me to the finish line, and the countless hours and late nights; my friends for their kind words of encouragement and support; Microsoft Corp and my coworkers for their support and encouragement; and above all God for giving me the strength and health to push forward. I realize without all their help I couldn't pull through.

Finally, I thank you for picking up this book and letting me help you learn Excel 2007 and incorporate it into your daily life. I hope through my passion and creativity I will help you learn the amazing world of Excel 2007 and join me and other women in technology. I wrote this book in hopes of encouraging more of my sisters to enjoy technology and to grow our numbers in the technology world. I hope to see more of you in the technology conferences, where I hope to see the same long lines for the women's restrooms as I see for the men's.

Publisher's Acknowledgments

Some of the people who helped bring this book to market include the following:

Acquisitions, Editorial, and Media Development

Acquisitions Editor: Katie Mohr

Development Editor: Ami Frank Sullivan

Production Editor: Angela Smith

Special Editorial Help: Adaobi Obi Tulton, Jessica Bagar, and Rebekah Gholdson

Copy Editor: Kim Cofer

Technical Editor: Julie Yack

Editorial Manager: Mary Beth Wakefield

Production Manager: Tim Tate

Media Development and Quality Assurance: Angela Denny, Kate Jenkins, Steven Kudirka, Kit Malone

Media Development Coordinator: Jenny Swisher

Media Project Supervisor: Laura Moss-Hollister

Editorial Assistants: Rebekah Gholdson, Jessica Bagar

Composition Services

Project Coordinator: Lynsey Stanford

Layout and Graphics: Carrie A. Cesavice, Ronald Terry, Erin Zeltner

Proofreaders: Cindy Ballew, Jessica Kramer

Indexer: Broccoli Information Management

Publishing and Editorial

Richard Swadley, Vice President and Executive Group Publisher

Joseph B. Wikert, Vice President and Publisher

Composition Services

Gerry Fahey, Vice President of Production Services

Debbie Stailey, Director of Composition Services

Table of Contents

'm not a big TV person, but I do like the show *24*. For those of you who haven't seen it, it's a show about how the fictional Counter Terrorist Unit (CTU), which is always trying to defuse a bomb using their crew led by Jack Bauer (Kiefer Sutherland). There is also a second major character, Chloe O'Brian (Mary Lynn Rajskub), who is the geek chick. She is single-handedly responsible for hacking all databases and getting Jack every access he needs to get his job done. Without her, Jack Bauer would be lost.

Personally, I have always enjoyed utilizing what I know for good and to impress. I know it goes against society rule number (whatever), but really ladies, who cares if you use what you know to impress people? Does it really hurt anyone? It makes you feel great and it makes others appreciate your brains. You impress people with your hair, nails, dress, and makeup all the time; why not impress them with your brain? And if you say you don't, then why do you dress up especially nice, or have your best friend come help do your hair before an important event, like a date, an interview, or something else? So just think of impressing people with your brain as the "brain makeup."

The next time you look at yourself in the mirror and are cleansing, putting on your moisturizer, the foundation and then finally the powder, eyeliner, and mascara, just think of your newfound technical knowledge as "brain makeup." You can use your knowledge to keep yourself feeling good, and as a bonus you might just impress others with your knowledge along the way.

By learning a few cool things and applying them to Excel 2007 workbooks, you can put on your brain makeup without much effort. The nice part about brain makeup is, it's permanent and you don't have to put it on every day. Once you put it on, it's there for good, and you can use the same information in different contexts to impress people you want to impress. After all, you can have bad hair days, run out of mascara, or your makeup might run one day, but your brain makeup will always look good, even if you're having an off day. Even if you are impressing yourself!

Not Your Typical Technology Title

What you're holding in your hands is not only a book, but an entertaining approach to achieving results (whipping out top-notch business reports with the best of them) and rewards (feeling great doing it). The authors, editors, and publishers take pride in presenting you with a reference written for women, by women. Yes, it's a technology reference, but no, it's not boring, stuffy, or overloaded with irrelevant details.

The point is to show you the other side of technology, which is fun, playful, and helpful. The goal was to write these books in a way that would make sense and to be fun to learn from. You can succeed and learn technology with this book, recommend it to friends and colleagues, and come back to this book time and again.

Along the way, at the end of every chapter, there's a personal element, not much related to technology at all—but instead related to encouraging the Diva within to live up to her fullest potential. Enjoy.

We Know This Much About You

You're an IT Girl! You're intelligent, interested (and interesting), active, and educated. And you want to learn about Excel your way, in your own time, and with a focus on results. This book was written with the mindset that you are new to Excel, but still incorporated enough expert material so you can come across as an Excel Diva from the start. You can have fun and be smart about Excel.

Because we know you defy (and perhaps detest) categorization, we end any attempt to describe you further and simply say, "Welcome to the party!"

How to Make the Most of This Book

Just to make things easy and fun for you, this book is divided into three sections: Learn IT! Live IT!, and Love IT!

In Part I: Learn IT!, you'll learn about the foundations of Excel. Not too much history, but a few vocabulary lessons are included with the basic details of getting started. We want you to know the Excel lingo so you can impress others.

In Part II: Live IT!, you'll jump right into it and get into the meat of it. Not only will you be creating spreadsheets, you'll be formatting them, adding mathematical formulas, adding pictures and clip art, showing off your design skills, using charts, and making prints. Excel in your hands will be beautiful.

In Part III: Love IT!, you will earn your Diva status. This part really takes it up a notch, and you'll put everything you've learned to good, practical use. You'll create a very helpful budget spreadsheet you can customize for yourself and be able to save money for that next shopping spree. You'll learn about macros and merges and making eye-catching and attention-getting Word and PowerPoint presentations by adding your Excel data to them. Finally, you'll learn how to keep your Excel documents secure, and where to look when you're ready to move to the next level.

Becoming an Excel Diva Takes Style

Someone out there started the thought that women are either fashionable or smart. How many dumb-blonde jokes have you heard over the years? Well, I take issue with that. I think it's entirely possible to be both stylish and smart, both powerful and pretty, both feminine and strong. That's what this book is about. You will find more than one fashion analogy in this book, and that's because I like feeling like I look good. Your own approach to fashion might be very different, and let me be the first to say, "You go girl!" The point is the same: you can be just who you are without sacrificing anything for your career or for the sake of knowledge.

A true Diva is strong, balanced, smart, and beautiful. To most people, beauty is external, yet the beauty of the mind is the most important to an Excel Diva. And like any Diva, an Excel Diva knows her worth.

My own path to becoming an Excel Diva started when I was very young. After leaving Iran and traveling through two continents, four languages, and 24 schools before ending up in Denver, Colorado for a second year of fifth grade, yet another language, and yet another culture, one thing remained constant: mathematics and computing was the same, no matter which continent I was on, culture I was living, or language I was speaking. I saved up my babysitting money to buy my first PC, one piece at a time.

After a year I finally put together my first PC, just to play "Wolfenstein." I remember being upset at my parents because they had bought a dishwasher but no computer for me. After all, that is what all the hot geeky (not an oxymoron, ladies) guys at school were playing and I could not be left behind. I put together my first PC before I knew how to type, then I took typing, datasheets (Lotus 1-2-3), and finally programming. I enjoyed my PC but found mathematics more appealing, so I attained my BS in Mathematics and loved it enough to pursue a Ph.D. I never finished the Ph.D.; instead I studied Computer Information Systems and Business. After school I wanted to learn more, be more, and create more. I wanted to take everything I had learned in school, enhance it, and help others learn it, because after having to learn so many languages, at times I couldn't make sense of my own dreams. When things get complex I always relate back to the things I know: hair, makeup, and all the things I need to look and feel my best, and Excel, because it keeps me organized.

I don't know where you are on your journey, but I'm grateful you came here, to this book, to learn Excel.

What Are You Waiting For?

If you are totally new to Excel, here is your chance to become a Diva one chapter at a time. Begin with Chapter 1, where you will learn about the history of Excel, and as you progress the chapters will include Do It Herself sections that will guide you through accomplishing the actual tasks that I use every day to create my spreadsheets. These steps are done in such a way as to guide you so you can do the same things for your worksheets.

If you are already an avid Excel Diva, then feel free to skip ahead to other chapters and perhaps to the chapter where you can build an expense budget for yourself and begin saving for that next shopping spree.

I know there is a Diva in you, so come on, pick up this book, give me a shot, and allow me to guide you in becoming the Diva we both know you can be. Ready, set, let's go....

I Learn IT!

"We are not what we know but what we are willing to learn."

– Mary Catherine Bateson

The Four-One-One of Excel

To Do List

- Figure out where Excel came from (yawn!)
- Beautify the data
- Share the work of art
- Satisfy yourself with a Soy Chai Latte

If you looked up "Excel" on Wikipedia, you'd find a blurb about a spreadsheet program called "Multiplan," released in 1982. Excel has come a long way since then, thanks in part to competition from Lotus 1-2-3.

By 1988 Excel started to outsell Lotus 1-2-3, and since then Microsoft has regularly released updates. Soon, Microsoft became the leader in personal computer software development.

You, too, can become the Excel Diva with a bit of practice and consistent application. I won't lie to you, and I will not add yet another 10-minute routine you have to do every day to enhance your Excel skills. (I think the 10-minute routines are best kept for personal primping.) I will, however, say that no matter what you want in life, you still have to put some time in. You're a busy IT Girl and will put the time in when it is necessary for you to do so at work or otherwise, and I will be here to guide you when you need it. I hope this chapter (and this book) builds the Excel Diva-like intuition in you, so you can think it, and it will happen.

Excel 2007: The Louis Vuitton of Spreadsheets

So are you ready to look at Excel 2007 with new eyes? You should look at Excel the same way you look at the shoe department in Nordstrom's or the feeling you got when you went to a candy store as a kid. There is no other way. The enhancements in this version are so COOL you can't help but be excited about it and share with your friends. (At least, if you're an IT Girl you can't!) The gist of it is that you can do more with less time. If done right, Excel 2007 will give you some of your much-needed time back.

Do you remember when you purchased your first name-brand handbag? The feel of it, how it smelled, and how you knew it would be perfect with every shoe in your closet and it would go with the dresses you had not yet bought, because in its entirety that handbag is perfect? Well, in the software world, there really is no Louis Vuitton spreadsheet program, but Microsoft's Excel 2007 comes pretty darn close. Sometimes new versions of software just don't seem complete enough to worry about. When you walk into a department store, you're usually not looking for a purse because you want something, anything new; you want a specific function. You walk into your favorite department store and you will see a lot of handbags that are all new. You don't buy just any new handbag, you find just the right one, built in a way that makes sense: the zippers work well, the pockets were made with your needs in mind, and it comes with an extra bag to protect it when you don't use it and a lock or some other feature for the cutesy look. Well that's a top-shelf company: they keep everything in mind and put your needs first. Maybe you're not a Louis Vuitton kind of girl with a fancy purse; you're more of an Eddie Bauer backpacker—it matters not. The point is still the same: you're looking for improved functionality, and Excel 2007 has it.

Who knew?

Out in the courtyard of Building 17 on Microsoft's campus there are tiles in the ground with all the product names and dates they were released.

For those of you who have used Excel in the past I would say that Excel 2007 is truly close to the "Extreme Makeover" or the "Swan." There was great substance there before but it really wasn't apparent until an extreme makeover enabled us to have access to more of the functions with less effort and time to find it. After all, I promised we would be spending more time utilizing the functions and keeping the 10-minute routines for your abdominal workouts and your skin care, to give us time back to do the important things, like take care of our family and friends, and shop for fancy handbags. The best part about the whole thing is, despite the "Extreme Makeover," Excel 2007 still feels and works like a spreadsheet should. So for those of you who have been using Excel for a while now, it will take some time to get used to the new layout, but after the initial bumps you will be up and running in no time making your spreadsheet beautiful and effective.

What Excel Can Do for You

With all the changes in Excel 2007 it's important to bond. It's important to spend time with Excel 2007 and learn a few key terms. Let's begin with the "Office Pearl." It's not just another pearl to add to your necklace, it's the Office logo on the top-left corner of the Microsoft Excel 2007 screen (Figure 1-1).

Figure 1-1

Did you know?

The most commonly used function in all of Microsoft Office is the Paste function, followed by Cut, Copy, and Format Painter. These common functions have been put on the first tab on the farthest left corner where you are easily able to use them.

When you hover over it, you can learn more about what it does. It is where you will find the most common items such as printing, saving, and others. We will get into that more later. The next big item is the Microsoft Office Ribbon. Microsoft has spent a lot of time learning from users how and which features they use most when using Office. From this they have organized the Microsoft Office Ribbon, which is what sits on top of Excel 2007. The Microsoft Office Ribbon is shown in Figure 1-2, where you can see several tabs organized from left to right with several of the most commonly used buttons on each tab.

Figure 1-2

The tabs are also organized per utilization order. If you notice, Paste is the first item on the left corner; that is because Microsoft has found that Paste is used most commonly across all the users they studied. You'll notice this spreadsheet application was designed with you in mind. It has what you need, where you need it, and you can hover on any of the items on the Ribbon and a pop-up window will explain what each logo does as well as where to get help (Figure 1-2).

Excel Can Beautify Your Data

We all like to spend more time with things that are beautiful or pleasing to the eye. We ladies already know this. So Excel 2007 has just the thing. New key features, such as Format as Table located on the Styles section of the Home tab (Figure 1-3), allow you to make your work look beautiful and helpful, impressing your boss and your coworkers while making complex information easier to understand. Managing printed headers and footers is very easy with the use of Page Layout view. I love the new Themes feature, which lets me have access to colors, fonts, and even make my data look flashy and sharp. I use this feature throughout Office 2007 and my manager always wonders how much time I spent on that thing. But to tell the truth in most cases I spend 1–2 minutes more, which buys me 5 minutes of kudos, and no rework needs to be done so I always get a great deal of my time back, making it a great investment.

New feature styles cells into a table.

Figure 1-3

For those of you who want to understand the data you are looking at right away, there is *Conditional Formatting*, located on the Styles section of the Home tab (Figure 1-4). This is a new feature added to Excel 2007, and the enhancement makes it much easier to find and use. Conditional formatting helps you see what your data is telling you right away. Rather than having to graph the block of data to see where the highest or lowest numbers are, this little function tells you that in real time. You can add graph bars to the numbers in each cell to better understand the trends of your data. You know that cool feature on the Home Depot site that allows you to pick the color of paint and it shows you what a room with that color of paint and the certain color of backsplash you picked looks like? Well this is very much the same thing, but instead it shows you information about the data you're trying to digest. Once you select the Data Bars option from the Conditional Formatting button in Figure 1-4, you can easily see the highest and lowest values, as shown in Figure 1-5.

Select Data Bars or other formats here.

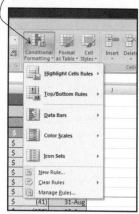

Figure 1-4

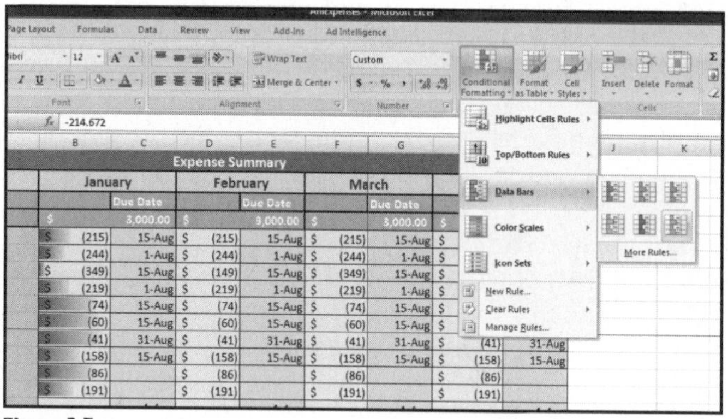

Figure 1-5

There are so many new things, and old things that are now done better, that it is hard to pick and choose. By far my favorite, and probably the most important in terms of improving the look of your data, is the robust *SmartArt* feature (Figure 1-6). All the guys in the office always wonder how I make my presentations look so good. All the well-known diagrams are there, but now they have a more sophisticated and chic look. Divas, if you want to learn more about SmartArt, also read through Chapter 9.

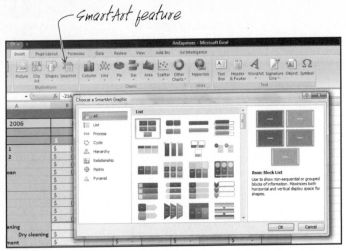

SmartArt feature

Figure 1-6

The presentation piece of Excel has always been a bit hard and frankly most of the tools were not really there, or if they were they were hard to find. In Excel 2003, you could have a maximum of 56 different colors in your workbook (see the Geek Facts 1.1 sidebar). Also, there was just no easy way to make sure the colors looked good together, unless you spent countless time and had your graphic artist friends help you. Well, Excel 2007 includes a great number of improvements and new formatting options. You can have as many different colors as you'd like. Also, the cool part for those of us who are not color coordinated but want to be, is that we can assign a theme to the workbook (mine are always magically pink if I spend time to change it). The nice part about assigning a theme is that you get the complementary colors to assign inside your workbook. But if you want to make sure certain data points still show up clearly and you don't really care about color coordination, you can of course do that as well. Just be mindful that you might be questioned by the fashion police. And for those color Divas out there you can create your own themes. Really, a theme is a group of colors you choose; this way the reader of your data knows all your expenses will be a certain color, and your total income a certain color—you can also think of it as formatting. This is something you can define for yourself or use pre-created common themes (Figure 1-7). To learn more about themes, take a look at Chapter 7.

Excel 2007 also gives you time back by including a lot of new chart types, cool graphics, and new Chart Tools that make looking at data very easy. You now have more graphic ability and can apply shadows, bevels, and most anything else you can do with other types of graphic elements. We can now all become our own Excel Divas. What's amazing about this is that Microsoft Word 2007 and Microsoft

PowerPoint 2007 now use the Microsoft Excel 2007 charting engine, making creating charts much easier and more powerful within those applications too. So you can take the charts you create in Excel 2007 into PowerPoint 2007 and Word 2007 for great presentations and reports. You heard it here first!

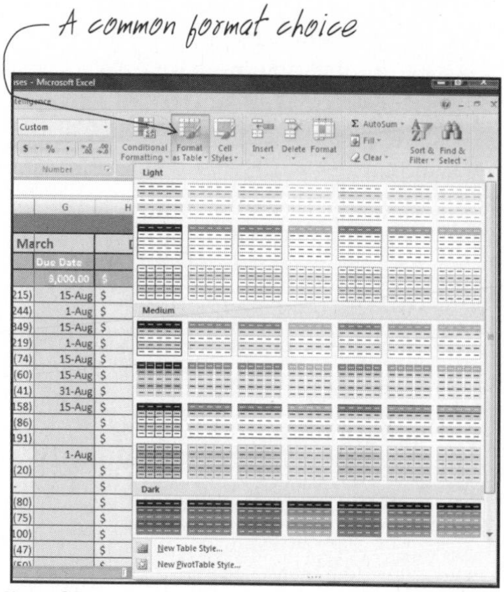

A common format choice

Figure 1-7

Geek Facts 1.1

How about the geeky cool things? Now you can show off your geek-skills: Excel 2007 can hold more than 1 million rows of data. Want more?

- Total number of columns in Excel 2007 is now 16,384; it was 256.
- Total number of rows is now 1,048,576; it was 65,536.
- The number of unique colors allowed in a single workbook is now 4.3 billion; it was 56. But please follow your good sense and use color coordination.
- The number of levels of sorting you can perform on a range of tables is now 64; it was 3.
- The number of items allowed in the Filter drop-down is now 10,000; it was 1,000.
- The maximum number of characters allowed in formulas is 8,000; it was 1,000.
- The maximum number of arguments allowed to a function is now 255; it was 30.

Excel Formulas: It All Adds Up!

Ever remember getting frustrated trying to type Excel functions? If you are new you probably don't even know where to begin. Well, never fear! You get a new AutoComplete feature in all the equations you will use, and now you have it in Excel 2007. When you type an equal sign followed by any letter you get a drop-down list of functions that start with that letter, and as you type more letters the list narrows down to finally what you need.

A few items AutoComplete offers are:

Excel 2007 functions: As you can see in Figure 1-8, when you type the "=s" you can see a lot of equations from "SUM" (which is the total) to "SQRT" (which is Square Root) and more.

User-defined functions: These are the special functions that you (yes, you will create some of these later on), or someone else has created in your workbook or macro code.

Defined names: These are user-defined (defined by you) nicknames for specific cell ranges (so if you had cells A1 to A30 on your monthly bill worksheet you could call them February Bills).

Notice these windows pop up as you begin typing in the cell.

Helpful hints conveniently pop up.

Health (Dentist, Doctor, etc.)	$	(47)	$	(47)	$	(47
other	$	(50)	$	(50)	$	(50
Education	$	-				
Vacation	$	(75)	$	(75)	$	(75
House/Investment Expenses	$	(100)	$	(100)	$	(100
Total Spent	=SUM					

Adds all the numbers in a range of cells

- *fx* SUM
- *fx* SUMIF
- *fx* SUMIFS
- *fx* SUMPRODUCT
- *fx* SUMSQ
- *fx* SUMX2MY2
- *fx* SUMX2PY2
- *fx* SUMXMY2

| Gifts | | | $ | (44) | $ | (44 |
| donation | | | $ | (140) | $ | (140 |

Sheet2 Christmas Expens   s 200

AutoComplete shows many different equations from SUM.

Figure 1-8

One of the most common requests from corporations that have utilized Excel was to find the average value of cells where the cell met a certain criteria. So for those of you looking at your monthly budget and you want to find out where you spend more than $500 every month (probably at the Louis Vuitton store!), this is a great place to start. After you enter all your expenses you can use the cool new formulas the Excel 2007 team has created to summarize your data given a certain condition. In the following list you can find a couple of the new added functions with Excel 2007 that enable you to get the most out of your data. If you want to find out more about functions, please read Chapter 6.

> **AVERAGEIF:** Helps you to find the average value of cells in a range for cells that meet a single criterion. So in this case if you want to find out where you spend more than $500 in monthly expenses, this function is how you would do it. You would start by typing "**=AVERAGEIF(**" (including the quotes, of course) into a cell and continue by selecting the cells you are looking at.

> **AVERAGEIFS:** Helps you find the average value of cells in a range of cells that meet multiple criteria. So if you wanted to find out in which month you spent $500 on your shopping bill that would be two criteria: shopping and $500 minimum. So you would select the shopping column and then the cell for each month where you spent your shopping money.

File Formats and How to Share with Your Friends

With the new Microsoft Open Office file format XLSX (.xlsx) you can integrate better with other programs such as Open Office or other types of comparable office products. You can also integrate better with other types of data, such as if you want to copy pictures or your Christmas wish list to a blog, Amazon.com, eBay, or other places. As you grow your Excel 2007 skills and want to connect to data sources such as Access, SQL database, or others, it is easier than ever with Excel 2007. You can even begin by clicking on the Data tab of the Office 2007 Ribbon. So what this means, ladies, is more room for pictures of all the wish list items you have and room for music and video lists. So the next time you make a wish list on Overstock.com, you can put that list on your desktop and save it for later use. But this also means that if you want your friends and coworkers (who may not have been as lucky as you to have gotten a copy of Excel 2007) to be able to read the spreadsheets you create, you will have to save in the 97-2003 format. Some things might change (such as shading or font styles that were unavailable in older versions of Excel) but most of what you see, they will see.

In order to save properly, click on the Office Pearl from Figure 1-1 and choose the Save As option (Figure 1-9) from the drop-down menu. Once you click on the Save As option, you will see a window like the one in Figure 1-10 come up. This window is where you can make sure you are saving to the right location, with the right name, and to the right format (pay close attention here or your friends can't see it!), as shown by the bottom arrow of Figure 1-10.

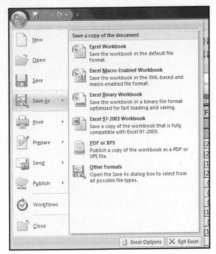

Figure 1-9

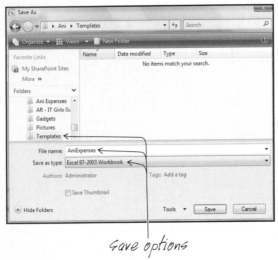

Save options

Figure 1-10

Review Before You Print

Now you know the value that has been added into Excel 2007, but how about printing? After all your effort you'd like to share your work with your colleagues and manager. With Excel 97 there was something called Page Break Preview view, which helped you see (in a small font, which you couldn't really read) what your work would look like. Well, when you take a look at your workbook with Page Layout view you see exactly what your work will look like. The cool thing with Page Layout view (Figure 1-11) now is that you can change your workbook's margins, so they fit better on a printed page; and add and edit headers and footers, so you can put the confidential lines, page numbers, and dates in that you forgot. And most importantly, edit your data.

Click here to see the Page Layout view.

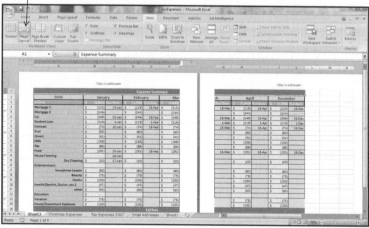

Figure 1-11

Online Help

There is ample help inside Excel 2007, but if you need more for the project you are doing, there is also ample help online. You can click on the question mark on the top-right side of the screen (Figure 1-12).

Find help here.

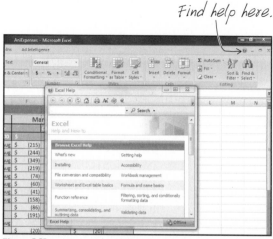

Figure 1-12

Figure 1-12 shows a great place to find help about anything you are trying to do. You can also visit http://Office.Microsoft.com, where you will find the same Ribbon feel and be able to navigate to get the updates and help you need. For updates you can click on the Office Pearl and go down to the Excel options. When you click on Excel 2007 Options, the Excel Options window appears (Figure 1-13). From this window you can select Resources from the left side and check for updates online. In most cases you will be automatically notified that updates are available from Microsoft for your product. What you can expect from these updates are mainly bug fixes, so when you find something and let Microsoft know, the Excel team captures the most important ones based on number of occurrences and amount of impact, and fixes them and sends out updates.

Click on the Office Pearl to open the Excel Options window.

Check for updates.

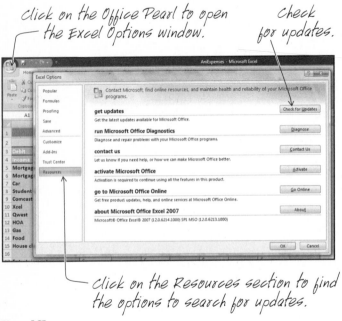

Click on the Resources section to find the options to search for updates.

Figure 1-13

Relax, Refresh, Reward

You have made it through the first chapter. Hopefully you're inspired and looking at your favorite handbag with a whole new perspective. You've learned about some of the coolest new features in Excel 2007 and are ready to move on to something new. Reward yourself with a soy Chai latte.

Did you know the word Chai is Farsi, and it means tea? For those of you who have seen it with the Indian culture, yes, the same word in India is used to mean "tea with milk." So the truth is when you order Chai tea, you are actually ordering a "tea tea," kind of like a mahi mahi. Funny thing is in Farsi Mahi means fish, so you are then saying "fish fish."

So why soy and not regular Chai? Because it's fat free and very low in calories. After all, soy is a bean. The cool thing is, you have to walk somewhere to get a soy Chai, and not too many places have it either. So as you walk around trying to find your soy Chai, you get the exercise too, and that keeps good oxygen flowing in your body and burns extra calories, and you may meet a lot of nice people along the way. When you look at the calories of a regular latte, compared to a soy Chai latte (this is what most places call it), you will see a big difference.

2

To Do List

Install and activate Excel 2007

Learn to speak the Excel 2007 lingo

Create a workbook

Balance yourself with a little yoga

Where to Begin with Excel

Most people have been in situations where they moved to a new school, neighborhood, or workplace and felt they just didn't fit. But that feeling was just temporary. After a few months, and a couple of social gatherings and some gossip, they learned the "lingo" used by everyone else, which helped them feel like they were part of that crowd. Well this is no different. There is an Excel 2007 crowd, and my goal is to help you learn the lingo to communicate with that crowd and know what you're talking about.

In recent years I have learned there is something specific about Microsoft; we have our own culture and have a set of vocabulary we like to use. That set of vocabulary and set of acronyms helps us feel connected and provides better understanding of each other at work and outside. I have noticed that other professions (dentists, yoga instructors, personal trainers) have the same practice of using the same set of vocabularies and follow the same cultural behaviors. This helps everyone feel more connected to these service providers and utilize their service more.

Technology Smarts

Ladies, I know some of you are new to Excel, so take a few minutes and get up to speed. For those of you who already know this, you can skip this section only, and pick up reading again at "Do You Need to Register?"

So how do you start Excel 2007? Well, it's so easy, any IT Girl can do it:

Figure 2-1

1. Using Microsoft Windows, go to Programs→Microsoft Office→ Microsoft Office Excel 2007.

2. If you are lucky to have Windows Vista, just click on the Vista Pearl (Figure 2-1) on the bottom left-hand corner of your screen.

3. Type the word **Excel.** You will see that Microsoft Excel is the first one that comes up. Click on it and Excel 2007 will launch.

Do You Need to Register?

So when you click on Excel 2007 for the first time, you will be asked to register your copy of Excel 2007. If you had someone else install Excel 2007 for you, they may have done this already and you don't have to worry about it. For those of you Divas who are installing your own, fantastic! This is pretty self-explanatory when you first put the CD into the computer and begin installation; at the end the CD will ask you to register using an online method or you can choose to call in. Whichever method you choose is great; do, however, make sure you register so you can take advantage of the latest fixes and changes that Microsoft will provide.

Waiter, I Think There's a Bug in My Software

I know many of you buy various things that ask for registration, such as hair dryers, mixers, and blenders. I can see you not wanting to take the time to register those items. But, most things in life are not perfect. So when bugs come up in Excel

2007, Microsoft fixes them and wants to let you know so you can download the fixes, and they need you to be registered so they can keep you informed. These downloads are free and help you perform better. This enables you to keep producing beautiful charts and being productive while Microsoft worries about the bugs and how to fix them.

If you are paying good money for this great software, why would there be bugs in it? That's a great question. Keep in mind that software doesn't ship with big, problem bugs anymore. Most companies follow the development life cycle that develops code and testing side by side, so all major bugs are taken care of by the time the software ships. That said, testing for all bugs is impossible since there are cases that only come up during certain times. There are many reasons why products need updates, but the most common one is that the planning was rushed to have a product out the door and into your hands before the competition. Getting the latest features into your hands might mean getting you the product faster, yet perhaps with a few bugs. The more features a product has, the more lines of code it takes to write, and the more lines of code written, the more room for bugs. Think of it like making a soufflé compared to a basic cake out of the box. With the cake out of the box, you add eggs, water, and oil and mix them all. Even if you were to make a mistake you would be able to fix it next time around. But with a soufflé there are a lot more factors, such as the right amount of heat and the right time to take it out of the oven. Also, being on different sides of the equator and having convection ovens, electric, or gas can play to your favor or detriment when it comes to making a soufflé. You get the idea. The beauty of registering is that bug fixes are delivered to your door unsolicited by you.

These bug fixes are free, but they are never advertised. To get a bug fix without being registered, you must remember to click on the Check for Updates button or go to your favorite search engine and search for the keywords "Windows Update."

With Office 2007 you will have to register at some point. This has been the case for a while now. You can call in, mail a post card and wait a while, or just connect to the Internet and register your version of Office. There is an Activation Wizard to help you through the process. This Activation Wizard will come up as soon as you put the CD into your computer. Once the CD is in your computer, it will in most cases begin playing automatically and start the Installation Wizard. In some cases with older computers you may have to find where your CD is and begin this process manually. In those cases ask someone in your circle of friends who has installed or played music before on their computer to help you. You always do have the choice to activate later as well. Nevertheless, at some point you will have to go through the activation process. It really doesn't take very long. For those of you sticklers, I have Comcast cable at home and it took me five minutes.

All you need to have is the package Microsoft Office 2007 came in. In that package you will find the serial number, which is what you will need to get Microsoft Office 2007 installed and working as well as run Microsoft Excel 2007 for the first time. If at any point after you run Excel or any of your Microsoft Office 2007 products for the first time you run into problems and need help or want to find out if there are updates available for your version of Microsoft Office (in this case Microsoft Office 2007), you can use your help menu. Just simply click on the question-mark-in-a-circle button on the top-right side of any of the Microsoft Office 2007 applications (Figure 2-2) and the help menu will come up (Figure 2-3), inside which you can type the keywords "Customer Service" and then press Enter. After a brief search several results will return in the same pop-up window, as shown in Figure 2-4. You might notice you are getting the same results shown in Figure 2-4. That's because Excel 2007 learns from you every time you search for something and tries to help identify what you need. One of the results will be titled "Get help from Microsoft Support Service." Be sure to look through all the results shown.

Click this for help.

Figure 2-2

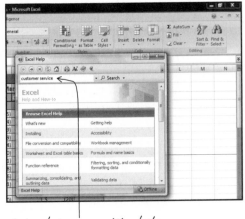

Search for specific help.

Figure 2-3

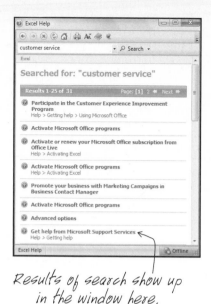

Results of search show up
in the window here.

Figure 2-4

Example of a first step

Figure 2-5

Once you select the first result by clicking on it, another window will open that will guide you through the steps of how to get help, as shown in Figure 2-5. Note you do have to be connected to the web to be able to access this help page. You can see Figure 2-6 and follow the steps without being connected to the web; however, the final steps will require you to be online. The steps will guide you to click the Office Pearl as shown by the top arrow in Figure 2-6, which will open a drop-down menu from which you will select the bottom option, called Excel Options, as shown by the bottom arrow in Figure 2-6.

Once you select Excel Options, a new menu will pop up where you can click Resource, which will bring you to a page where you can click the Contact Us button (Figure 2-7). By clicking this button you will be routed to the online help center (Figure 2-8). You can always go to the website for other information as well by opening the Internet Explorer browser window and typing **http://office.microsoft.com**. If you do not have access to the web you can always call 1-800-MICROSOFT to "find the right number for your specific issue."

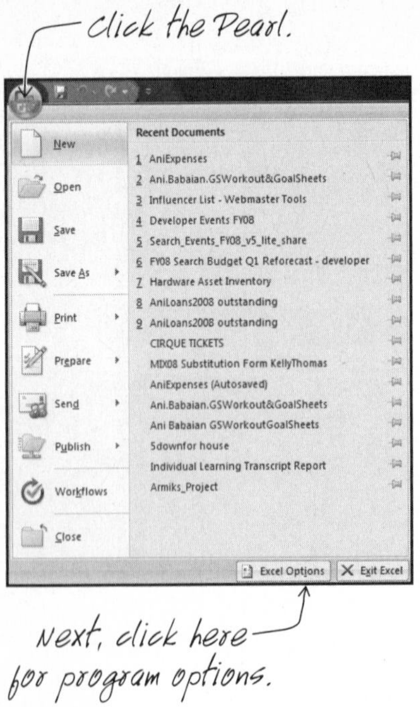

Click the Pearl.

Next, click here for program options.

Figure 2-6

Click here

Contact us button

Figure 2-7

Online help center web address

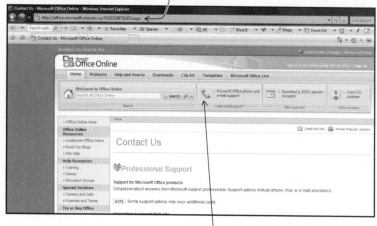

Click here for phone or mail support.

Figure 2-8

Excel Lingo

If you want to talk the talk, you've got to walk the walk, right? Well, this section is here to help you talk the talk. Or rather, to understand the Excel 2007 talk. You'll figure out all those confusing terms, such as ...

What a Worksheet Is; What a Workbook Is

Let's begin with a few important pieces of information. The grid-looking Figure 2-9 shows what is called a *worksheet*. (You'll notice some new formatting to the worksheet example shown here. Keep reading; this book teaches you how to make all those changes and more.) You can have multiple worksheets in a *workbook*; as a matter of fact, there is no limit. The only limit to the number of worksheets in a workbook is how much random memory your computer has.

RAM is . . .

Random Access Memory (RAM), which works very similarly to short-term memory. You can only keep a few things in your short-term memory, and there is a limit to how much you can keep track of.

The workbook is a collection of worksheets. So think of it as a manila file you might have in your home or office. The file is the workbook and the sheets of paper inside it are the worksheets. In this case the worksheets inside the workbook have a grid on them. They range from columns A to XFD. Okay, so how did Microsoft come up with XFD? The order goes as follows: A to Z, then AA to ZZ, then AAA to AAB to ABB to XFD. The rows range from 1 to 1,048,576.

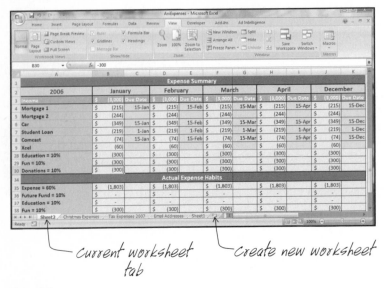

Current worksheet tab   *Create new worksheet*

Figure 2-9

Go here for spreadsheet humor!

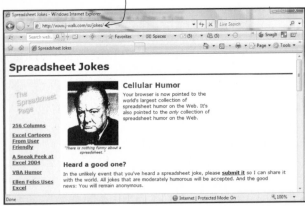

Figure 2-10

Let's spend some time and define a few other important words we will be using throughout this book and you will need for your Excel Lingo list:

- **Cell**—Each rectangular box is referred to as a cell. You can only put one piece of text or data into this rectangular box.

- **Row**—Rows run horizontally and have a number assigned to them. The combination of the row number and the column letter can help you or others pinpoint the location of data you are referencing.

- **Column**—Columns run vertically and have an alphabetic letter assigned to them. The combination of the row number and the column letter can help you or others pinpoint the location of data you are referencing.

- **Scrollbar**—In Excel 2007 scrollbars are on the far right of the screen and to the bottom of the screen where you can use the bar to drag the worksheet up and down or sideways, as shown in Figure 2-11.

- **Tab**—If you use the right or left arrow keys or the up and down arrow keys you can move up or down, left or right through the cells. This is also called *tabbing over* to other cells. As confusing as it might sound, you can also use the Tab key to move to the right or use the Shift key and Tab key together to move to the left.

- **Sort**—Excel offers various ways to arrange data, whether it's numeric or alphabetic, ascending or descending. You can select how you want to sort the data in your row or column by clicking the Sort & Filter button to the far right of the Office Ribbon on the Editing section, as shown in Figure 2-12.

Funny strange or funny ha-ha?

I don't know if anyone has ever used all the rows or columns in an Excel 2007 spreadsheet, or other Excel spreadsheets for that matter. I do know there is a pretty funny place I like to go to for spreadsheet humor (Figure 2-10). If I ever need a bit of a break or want to brush up on my Excel 2007 funny lingo, this is a great little treat to keep me good-humored and keep me going. You can also access it online at http://www.j-walk.com/ss/jokes/.

Figure 2-11

Scrollbars

Sort & Filter button

Figure 2-12

No GPS Necessary

So, when you're referring to a certain cell in a memo or email, you might say, "The data in cell 7C demonstrates the highest figure count in all 12 months." Cell 7C isn't a jail cell; it's the cell that's in the seventh row, in column C.

- **Sum**—A well-used function (more about functions in Chapter 6) to add the values of a selected set of cells in a column, row, or a variety of columns and row-based cells.

- **Zoom slider**—A new feature of Microsoft Excel 2007 located on the bottom right-hand corner of the screen. If you are unable to see the zoom slider, you can add it (see the following section). By sliding the arrow in between the "+" and "−" bubbles you can zoom in (more toward the "+") or zoom out (more toward the "−").

- **Active cell**—In an Excel 2007 worksheet this is the cell with the darkest black border where the selector rectangle is. As you use the arrow keys to move left to right or top to bottom, this dark rectangle will change positions (Figure 2-13).

Active cell—
see the border?

2006		January	
Debit			Due Date
Income	$		3,000.0
Mortgage 1	$	(215)	15-A
Mortgage 2	$	(244)	1-A
Car	$	(349)	15-A
Student Loan	$	(219)	1-A
Comcast	$	(74)	15-A
Xcel	$	(60)	15-A

Figure 2-13

- **PivotTable**—A table with many criteria. For example, if you want to keep track of your family expenses per month, per type of expense, and per person, you would use a PivotTable.

This would not be easily done by just a regular table. Take a look at Chapter 11 for more information.

- **PivotChart**—A chart (a graph) with many criteria. For example, if you want to keep track of your family expenses per month, per type of expense, and per person in a chart (instead of a table), you would use a PivotChart. This would not be easily done by just a regular chart (that is, graph). Check out Chapter 11 for further details.

So why would you use a workbook of worksheets? Well, it's all based on how you organize things. Sometime it makes sense to only have one worksheet in a workbook. It might help to think of a workbook as a manila folder and a worksheet like the paper(s) you keep inside the manila folder. Other times it makes sense to cram as many worksheets as you can in one workbook. In my case I like to have an expense workbook with all my expense worksheets in it, and an exercise workbook with my exercise log and calorie intake worksheet in it. In Excel 2007 workbooks start with three worksheets, indicated by tabs located on the bottom left of your worksheet.

The tab area in the lower-left corner of the worksheet enables you to make several changes:

- **Add more worksheets:** Click on the star on the tab of the sheet next to Sheet 3 to add more (Figure 2-14).

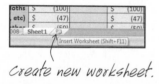

Create new worksheet.

Figure 2-14

- **Change the name of a worksheet:** By default the sheets will be titled Sheet 1, Sheet 2, and so on. To change the worksheet name, take your mouse and right-click on the sheet name where the arrow is pointing in Figure 2-15. A menu will show where you can select Rename from the options. Once you left-click on the Rename option you can begin typing the new name (Figure 2-16).

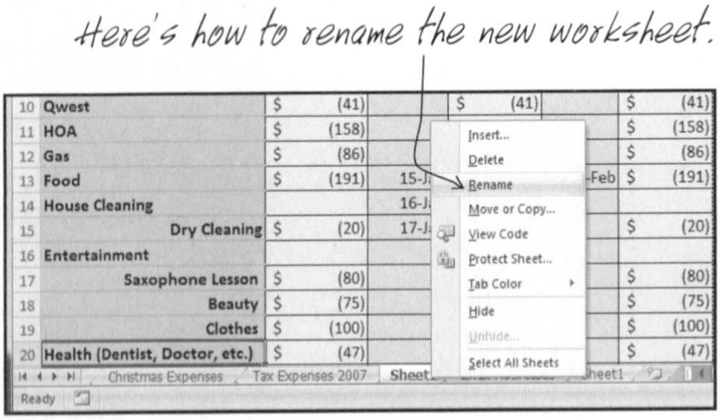

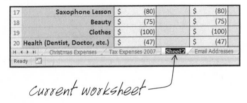

Here's how to rename the new worksheet.

Figure 2-15

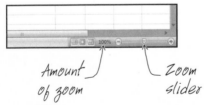

Current worksheet

Figure 2-16

- **Zoom in on a few particular cells:** For those of you who want to zoom in and out and see your data bigger and/or smaller you can use the Zoom slider on the bottom-right corner of the screen shown in Figure 2-17. If you do not see the Zoom slider you can choose the options shown in Figure 2-18.

Amount of zoom *Zoom slider*

Figure 2-17

You also have *scrollbars* on the bottom and the right side of your worksheet so that you can scroll side to side and top to bottom to see all your data, as shown in Figure 2-11.

In addition to scrollbars, your worksheets also include *scroll buttons*. They sound similar, but are not the same thing. A workbook only displays four worksheet tabs at a time. If your workbook grows to more than four sheets, you need to use the *tab scrolling buttons* to go from the first four sheets to the next four and so on. Figure 2-19 shows the tab scrolling buttons that you can use to move forward or back through all the worksheets. The single side arrows will go through one worksheet at a time, whereas the arrows with a line next to them will scroll all the way over to the last or first worksheet (Figure 2-19). These buttons look very similar to your CD player—when you want to forward into a song you hit the arrow keys and when you want to skip to the next song you use the arrow-plus-line keys.

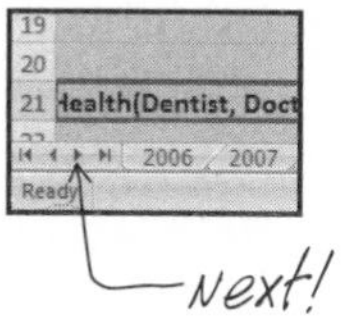

Add the zoom slider in.

Figure 2-18

—*Next!*

Figure 2-19

Inside a Cell

Now, looking at Figure 2-20, you'll see a selected square on the top right. Each of these squares that can hold self-contained data is called a *cell*. Each cell in a worksheet has an address. You can refer to it by its column heading and row heading. So the cells on a worksheet are organized like addresses in a city block. If you live on the 1300 block south and 400 block west, we know exactly where your house is located. All city streets have these block addresses; however, the public typically uses street names to make it easier.

Cell A2

Figure 2-20

If you begin selecting multiple cells, only the one on the top-left side will be considered active; it's called the *active cell*. You can also call this a *mother cell*. I think of it as the mother cell, since in my church and community everyone knows me by my mom. I can tell them who my mom is and they will know who I am. Same thing happens here, the contents of the upper-left cell (a.k.a. active cell) will be displayed in the Name box on the right end of the formula bar as shown in Figure 2-21. In Figure 2-21 you will see two arrows. The bottom arrow is pointing to the mother cell and the top arrow is pointing to the right side of the Name box where the value of the mother cell is.

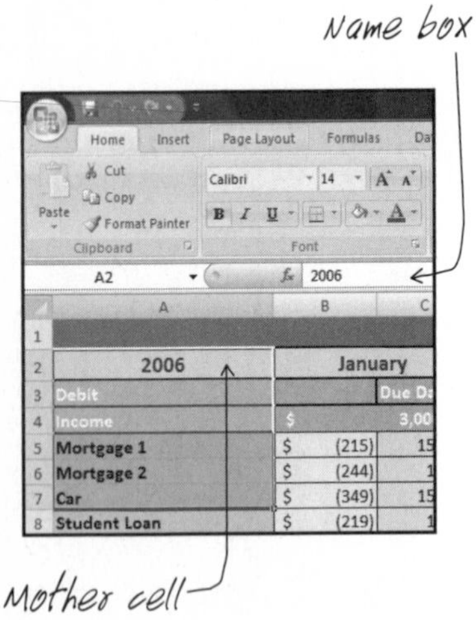

Name box

Mother cell

Figure 2-21

Shortcuts Aren't for Everybody

For those of you who don't really like the mouse or would rather do everything with your keyboard, there are a few shortcut keys that will help. But mice can be nice; they come in all colors and sizes and you can even get one like mine made by Targus that changes colors very slowly. It's a great conversation starter and helps you get your work done. Table 2-1 lists some of the more common shortcuts.

Oldies But Goodies

All of these shortcuts have been around since before mice were commonly used in computing.

So what happens when you have a few coworkers walking by and you don't want them to see what you are working on? In the top right-hand corner of the screen there are four items (Figure 2-22, from left to right):

- **Help button**—The Help button opens Excel 2007 Help much like in Figure 2-3 where you can type a set of keywords to search for a topic.

- **Minimize**—The Minimize button minimizes the size of the worksheet you are working on to the bottom-left corner of the Microsoft Excel 2007 workbook.

- **Maximize**—The Maximize button maximizes the size of the worksheet from minimized to full workbook size.

- **Close**—The "x" at the rightmost end of the Excel 2007 workbook screen closes the worksheet.

Your friends or coworkers can still tell you are working in Excel 2007 but will not know what worksheet you are working on. (No one needs to know your purse-shopping budget anyway! Now get back to work!)

Don't Mess with X

Note that if you have made any changes to your spreadsheet (and haven't saved recently, tsk tsk) you'll get a prompt asking if you want to save changes. So X-ing out might not be the fastest way to remove a secretive spreadsheet from your screen.

Minimize all worksheets.

Figure 2-22

Table 2-1   Give the Mouse a Break

Shortcut Keys	Function
Ctrl + Page Down	Takes you to the next worksheet in the workbook.
Ctrl + Page Up	Takes you back to the prior worksheet in the workbook.
Ctrl + Home	In case you get lost and don't know where the first cell is, this takes you back to the first cell on the first worksheet page (that is, Column A and Row 1).
Ctrl + C	Copies a selected set of text or data from a worksheet.
Ctrl + X	Cuts a selected set of text or data from a worksheet.
Ctrl + V	Pastes previous cut or copied text or data.
Ctrl + A	Will select (highlight) everything in the worksheet.
Ctrl + Z	Is the magic undo key; in case you make a mistake you can use this combination to undo your mistake. You can also use this multiple times in a row to go back a couple of steps.
Ctrl + Y	Is the magic redo key; in case you make a mistake and undo too many times, use this shortcut to redo, and get back what you just un-did.
Ctrl + P	Pops up the Print window to print your current worksheet.
Ctrl + S	Saves your current worksheet.
Ctrl + F	Pops up a window in which you can type text to search for in the worksheet.
Ctrl + G	Pops up a window that can take you to a specific place in your worksheet.
Ctrl + O	Pops up a window that can help you choose a file to open.
Ctrl + N	Opens a new workbook.
Ctrl + U	Underlines the text you are about to type and if clicked again, it will turn off the underline.
Ctrl + I	Makes the text you are about to type *italic* and if clicked again, it will turn off the italics.
Ctrl + H	Finds a set of data in a worksheet and replaces that set of data with new data.
Ctrl + Scroll on mouse	Enables you to zoom in and out of the worksheet you are working on.
Ctrl + end	Takes you to the end of the worksheet.

For those of you who don't even want anyone to know that you are working in Excel or just want to minimize your work to open something else, you can use the workbook Minimize, Maximize, and Close buttons located on the top right-hand corner of the Microsoft Excel 2007 workbook (Figure 2-23, from left to right) to close Excel 2007 altogether.

Multitasking Maven!

As you advance you might have multiple worksheets open in a workbook, and, by minimizing them all, you will be able to see them all and maximize the one you need, or just close the ones you do not need.

Minimize workbook here.

Figure 2-23

This Ribbon Isn't for Your Hair: Introducing the Excel Ribbon

Now that you're a walking, talking expert on the spreadsheet basics of cells and columns and rows and workbooks and worksheets, it's time to start talking about what you do with all the data in these worksheets.

Use whatever means necessary to get the data into Excel. You are welcome to enter it yourself, get it from data sources such as Access or another Excel worksheet, or pay your children to enter it. (Who said this book will not give you family time?) Once that data is in, you will be spending a lot of time using the Office Ribbon, shown in Figure 2-24, to make changes to your data and get the look and feel that will make you the Excel 2007 Diva you know you are.

The Office Ribbon is not specific to Excel 2007; all Microsoft Office 2007 products have the Ribbon. You can also find it at http://office.microsoft.com, the official help website for Microsoft Office 2007. After a long study of how most people used previous Microsoft Office products, Microsoft found that most of the functionality people were asking for in the next version of Microsoft Office was already inside

Microsoft Office, it was just very hard to find. Many of you might remember the drop-down menus, which opened other drop-down menus, which opened other drop-down menus (you see where this is going). From the conducted studies, the idea was born of the Office Ribbon, where you can find the most common functionality on a tabulated part of the top of any Microsoft Office 2007 application (Figure 2-24).

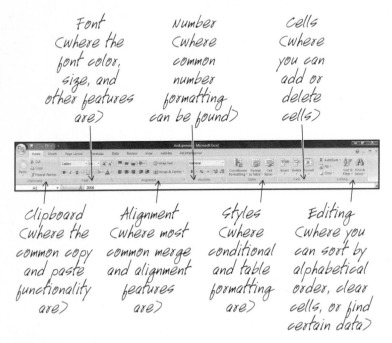

Font (where the font color, size, and other features are)

Number (where common number formatting can be found)

Cells (where you can add or delete cells)

Clipboard (where the common copy and paste functionality are)

Alignment (where most common merge and alignment features are)

Styles (where conditional and table formatting are)

Editing (where you can sort by alphabetical order, clear cells, or find certain data)

Figure 2-24

The Excel 2007 Ribbon is the best facelift anyone ever attempted and the best part is, it was painless. I hate to say it, ladies, but it's time for some terminology. Yawn, I know, but it's critical to achieving that Diva status. Figure 2-24 showed the *Office Ribbon,* and each tabulated section such as (from left to right) Home, Insert, and so on, are the *Ribbon groups.* Each Ribbon group has related controls. The order of the items on the Ribbon and the tabs was taken from a usability study that was done on previous versions of Microsoft Office products, where each click was taken into account. Microsoft learned from the users which features they use most and put them first. So ladies, this was customized for you by other Excel users.

There is a certain workflow designed into the Ribbon tabs such that you begin with the Home tab, where you find most of the items needed to create a worksheet, and as you progress right on the tabs you reach different items you need, such as previewing your document and viewing how the final worksheet will look. So what do I mean by workflow? In most cases we are multitaskers; we can get dressed and apply our morning moisturizer at the same time. Some of us can also drive and

Flying High with Excel

You may have heard that you can run a flight simulator in Excel 97. (This might be a way men would love to use Excel.) I am not certain this trick still works with Excel 2007, but if you are really interested, what worked in Excel 97 was to restart Excel 97 and then open a new blank worksheet. Press the F5 key and a reference box opened, inside which you would type X97:L97 and press Enter. Pressing the Tab key took you to cell M97. Clicking on the Chart Wizard button while holding down the Ctrl and Shift keys put you in Flight Simulator (the game), using the mouse to navigate. Hitting the Ctrl and Shift and Esc keys ended the game.

apply our makeup and come out looking fantabulous (although the car might not end up looking so great ... maybe we better rethink that). Excel 2007 works with us. It helps us have access to what we need when we need it so we can multitask and view what our data looks like and put the finishing touches on it all at the same time. In summary, you can insert data and change the font if you want to, or insert all the data and then change all the font at the same time. The Office Ribbon enables you to work how you want to work.

Using the Office 2007 Ribbon for Formatting

Let's start with changing the font of data (Figure 2-25) and looking at what's possible. The arrow is pointing at where you can left-click on the drop-down arrow next to the font name and a drop-down menu will appear from which you can select the font style you want (Figure 2-26).

Hover Changes

When you select the font type from the drop-down menu on the Ribbon, the data you have selected changes as you hover over the different font types. This is a new feature added in Excel 2007. The same works for font color, bold, italic, font size, and other formats.

Use the drop-down arrow to see all the font styles.

Figure 2-25

Don't like change?

For those of you who liked how Excel 2003 worked, you can double-click on the bottom-right corner of the Font group and get the old window (Figure 2-27) back. Once you are done with this window just click the OK button if you want to keep the changes or the Cancel button to reject the changes and exit that window.

For those who love shortcuts, there is one more way to access quick font help and frequent task help. If you select the cell (a.k.a. active cell) and then right-click, two separate menus (Figure 2-28) pop up that can help you further. In Figure 2-28 you see a small menu on the bottom and a bigger one on top. The arrow points to the active cell. You can use the smaller menu on the bottom to change the font of the text inside the cell you have selected. Or you can use the bigger menu on top to make other changes to the active cell. The location of the big and small menu might change based on where the active cell is located in your worksheet. You might see the small menu appear on top of the big menu.

use the drop-down arrow to see all font styles.

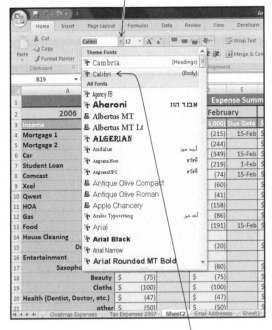

use your mouse to select the font style you like.

Figure 2-26

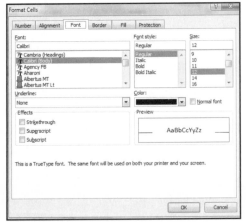

Figure 2-27

Style the text in the active cell.

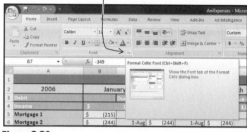

Figure 2-28

The best part of it all is the hover screen that pops up to tell you more about the Office Ribbon features (Figure 2-29). As you hover over each section of the Office Ribbon and point your mouse to the bottom corner of each section, as shown by the arrow in Figure 2-29, a pop-up window appears that tells you more about each section and what it does. For more help you can go back to the online help or at anytime press F1 (the function keys on top of your keyboard). This will open a search window where you can type what you are looking for.

Point mouse here for more font options.

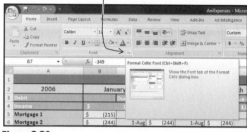

Figure 2-29

One At a Time

Another great shortcut I use when I want to apply a change to cells that aren't in the same row or column is to hold down the Ctrl key and select certain cells in the worksheet. This way I can select any fields I need to include in my equation, my graph, or to which I want to apply font changes. Of course, if you want to change a whole range of cells inclusive from start to finish, you can press Shift while you select. The Shift key allows you to select all the columns and rows between the two cells you click, whereas the Ctrl key allows you to pick and choose.

X Marks the Spot for Help

At any point you can turn the help screen off by simply clicking the small "x" button on the top right-hand corner of the screen, as shown in Figure 2-30 by the bottom arrow. The top arrow in Figure 2-30 shows how to open help by clicking on the blue circle button with a question mark inside.

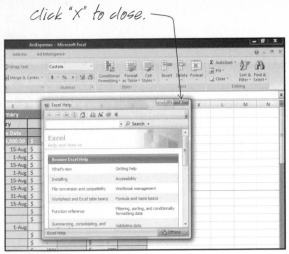

Click "X" to close.

Figure 2-30

Finding the Special Tools

There are a lot of exposed tools on the Ribbon, but what about when you need to do something a bit more special? What if you are trying to change the design and the shading of a graph? Well, there are extra tools that come up at the end of the tabs you already have on the Office Ribbon. So currently if you look at your Office Ribbon, you will see that the View tab is the last one you have. However, if you were to begin working on charts (see Chapter 11 for more details on charts) or SmartArt (see Chapter 10 for more details about SmartArt) extra tabs would appear next to the View tab that would better enable you to format your chart, or whatever the case may be. Ladies, we can relate to this: When we are putting on our work makeup we are just putting on the basics of what makes us more beautiful, but we do have a few very special blushes, shadows, and that long-lasting, extra-long waterproof mascara for special occasions. You would only put on the special stuff for the special nights or times when you are dressing to impress. Likewise, the Office Ribbon is smart enough to save the extra tabs for those occasions only when you'll need them. So let's take a column from a worksheet and graph it to see what comes up (Figure 2-31). As you can see, the tabs Design, Layout, and Format appear after the View tab where the arrow is pointing in Figure 2-31.

Special charting tools

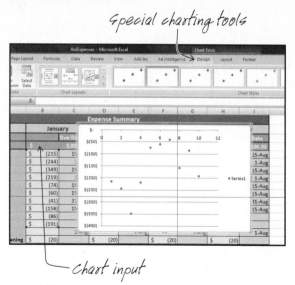

Chart input

Figure 2-31

Having extra tools allows you to take the simple graph and make it better and easier to read. Figure 2-32 shows a basic chart (to find out more about how to create charts, see Chapter 11). However, with about 20 clicks you can take a simple graph and without much work give it a great glow.

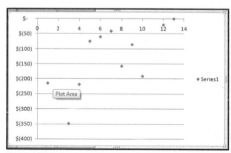

Figure 2-32

Chart tools can take a little bit to get used to, but what helps most is, as you begin to use the tools your graph changes take effect in real time, so you can see what your changes are causing the graph to do. In previous versions of Microsoft Excel you had to wait until all changes were done and exit out of the Change Tools window before you could see the changes in effect. In the past versions it was a bit like putting on your makeup in the dark; you don't really know where you put the eyeliner and the mascara until you see yourself in the mirror. But now it is more like having the best-lit mirror to help you apply your makeup. So as you can see in Figure 2-33 the chart looks prettier and has more character than the one in Figure 2-32.

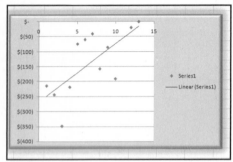

Figure 2-33

A Quick Save Tip

So now that you have made a graph, you want to save it. On top of the Office 2007 Ribbon next to the Office Pearl there is a small picture of a disk, which you can click on to save your work. After all, the best practice to follow is to make sure you always save everything. Save often! You can either hold down the Ctrl key and press the letter S key, which will save automatically, or you can use the Office Pearl which drops down a menu much like in Figure 2-34.

Save Save Save! use the Save option in the drop-down menu that comes up when you click on the Office Pearl.

use the little disk slymbol to save.

Figure 2-34

This is where you find the most common tasks you do when working with worksheets and workbooks, such as Save, Save As, Print, New, Send, Publish, Close, or others. You will also find a quick view of all the latest Excel 2007 documents you have worked with, which I find very helpful when working with multiple Excel 2007 workbooks. Rather than having to find where these workbooks are in Windows Explorer and open them, I can view the latest workbooks I have worked on and open them and begin work again.

Kickin' it Old School

What if you just want to save the work you have done so far and not really have to work through this menu? There is a small save icon next to (to the right of) the Office Pearl that you can click to quickly save your work. Of course for those of you who are old school the Ctrl+S keys (as popped up in Figure 2-34) pressed together still works as well.

Creating a New Workbook

What if you want to create a new workbook?

Here's how to do it yourself:

I. Just Click the Microsoft Office Pearl on the top-left corner of Excel 2007 and select New (Figure 2-35).

Open the New Workbook menu.

Figure 2-35

2. Once you click on the Microsoft Office 2007 Pearl, which is shown by the arrow in Figure 2-35, a drop-down menu appears from which you can select the "New" option (Figure 2-36).

3. Once Figure 2-36 comes up you can select Blank and Recent from the Templates section on the leftmost side.

4. Now click on the Blank Workbook in the middle section of the window, which looks like Figure 2-36.

5. Finally, click on the Create button on the bottom right of the screen, which will make a new blank workbook appear.

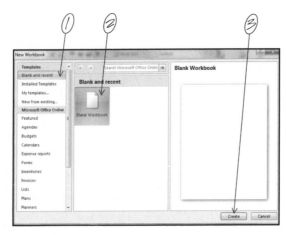

Follow steps 1, 2, and 3 to create your blank workbook.

Figure 2-36

This is where you can get really creative. You can utilize templates other people on your team might have. Or you can just create a blank workbook by selecting the workbook and clicking Create on the bottom of the screen, or just double-click on the workbook icon.

So let's spend some time and define a few items here:

   Template—A preformatted, structured workbook or worksheet. This a workbook or worksheet where you can insert some text in the highlighted areas and an Excel 2007 report will be generated. You can either download one of the many templates Office 2007 comes with from online, create your own, or follow someone else's.

Blank and Recent—Clicking on Blank and Recent creates just that: either a blank workbook, or uses the most recent template you have selected and creates a blank workbook based on that template.

My Templates—Clicking on My Templates creates workbooks that follow your predefined templates.

New from Existing—Clicking New from Existing opens a new box much like Figure 2-37. So now you can open any existing Excel 2007 file as a template. After that point, it only opens copies of workbooks and if you try to save your work, it will save it with a number following the name that was previously given unless you use the Save As option from the Office 2007 Pearl drop-down menu (Figure 2-35) and give it a new name. So, therefore, the original is really used as a template and it's hard for you to overwrite the original.

Creates a new workbook with the same template as the old.

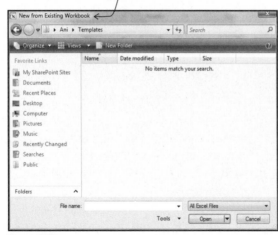

Figure 2-37

Installed Templates—If you have used any templates, the New Workbook dialog box adds another group in the Blank and Recent area, which helps you see your recently used templates and you can select from them to begin a new workbook.

Microsoft Office Online—You can always check the Microsoft online (http://office.microsoft.com) website for templates if you are connected online. You can also look at this website if you need help with certain topics inside Excel 2007. After all, the online help in Excel 2007 connects directly to this website in the background.

Relax, Refresh, Reward

"When the Breath wanders, the mind is unsteady, but when the Breath is still, so is the mind still."—Hatha Yoga Pradipika

You made it through Chapter 2; all that Excel vocabulary, new features, templates. It's time to reinvigorate yourself with some yogic breathing.

The next time you breathe, notice if you are breathing a shallow breath or an actual full-body breath. Most of us breathe very shallow and only bring small amounts of oxygen to our lungs due to stress, poor posture, and our observations of others. With full Pranayama breathing you not only bring full oxygen to your lungs and feel better, you can also reduce your stress level and set a new habit for yourself: one of full breathing and using your abdomen to breathe. Have you ever noticed how babies breathe with their full stomach? They don't care if their belly fat hangs out a little, they are taking full-body breaths and feeling good. You can do the same; after all—breathing is life.

The exercise is as follows:

1. Sit in a comfortable place, whether in your office or my favorite, outside!

2. Just observe how you are breathing for a short while.

3. Begin with a strong exhale as you bring your belly button toward your spine. And as you inhale fill your stomach with air. Try to go as slowly as you can. It might help if you place one hand on your sternum and the other on your belly. This allows you to focus on where the breath is filling and leaving your body and helps you focus your efforts.

4. Do this 10 to 20 times, based on how much time you have. Also, if you do work your way up to 50, give yourself a pat on the back . . . you are a true Diva and ready to take on yoga. But you obviously have to consult a doctor first.

We are where we are today because of where we have been. I know this might be a bit obvious. However, it is important to understand this concept if we want to re-create or change our future.

So with that in mind, as you sit there and breathe (I know most of you Divas love to multitask) you can concentrate on what you want in your life. Keep in mind that good, kind thoughts bring goodness to you and everyone else, and bad thoughts hurt you and others. The best thing to do is to do the exercise with friends. That way you don't look out of place and you can use each other's energy. Believe me, this will make more sense when you do it. It will definitely make sense to my fellow yogis (girls and guys). Don't get me wrong, though, I too have days I lose control:

3

Make Minor Alterations

To Do List

Know the fashion basics about Excel

Undo and redo cuts and pastes

Glorify your cells

Enjoy the vista

to Your Data

D on't wear white shoes after Labor Day, and stripes don't go with plaid. You will also see fashion sensible Divas matching their purse with their shoes and always dressing in ways that complement their figures. This year the thick eyebrow has been in fashion. Well, not everyone looks good with thick eyebrows. Some people even shave their eyebrows and tattoo eyebrows in. I think tattooing eyebrows is just fashion suicide, never mind what that does to your face. But it's all up to the person who is wearing it. The same can be said about your worksheets. This chapter gives you all the fashion basics you need to know. (Excel spreadsheet-wise, anyway!)

In Excel 2007, spreadsheets are a gathering of worksheets and, at times, workbooks. Just like fashion has a trend and a way things are suppose to be, worksheets do as well. There is a certain way those in the technology industry have come to display data. And there's a certain way the human eyes and brain can process data. So, just like you pay attention to fashion and spend time to dress for work, you should spend time on your worksheets. Before you dress you always keep in mind what time of year it is, who you will be meeting, and whether it is morning, for drinks after work, with friends, or with your favorite person. With your worksheets you will do the same. Keep your audience in mind and you are 70 percent done.

It's All about the Data

The first thing to think about when starting your worksheets is the data. It's all about the data—what information needs to be conveyed, to whom, and why do the care about it? Then, what's the best way to get that information to them, so they can process it easily? It's like dressing up for an occasion; you wouldn't show up to an interview wearing a nightgown and you wouldn't show up to a black-tie dinner wearing an interview suit.

Be sure you take into account what the purpose of this data will be. Will it be used in a Microsoft Word document, a PowerPoint presentation, or a printed report? In each case there are various things that you need to keep in mind.

You will also need to answer the question: Who is your audience? That is always a very important question to answer as you get ready to create any worksheet. Are you just dressing to stay home and do a few chores? Or do you need to look marvelous because you are going on the date of your life? You have to take the same consideration for your data. At times you might be asked to share your data with coworkers, other managers, over the web, and in various other places. For those times you'll want to make sure your data looks fantastic.

Fashionista Tip

When you're designing a worksheet for others' eyes, it's helpful to know what they will see. Here's where the Print Layout on the Print tab comes in handy. First select the printer you will be printing to so Excel 2007 has a chance to figure out what the printer schematics are from your printer. Then you can see in a quick glance how your printouts will look. If you know for certain you will be printing the worksheet, keep using Print Layout to ensure you have exactly the look you want. It is very easy to make mistakes when you are just looking at the home screen.

A common best practice is to have fewer columns than rows, merely because at some point you will have to print this puppy and you don't want to spend time using scotch tape to paste the pieces together—that's tacky. Having fewer columns than rows allows you to scroll up and down and perhaps freeze panes (this is covered later in Chapter 4) to see more of the data you need to see. However, if you do feel it makes better sense to paste your datasheet together because it conveys your point, then go ahead and make more columns than rows. In most cases I put my graphs on a separate worksheet, so I don't have to worry about what will happen when I print it. Also, most people are not interested in the data, are much more interested in what the data tells them, so the charts and graphs are more useful in those cases. This is a good way to keep things tidy and always know where your graphs and charts are.

However, if the worksheet is only for your use, you can make it as nice or plain as you would like. If you know your worksheet might have different audiences, you might think about creating different summary sheets. Summary sheets are a great way to share only the information you think the audience should know. We almost always have way too much data (Figure 3-1) for anyone to consume in our worksheet. A good way to make this information consumable is to create an easy-to-read summary sheet (Figure 3-2).

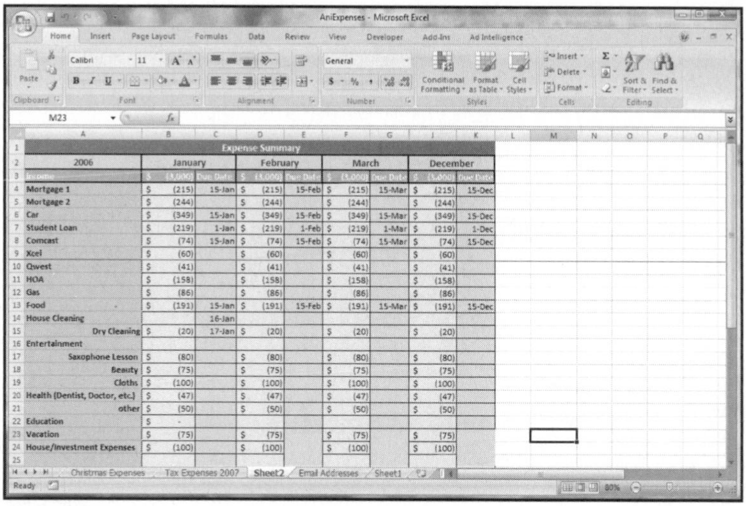

Figure 3-1

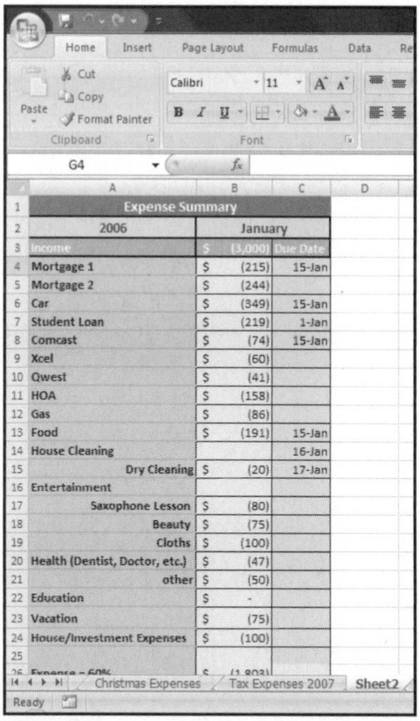

Figure 3-2

Entering and Editing Data—Copy and Paste Is Our Friend

Some of the most commonly used functionality in Excel 2007 (and my life) are: Copy and Paste, Insert and Delete, Cut and Paste, Undo and Redo. I would say these select features are the things that either make your life easier or cause you stress—sometimes both. If you know how to use the combinations properly, you become the heroine (that is, the Diva) you are, and if you don't, well life just doesn't seem as neatly organized as it can be.

Why make such a big deal out of copy and paste? These are simple keystrokes that make data look and act the way you need it to, and put you in the Diva seat in front of your Excel 2007 program, or they make you cry and your makeup runs. As Divas we don't let things get the best of us, and if they do we put up a good fight.

Copy (and Paste) Is Key

So let's begin with the Copy command. When you copy in Excel 2007 the contents of the cell and any equations inside that cell are kept in memory on a temporary area called a Clipboard (Figure 3-3). Once you click on the Copy button on the Home tab (Figure 3-4), you will get the dotted lines going around the cell or cells you are copying (Figure 3-5). In order to see the Clipboard, click on the bottom-right corner of the Clipboard section of the Home tab on the Office 2007 Ribbon.

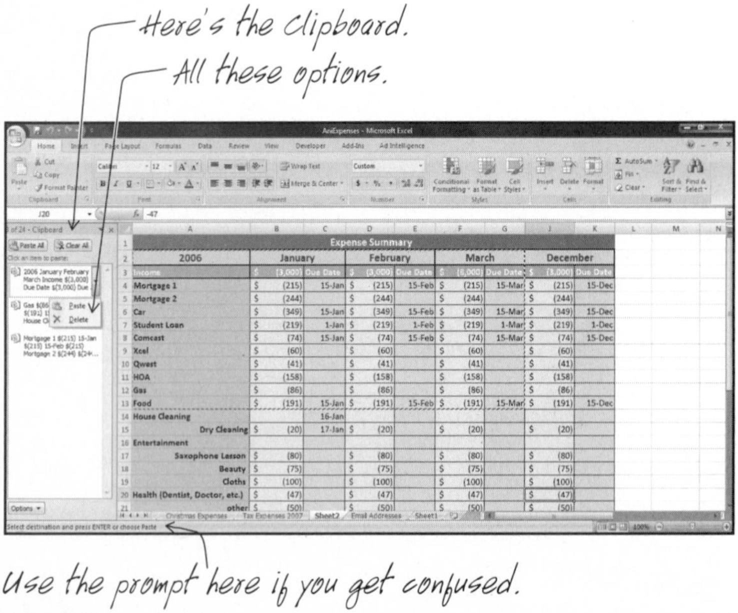

Here's the Clipboard.
All these options.

Use the prompt here if you get confused.

Figure 3-3

You will learn to love the Copy button.

Home Insert Page Layout Formulas Data

Cut
Copy
Paste
Format Painter

Calibri 12 A A

B I U

Clipboard Font

Copy (Ctrl+C)
Copy the selection and put it on the Clipboard.

	A	B	C
1			Exp
2	2006		January
3	Income	$	(3,000) Due Date
4	Mortgage 1	$	(215) 15-Jan
5	Mortgage 2	$	(244)
6	Car	$	(349) 15-Jan
7	Student Loan	$	(219) 1-Jan
8	Comcast	$	(74) 15-Jan
9	Xcel	$	(60)
10	Qwest	$	(41)
11	HOA	$	(158)
12	Gas	$	(86)
13	Food	$	(191) 15-Jan
14	House Cleaning		16-Jan
15	Dry Cleaning	$	(20) 17-Jan
16	Entertainment		
17	Saxophone Lesson	$	(80)
18	Beauty	$	(75)
19	Cloths	$	(100)
20	Health (Dentist, Doctor, etc.)	$	(47)
21	other	$	(50)

Christmas Expenses   Tax Expenses 2007   Sheet2

Figure 3-4

The Clipboard is where you can see all the items you have currently copied. You can get to it by clicking on the bottom-right corner of the Clipboard area on the Home tab (Figure 3-6). Once you click on the Clipboard section, you will see the side menu that shows you what you have on your Clipboard. (This might be a great time to clear out your Clipboard as well. Go ahead, I'll wait a second.)

Helping You Out

If you're detail-challenged, Excel 2007 provides a nice accessory feature: A little reminder about what to do next! A message on the bottom of your Excel 2007 screen appears that says "Select destination and press ENTER or choose Paste." See Figure 3-5 for an example.

By hovering over each item in the Clipboard (Figure 3-3) you will eliminate the item you have selected and a down arrow will show up. By clicking on the down arrow you can then select from the two options (Paste or Delete). You can also use the buttons that appear on the right side of the Excel spreadsheet to "Copy All" (which is used to copy all items to your Excel datasheet), or "Delete All" (to delete all items on the Clipboard and clear everything) to get ready for a new set of copying and pasting.

Your border will change once you've selected cells to be moved.

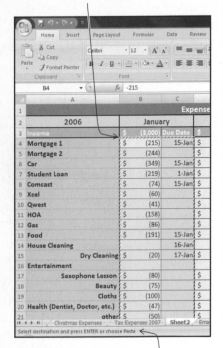

Here's the handy prompt again.

Figure 3-5

You also find the clipboard icon for Paste, the scissors for Cut, and the brush for Format Painter all in the same location (Figure 3-7). If they are not already, these icons will become your best friends. These are not like the friends you had in high school that you liked and then parted ways later; these little gadgets become your friend for life.

Click on the bottom-right corner of the clipboard area on the Home tab to open the clipboard.

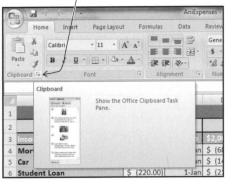

Figure 3-6

All in the same place, isn't that handy?

Figure 3-7

Cut and Paste

So let's talk about Cut. If you are sure you want to cut something out and paste it someplace else, I strongly suggest you just use Copy. Because once you cut you can't go back. If you do cut and go into another application and use Cut again, your data is lost forever.

If you insist on using Cut, here's how. However, know that using Cut is pretty risky! In order to use Cut, execute the following steps:

1. Take your mouse and click on the cell from which you want to cut information.

2. Go up to the leftmost corner of the Office Ribbon as shown in Figure 3-7 and click on the scissor icon. This will begin a jagged line going around the cell you just cut.

3. Go to the new location where you want to paste this data and right-click, which brings up a menu from which you can select Paste.

4. Alternatively, you can go to the new cell where you want to move the cut cell and use the Office Ribbon (Figure 3-7) and click on the Paste button. You can also use the short-cut key Ctrl+P to paste.

Back Out Now

You can always hit the Esc key to stop the cutting (and the jagged line from going around the cell you just cut) in case you made a mistake.

Safety First

Just copy the cell you want to cut, paste it into the new cell, and then come back and delete the old one. I think this way is much safer.

Paste, But Not Paste-y White

With Paste you can go to the new cell you want to move the information into and use the Paste button on the Home tab of the Office Ribbon (the button all the way to the left side) to paste. For those of you who are selecting multiple cells or holding down Ctrl and right-clicking to select certain cells, keep in mind you will need to copy the cells you selected into just as many cells. So, if you are copying four cells, you need room for four cells to copy into. You can either highlight the four cells you want to paste into, or just the first cell and the paste will flow down (or over, depending on what was copied) into the other three. If there is not enough room for four cells, you will see a pop-up window, which asks you if you want to replace the contents of the cells it has selected to open up room for you. If those cells Excel 2007 has selected for you are free, then go ahead and say "Yes." However, please pay attention to which cell Excel 2007 has selected—otherwise you might overwrite your work of art.

Special Pasting

When you copy a cell you copy the whole cell, the hidden information and all, which means you bring formulas with you from one cell to another when you execute a standard copy and paste. There might be times when you want to copy the values of the cell (meaning just the answer, not the formula that gave you that answer) rather than the formula, which is kind of tricky. We will get into formulas later (see Chapter 5 to learn more about formulas), but for now let's look at how we can copy the value or various parts of a cell rather than copying the whole cell.

In order to copy just the value it would make sense to have a special copy, right? Well in Excel 2007 it's called Paste Special. Because there are more things I can do with Excel 2007 Paste Special, it reminds me that there are more options in this section than simply pasting (Figure 3-8).

For more complex pasting, check out the Paste Special option.

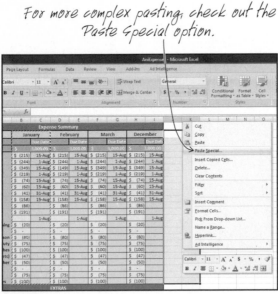

Figure 3-8

For those special jobs where you want to paste but need a little bit more hands-on work to make sure the data looks just right, try the following steps:

1. Select the area you want to copy.

2. Use the right mouse button to select the area you want to paste to and rather than clicking with the left mouse button to paste, use the right mouse button to bring up the menu shown in Figure 3-8.

3. From the menu in Figure 3-8 select Paste Special, which brings up another window, shown in Figure 3-9. By default the All option is selected under Paste.

4. In order to just copy the values, select the Values button by clicking on it. You can also find this menu if you click on the down arrow on Paste on the Home tab.

Figure 3-9

Did you know ...

If you want to paste a hyperlink, the web address to a page you want to include in your worksheet, the preceding steps work as well.

Introducing Cut's Best Friends, Undo and Redo

For those of you daredevils who want to use Cut, you will need the Undo and Redo buttons. The Undo and Redo buttons are always on top next to the Office Pearl (Figure 3-10). You can also always use Ctrl+Z to undo and Ctrl+Y to redo. The Undo button is always ready to be used. The Redo button only activates once something has been undone. So once you select the Undo button, at some point the Redo button will be illuminated and ready for use. In some cases your work may have autosaved, a feature of Excel 2007 that saves your work automatically so you don't lose much work if something happens to the file you are working with. If an autosave has executed, you will have to remember on your own what you did, and manually change it back. Those are the breaks.

The always-useful
Office Pearl
strikes again...

Figure 3-10

Have You Saved?

You can undo most things you have done in a worksheet unless you have already saved the workbook, in which case it cannot be undone.

Painting Isn't Just for Fingernails: Meet the Format Painter

The Format Painter button (Figure 3-11) is great if you have a cell or an area you like and you want to apply the same look, feel, color, and so on to other multiple areas in the same worksheet, a different worksheet in the same workbook, or a worksheet in another workbook you have open already. Wouldn't it be great if you saw someone's professionally decorated home and could just click a button and have that same look and feel in your home, instead of having to paint the walls, hang the pictures, and rearrange the furniture yourself? Well, Excel 2007 can't do that for you, but it does let you do the same thing with cell format. If you have one cell that has the right alignment, font size, font color, and style applied, you can make any other cells look just that way with a click of the Format Painter button, rather than having to apply alignment, then apply font size, then apply font color, then apply bold. It's really easy. First, select the cell that has the formatting applied that you want to apply elsewhere. Then click the Format Painter button. Finally, select the cell or cells to which you want to apply that formatting. Voila, it's magic! This does override all formatting from before and overlays the new formatting you are pulling in.

The Format Painter is a great time-saving feature.

Figure 3-11

One last thing before I move on to a new topic. I know many of you ladies prefer the keyboard shortcuts to the mouse clicks, so view Table 3-1 for a list of what will surely become some of your most-used shortcuts.

Table 3-1   Keyboard Shortcuts

Task	Shortcut Key
Cut	Ctrl + X
Copy	Ctrl + C
Paste	Ctrl + P
Format Painter	Click on Brush
Undo	Ctrl + Z
Redo	Ctrl + Y
Switch between programs	Alt + Tab

Inserting and Deleting Rows and Columns

Did you know ...

In most cases, a left mouse click is a selection or a decision, and a right mouse click shows you options that you can choose from. This rule holds true for most programs throughout Windows and Office.

You can do great many things with cells, but you might need to add or delete a few columns, and do the same with rows. You might also need to merge a few columns together to make things look nice and tidy.

So let's start by adding a few rows to the current worksheet because I want to track a few other types of expenses. For example, I need to keep track of how much I've spent on movies in a given month. In order to insert a row, first go to the row you want to insert on top of and right-click on the row number (on the far left side of the Excel 2007 screen). If you want your new row to appear at number 36, you'd right-click on row number 37. Then scroll down and select Insert from the drop-down items (by left-clicking on Insert), shown in Figure 3-12. Once you select the Insert option a row will automatically be added to the top of the row you started with. Note that where you select to insert a row is where Excel 2007 will pick up the formatting and the formulas from. So if the rows prior are formatted a certain color, font style, and size, that is what this row will look like as well. Also, if the rows prior and proceeding are involved in an equation this row will be added as well, unless you manually go to the function and remove it.

If you want to cut and paste an entire row you can do so similarly to inserting a row, with one little extra step. Once you have cut your row and you have selected which row you want to paste this new row in front of, you will have a menu pop up that will ask you if you want to paste your selected cut row in the row you just clicked. If you select Yes, then all the values you cut from the previous row will be pasted into this new row.

In order to delete a row you can follow the same steps as inserting and select the row you want to delete by right-clicking on the row number, and from the drop-down menu select the Delete option. Once you select the Delete option the row is deleted and all the remaining rows will automatically move up one. Keep in mind when you delete that you will not get any reminders or warnings that you are deleting a row. There will be no pop-up to remind you; the row will just be gone.

What if you wanted to work with columns? Well the same thing that applied to rows applies to columns. So in order to add columns to your worksheet you would go about it the same way. Select the column you would like your new column or columns to appear prior to, then right-click to get the menu (Figure 3-13). Keep in mind your inserted columns will look like your current columns (as far as format and colors). Once you click Insert you will then have the new column or columns based on how many you selected initially appear before the column you selected.

Use this option to add rows.

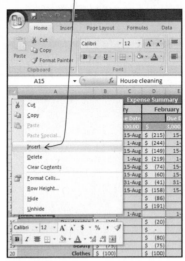

Figure 3-12

This menu pops up when you right-click the column; choose Delete, not Insert.

Figure 3-13

Location Is Everything

This is important: inserted rows and columns will appear prior to the row or column you have selected, so be mindful of which column you are selecting.

If at any point you want to delete an entire column, just select the column you want to delete by right-clicking on the top of the column (on the column letter) and a menu will pop up (Figure 3-13) from which you can select Delete (it appears under Insert) to delete the column. This will take effect immediately and the column will disappear.

You can also delete a full column by selecting a cell and then right-clicking and selecting the Delete option. You will get a pop-up menu such as in Figure 3-14, from which you can click on the radio button that has delete "Entire column," which deletes the entire column the cell you selected resides in.

Figure 3-14

Formatting Cells

You can also define the way text appears in a cell. Perhaps you want the text that is in the cell to wrap instead of continue outside the cell boundary, or you want to have the text display horizontally. Here is a list of some of the many things you can do with the formatting menu:

- Select what types of numbers you want to display, whether scientific with decimal points, $ values, date and time, fractions, and so on

- Align words or data (method covered shortly)

- Wrap the text in the cell, so that all the text will wrap onto a new line within the cell

- Choose the type and style of font

- Select a border style for the cell; choose between dotted or solid lines, pick their thickness, and select which sides of the cell they border

- Look at colors or patterns with which you can fill the cells

- Protect the cell so that no one except you can change the value

- Hide text so you can't see the data inside

Two Places to Change It

You'll notice most of the options in the Format Cells window are also on the Number group on the Home tab on the top of Excel 2007, shown in Figure 3-16. This is done on purpose. After running a very lengthy study of how most people use Microsoft Office (Microsoft Excel is a part of Microsoft Office), Microsoft and the Office team found that most people use a very minimal set of all the features Excel offers. This is because most of the functions and features were too hard to find.

There is an easy way to align data. On any cell you can right-click to get the menu in Figure 3-15 and choose the Format Cells option, which brings up the window shown in Figure 3-16. In the window you can then select various format options, such as font and numerical alignment. Remember this will only apply to the selected cells.

Right-click on any cell to get this menu, then choose whichever tab you need.

Figure 3-15

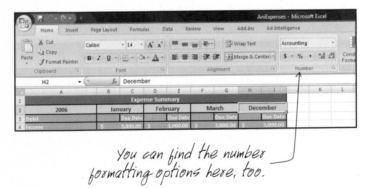

You can find the number formatting options here, too.

Figure 3-16

When you bring up the Format Cells window for the first time, by default you will be on the Number tab (Figure 3-15). If you or others have used this window before, however, then you will see the tab that was last used. From here you will want to click on the Alignment tab and begin work on the way your text looks in the cell. You will also be able to make changes to the font of your selected text, how the borders look in the Borders tab, if you want to fill the cell you have selected with certain colors, and finally, protection, which we will talk about later (see Chapter 16 for further detail), but this is a great place to hide a cell or lock it so no one else can make changes to it. But as you will see on the Protection box, it tells you that locking cells really doesn't do much until you use the worksheet protection options. Also, keep in mind that most of these options are on top of the Home tab. This is why Excel 2007 is superior to the versions before and worth the money, ladies; it's much easier to use. Easier to use means you get more done. Keep in mind that if you have data in a cell you are afraid you might overwrite, you will want to lock it by using the Protection tab in the Format Cells window. This window will come up as a drop-down window when you right-click on a cell. This locks the cell so you cannot make changes to it. If at any time you want to change the cell, you will have to go back to the Format Cells window and unlock it.

If you have used Microsoft Excel in the past, or want more options to format the data in the cell, you can right-click on the cell and click on the Format option to bring up the pop-up window in Figure 3-17, which will enable you to set other formats.

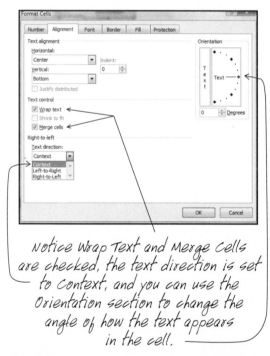

Notice Wrap Text and Merge Cells are checked, the text direction is set to Context, and you can use the Orientation section to change the angle of how the text appears in the cell.

Figure 3-17

Once you select the Alignment tab (Figure 3-17), you will have more options to change how the text in the cell you have selected looks (Figure 3-18). The sections are Text Alignment, Text Control, Right-to-left, and Orientation. The Text Alignment section will enable you to change the alignment of the text you put in the box, which are top left, top right, center, and so on from both vertical and horizontal sections, and you can indent (Figure 3-20).

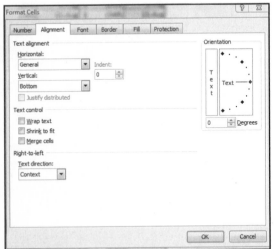

The Orientation section can help your text appear on an angle inside the cell.

Figure 3-18

In Text Control you can choose to have text wrap in the cell, which means the height of the cell enlarges to fit all the text you insert into the cell based on the existing width. In Text Control you can also select Shrink to Fit, which shrinks any text you put into the cell to fit into the size of the cell you already have. And finally, you can merge cells to fit one word or sentence across many cells. You can also merge cells using the Merge shortcut on the Alignment section of the Microsoft Office Ribbon on the Home tab (Figure 3-19).

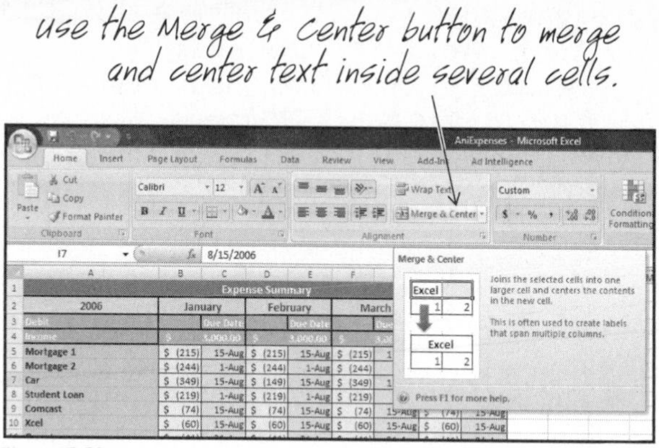

use the Merge & Center button to merge and center text inside several cells.

Figure 3-19

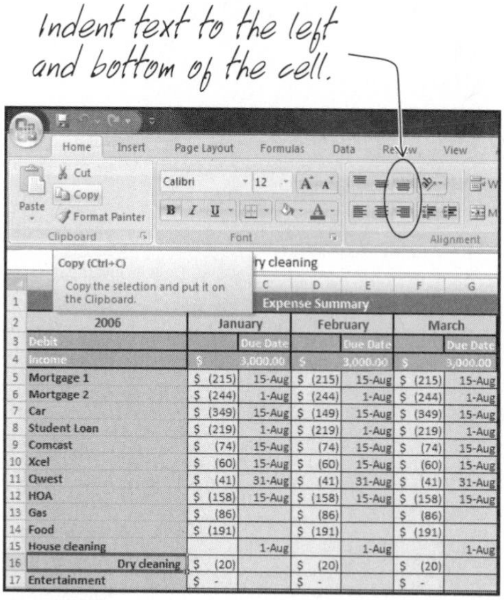

Indent text to the left and bottom of the cell.

Figure 3-20

The Right-to-Left section helps you set the text alignment from right to left or left to right or just center. And finally, the Orientation section helps you set the orientation of the text in your cell. If you want to do something creative with your text you can make each letter show up above each other and rotate to read on the side, or other options as shown in the Orientation box in Figure 3-18. The results can be pretty spectacular and will give your worksheet the Diva feel, as shown in Figure 3-21.

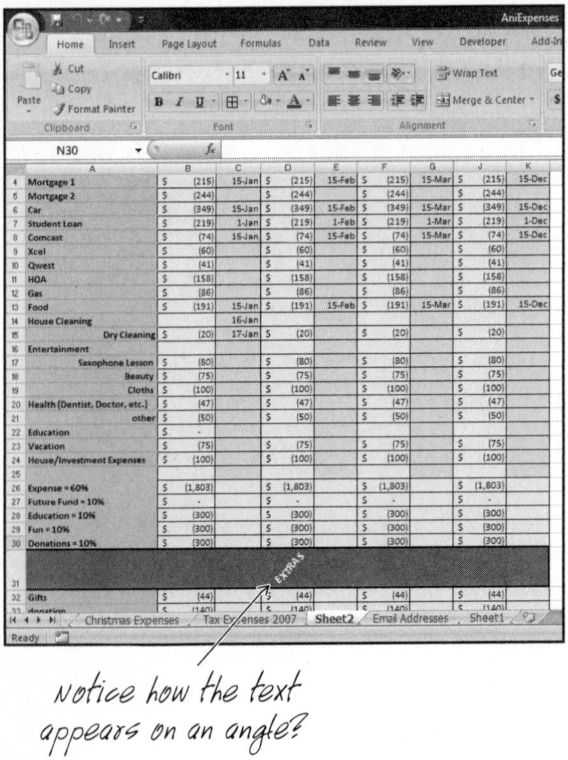

Notice how the text appears on an angle?

Figure 3-21

You have now seen a few examples of how much you can do by just staying on the same home screen and using the Ribbon. The Ribbon becomes your first place to go for anything you are trying to do. For those who have always used the menus, they still work, but it takes a longer time to find them.

Relax, Refresh, Reward

We end up doing so much in the 24 hours of a day that we sometimes forget to enjoy the little things about life that are free. I find when I am working on a project that is consuming my time and energy that there is nothing more fun than walking outside or sitting in an area where I can see outside. It seems like there is a certain level of energy every place has. For this chapter's self-reward, I want you to find somewhere that has an energy you like, and go there. For five minutes, just absorb the energy while you rest, people watch, or enjoy the view.

Recently I moved from Denver, where I'd lived for the past 18 years, to "Rainy Seattle." Seattle may seem like just another city, but to me it's amazing. I have been coming here since August of 2005, my first day with Microsoft. I arrived in Seattle at night and got to my hotel, slept, and woke up to a beautiful view of Puget Sound. I did my morning yoga, got ready, and walked to the Washington Convention Center where I met my manager. This was a 10-block walk, but I loved every minute of it. I drove with my manager over the 520 bridge to Redmond Campus to pick up my employee badge. This was one of the most magical moments of my life. To me Seattle is a great city because of its amazing energy. I love watching the people rushing to work, grabbing their morning paper and coffee as I walk by.

Currently I am staying in a temporary place while I find my new home. I am in the heart of downtown Seattle near the water, similar to where I was on my first day in Seattle. Just as I am typing this book now I am looking at the beautiful view of Puget Sound and at times when I need a break, I take a quick look outside or walk downstairs to sit at Tully's coffee shop and watch the people. This is the best way for me to reenergize.

Whatever vista it is that makes you happy, find it and absorb it, whether it's people watching, or looking at trees or flowers and daydreaming. These are actually the best times for your body and your brain. Your breathing slows down and goes to the level it should. In doing so, it gives your mind some time to wander out of the everyday box it is in. These are the times we can come up with the best ideas, because we are just relaxing and enjoying what we have for free.

II) Live IT!

"I could not, at any age, be content to take my place by the fireside and simply look on. Life was meant to be lived. Curiosity must be kept alive. One must never, for whatever reason, turn her back on life."

– Eleanor Roosevelt

Worksheet Presentation:

To Do List

Enter data into the worksheet

Stretch the cells to fit

Rearrange the worksheets for clarity

Rename the worksheets

Freeze that pane!

Choose a hero

Data Meets Intuition and Utility

You have probably heard people say, "You have a woman's intuition." (If not to you, then to someone else.) I think it's because many women are able to look past what someone is saying and read the body language that goes with the words that come out of a person's mouth. I think by nature we are social creatures, and part of that is being able to quickly realize what another person is feeling or acting out. Many women carry the same thing into their families and work. We are able to quickly see what our coworkers are feeling and if we are speaking in front of an audience we are able to recognize if we are on par, or have just lost the audience. Well, we need to apply the same sense to our worksheets. After all, when you create worksheets it is for other people (and often for your boss). So why not put this "intuitive" sense to use? This chapter will teach you all about applying intuition in the following ways: What type of data should be included, how the data should look, what colors would help emphasize the right data, and what type of title makes sense. Also, how to organize the data in the right order and make it accessible to everyone who needs to read it. You'll learn about stretching your cells to fit the data, you'll learn about moving your worksheets around, and you'll learn to freeze panes so you don't go crazy scrolling back and forth to remember what column you're reading.

Appreciate Your Selection

Choosing the right data, and choosing the right structure of rows and columns for your data helps you get the best results from your spreadsheet in Excel 2007. Getting your worksheet just right is like having the proof to make a case for your intuition. Well, with Excel 2007 worksheets you can pull the data you have together to perhaps be able to make the case for your intuition. There are so many ways to accomplish the same thing in Excel 2007. Therefore, it's up to you; if you find a way that works best for you, just stick to it. Before you are able to work with a cell you must select it. Once you do select it, the cell is now ready for your input. What you type in the cell also shows up on top of the page in an area called the *formula bar,* located right under the Office 2007 Ribbon on top of your Excel 2007 page. Even though you can select many cells at the same time, when you start typing only the active cell receives the data inside—just like you can have a lot of shoes in your closet but you can only wear one pair at a time. Typically the active cell is the first cell where the selection began. Sometimes when you're getting dressed it feels like you try out all the shoes only to come back to the pair you started with. In this case no matter which cells you highlight, you can only type into one cell at a time.

You Can Have it All

You can also select all cells in a worksheet by clicking on the Select All box located in the upper-left corner of your worksheet, or hold down the Ctrl key and press the letter A key.

Waltz the Regions

You already know how to work through a worksheet and scroll up and down the page. Excel 2007 offers a lot of ways to get around, including some really cool tricky ways.

If you work with large tables or lots of data you will appreciate this. I love the mouse because it makes my life easier and there's the added bonus of not chipping my nail polish. So let's get started. When you look at an Excel 2007 worksheet you *see* a sheet with a bunch of rectangles on it. The rectangles are called cells. If you take the mouse pointer (in most cases this is an arrow, unless someone has changed it on your computer's operating system) and slowly go to the bottom-right edge of the active cell, the pointer changes from a *big fat white* plus sign to a *small skinny black* plus sign. By hovering over any cell you will have the big fat white plus sign and by double-clicking it, you will be able to edit the contents of the cell. You can always select the cell by clicking once on it and going up to the formula bar under the Ribbon to input the contents as well.

You can also do the same with the keyboard. By using the up and down arrows you can go to the desired cell and begin typing. Also, the Home key will take you to cell A1 and the Page Down and Page Up keys will help you go 30 rows down or up. Ctrl + right arrow pressed at the same time will help you move right of the active cell, to the next cell with information inside. If there are only blank cells next to the cell that is active, Ctrl + right arrow will take you to the last possible cell in that row, which is Column XFD. The opposite will happen if you press Ctrl + left arrow.

Magic 30

Remember, a page in Excel is 30 rows.

Filling the Cells

Excel is very simple when it comes to accepting data. You can only enter two types of information: numeric and characters. So you can put names and sentences or numbers. The names and sentences can be different types like dates, time, letters and words, and numerals. Data that Excel does not accept are special characters (like a dollar sign, for instance). So to type things in a cell just select it and start typing. As you type in the cell you will see that what you type also appears in the formula bar under the Office 2007 Ribbon. After you are done typing in the cell you have to lock what you typed into the cell. You can do that by pressing the Enter key. What I mean by lock here is to complete the entering process. As you type data into the cell it only exists in the formula bar or in the cell temporarily until you press the Enter key. Once you press the Enter key the data is not considered locked into that cell until you come back later and overwrite it or change it. Also, another important thing to notice is, when you do hit the Enter key the active cell changes, which means you can begin typing in the next cell over from the cell in which you were typing before.

Did you know ...

There is more than one way to lock data into a cell. Some options are: the Enter key, down arrow key, up arrow key, the Tab key, and the Shift + Tab key combination. Basically, any time you move the cursor to another cell, the data in the cell you were typing into gets locked.

If you press the Tab key by mistake you will just start moving from one cell to another in the right direction (that is, moving to the right). The nice part is that whatever you typed in the cell before hitting Tab is not lost. If you press the Tab key you will skip to the cell to the right and if you hold down the Shift key and press the Tab key you will skip one cell to the left. What if you press the arrow keys as you are typing? That is okay too; anything you typed in the box will still be there and you will either go left, right, up, or down by one cell based on which arrow key you hit.

Three buttons (Cancel, Enter, and Insert Function) appear on top of the screen under the Office 2007 Ribbon (Figure 4-1) when you start typing in a cell. To enter a title or a name, just begin typing. For numbers you can just type the number. If you want the numbers to line up with your word text, you can put a single quote like ' in front of your number value in the cell. This tells Excel 2007 to treat this number like a word or as text.

If you want to type different types of numbers like percent, dates, times, or dollar amounts, you can use the fourth box from the left of the Office 2007 Ribbon on the Home tab titled "Number" (Figure 4-2).

These three buttons, which appear on the bottom of the Font box, let you delete, cancel, or enter a function.

Figure 4-1

$ is not a dollar ...

In Excel 2007 when you type $1 into a cell, Excel sees that as text rather than the value of $1.00. If you want Excel to regard your $1 as a value of a dollar, then use the Number part of the Home tab and click on the $ sign, which will change the way the number appears in the cell and add a decimal point and two 0's (that is, .00) at the end.

The drop-down box, which shows you the most commonly used formats.

Click here for more formats if what you need cannot be found in the other list.

Figure 4-2

Making the Information Fit

What if you type numbers or text that is too long to be in the cell and runs into another cell? Then you need to change the shape of the cell to fit your input. The cells are like stretch pants. When I have that pesky extra water weight I love stretch pants because they stretch with me; well, so do the cells when they need to hold more data. After you type what you want and hit Enter go back over the same cell, click once on it, then right-click to get the Format Cells menu (Figure 4-3), which helps with formatting cells to fit the data you have. Or you can also use the second box from the right called Cells on the Home tab in Office 2007 Ribbon Control in Excel 2007.

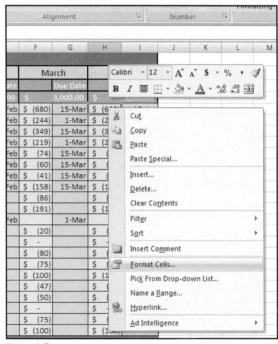

Figure 4-3

To format the full columns for rows you can right-click on the column letter (Figure 4-4) or the row number (Figure 4-5) to bring up the same format box as you saw in Figure 4-3. You'll also notice the full column and row being highlighted when you do this. That is because any changes you make will take effect for the full column or row.

Notice the full column is highlighted when you do this. That is because any changes you make will take effect for the full column or row.

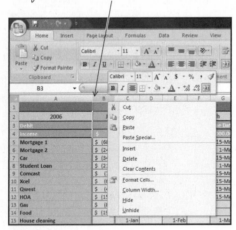

Figure 4-4

What you'll notice immediately is that you have more options on the cell formatting than the column or row formatting. This is because what you change about the cell is only for that cell, rather than causing changes to columns or rows.

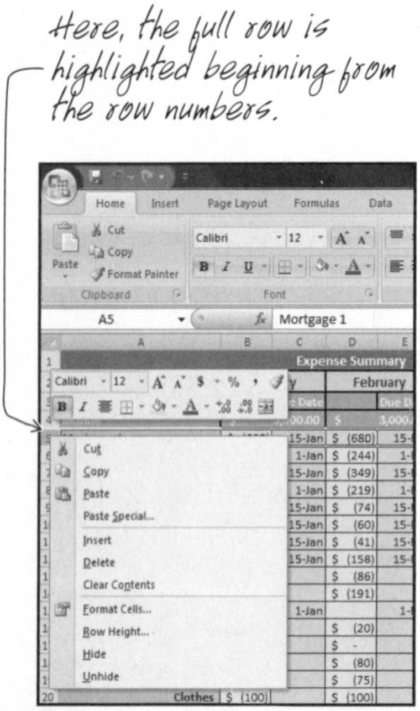

Here, the full row is highlighted beginning from the row numbers.

Figure 4-5

By fitting the cells to what you need, you can make your worksheet look and act how it should, intuitively. To give you a few words so you sound like an Excel 2007 Diva, remember that the values you type are called the *underlying values* and the values you see are the *displayed values*. Once you're done typing the underlying value you are ready to work with how the displayed value looks. Sometimes stretching the box up or down is just not enough and you want the text to wrap and fit. Well the formatting features are very helpful, so you can shrink your font size or choose a smaller font style. You can also merge cells, but in most

Fraction Fun

Here's a little Excel formatting trick. In most cases what you type and what appears in the cell are the same, but sometimes Excel is too smart and will change your values for you, even though you might not want it to. So if you are entering built fractions, start by typing zero followed by a space then the fraction and you will be fine. Otherwise Excel will show you the decimal value. So if you wanted to type 1/4 (one-fourth) in a cell, you would type it as follows: 0 1/4.

cases data in columns needs to fit the size of the columns and the data in rows at times needs to span over several columns. Once the menu comes up by right-clicking on the cell, you can choose the Format Cells option from the drop-down menu shown in Figure 4-3 to bring up the Format Cells window to format the cell to your liking (Figure 4-6). Once the Format Cells menu comes up, by default it will take you to the Number tab.

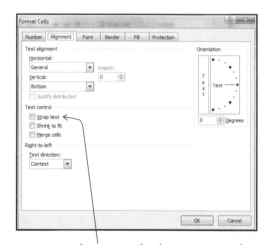

Click on the Wrap text check box to make your data in the worksheet appear on more than one line. Keep in mind sometimes you might have to adjust the cell size manually, by grabbing and dragging the cell bottom or sides.

Figure 4-6

By selecting the Alignment tab on the Format Cell's window, you bring forward the Alignment tab window. This is where you can select the text wrapping option shown in Figure 4-6, which wraps your text inside a cell as shown in Figure 4-7.

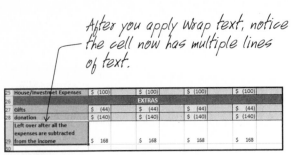

After you apply Wrap text, notice the cell now has multiple lines of text.

Figure 4-7

What if you want to add a title to the worksheet on top of the sheet and make sure it spans across all the columns? That is when the Merge Cells feature is very handy. You can find the Merge Cells Alignment box in the third box from the left on the Home tab on the Office 2007 Ribbon. First you select a cell and type what you want the title to be. In this case I typed Expense Summary.

Next select the cells you want the title to span across by left-clicking and dragging to select all the cells. (In Figure 4-8, you can see the cells highlighted in Row 1 will be merged together when the Merge & Center button is clicked.) Then go up to the Alignment box and click the Merge & Center button (Figure 4-8) to merge all cells together in one large cell. Once you click on the down arrow button next to the Merge & Center option in the Alignment section of the Home tab you will see a set of options as shown in Figure 4-9.

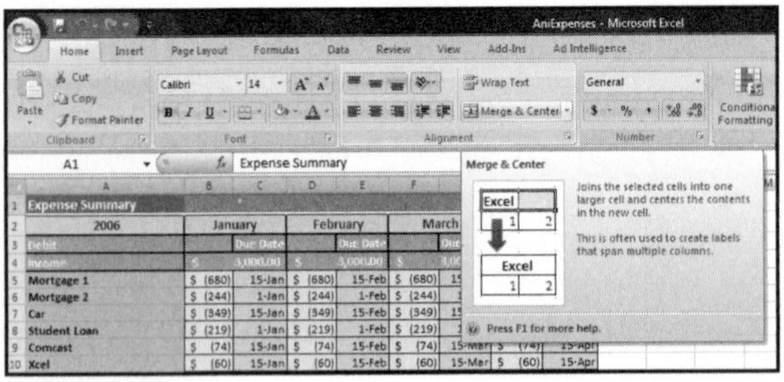

Figure 4-8

Figure 4-9

You can choose how you want to merge these cells (Figure 4-9). You can:

- *Merge & Center,* which is the most common task (Figure 4-10). You can merge the cells you select and center the content (the text) of the cell among the cells (that is, rows or columns).

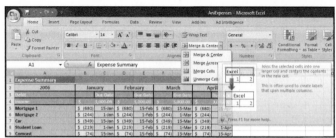

Figure 4-10

- *Merge Across,* so then you can merge the cells and place the content to the left across several cells (Figure 4-11) (that is, rows or columns).

Once you are done using the Merge Across, your cell will look like this one (as shown by the arrow to the left of where your current two cells are).

Figure 4-11

- *Merge Cells,* so you can take several cells and merge them into one, keeping the top leftmost text or data. Before this happens a warning will pop up asking you if that is what you want to do (Figure 4-12). Once you click OK, all cells selected from Figure 4-12 will collapse into one cell with the farthest left cell remaining and all others disappearing (Figure 4-13).

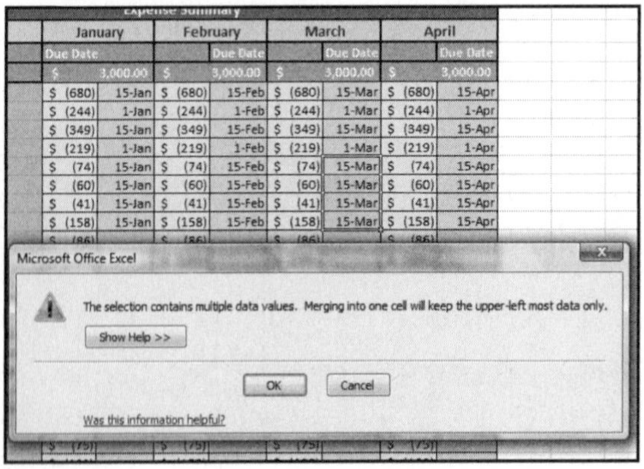

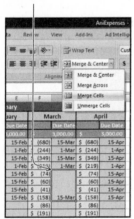

Figure 4-12

The merged cells have kept the top leftmost value and merged below it.

Figure 4-13

- *Unmerge Cells*, which will enable the cells to look like they were before they were merged in any way using the preceding options. However, if you had done any formatting of the text inside the cells or placed borders around the data you will have to redo that manually again. Figure 4-14 shows the cells that were merged in Figure 4-13 unmerged, and as you can see all the formatting that was done before is gone; the other dates are not there and the borders are gone. I will have to retype everything manually or use Ctrl+Z to undo changes (if they can be undone, that is; remember if autosave has executed or you have manually saved, undo will not work).

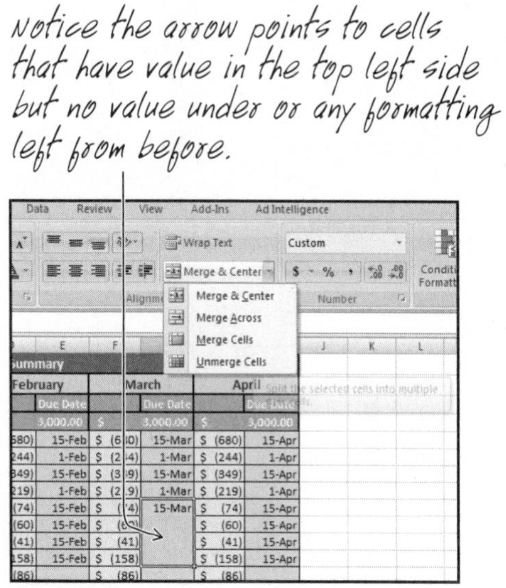

Notice the arrow points to cells that have value in the top left side but no value under or any formatting left from before.

Figure 4-14

Getting Symbolic: Entering Symbols in Your Worksheet

For some of you who need to enter symbols into your worksheet, Excel 2007 has made it very easy for you to get your work done and make it look exactly how you want it to look. Go to the Insert tab on the Office 2007 Ribbon (that's the second tab from the left, right after Home) and you can go to the Symbol icon all the way to the right. It looks like a Greek letter (Figure 4-15). Once you click the button, a Symbol box comes up with the list of all symbols installed and ready for your use (Figure 4-16). From the Font drop-down inside the Symbol window (which has just come up), you can select the font of the symbol and get to the symbol you need to get your worksheet just right. The Symbol window also contains a Special Characters tab, which lets you pick the symbols that are most commonly used, such as the non-breaking hyphen, Copyright (©), and more. In Figure 4-16 you will see two tabs: one for Symbols and the next for Special Characters.

Here's where you find the Symbol button on the Insert tab.

Figure 4-15

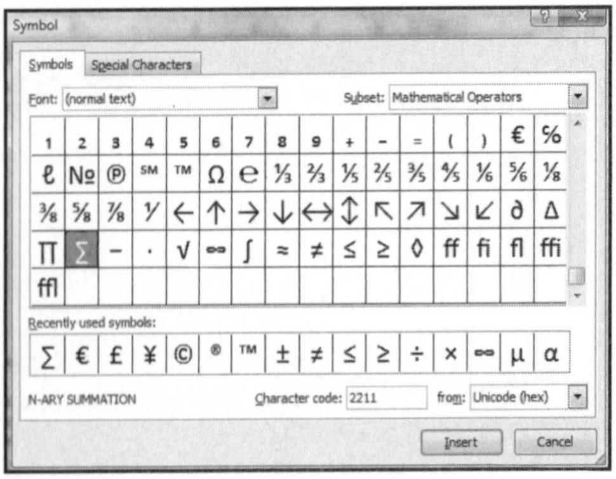

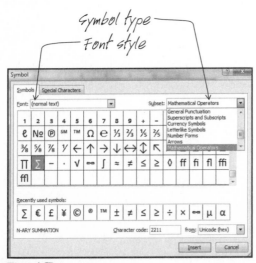

Figure 4-16

On the Symbols tab you can change the type of characters you see and the font you use as shown in Figure 4-17. However, by default you will only see the math symbols with (normal text) selected in the Font drop-down box (Figure 4-17). If you are looking for Copyright (©), Registered (®), and Trademark (™) symbols, you will find them on the Special Characters tab shown in Figure 4-18.

Symbol type
Font style

Figure 4-17

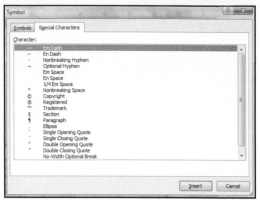

Figure 4-18

So You're Not Perfect: Editing Your Input

You're typing along and making a beautiful worksheet and your boss walks over and says, "You know after talking with you and thinking about what you had to say, I think you are right: Let's do the worksheet your way." I know for most of you this doesn't happen; it's more like your boss comes over and says: "You know after thinking about what you said, I have an idea!" then repeats exactly what you told her just a few minutes ago. But that's what the day at the spa is for, to forget all those silly things bosses say. After all, we all love our bosses because they make the days at the spa possible. Then you still need to make a change to your data so where do you start? It's easy, just go back to the cell that you need to make the change to and this time rather than just typing, you can double-click and you will end up inside the cell where you can make edits to what you have previously typed.

You can also click in the formula bar under the Office 2007 Ribbon after selecting that cell and you will now have access to make edits to your previous input.

Now that you've activated the correct cell, you want to change what's inside it. If you want to edit several characters at the same time you can use the mouse to highlight the characters and begin typing. If you ever need to erase what is inside a cell, just go to the cell and hit the Delete key. There is no need to highlight the contents, just press Delete.

Since we are on this topic let's talk more about Undo (Ctrl+Z) and Redo (Ctrl+Y). In case you do delete something by accident and want to go back, use Ctrl+Z (Figure 4-19). You can go as far back as re-creating how the document looked when you first opened it. And if you ever happen to go too far back, or you just change your mind and want to bring something back that you have done, you can use Ctrl+Y to redo (Figure 4-20).

Figure 4-19

The Great Escape

Another great shortcut to impress people is going to the cell that you want to delete and hitting the Backspace key. Hitting the Backspace key deletes the contents of the cell, but the real attention grabber is when someone watches you bring back the contents by hitting the Esc key.

Notice that redo tells you exactly what will be redone.

Figure 4-20

Worksheets Are Like Purses

I have a friend who has hundreds of pairs of shoes and a purse to match each pair. She would hold parties every time she bought another 20 pairs. I've known her since high school. She's in medical school now and the shoe buying parties are still happening; I hear she has over 500 pairs, and as the shoes multiply so do the purses. I have several, but I tend to buy multi-color purses, so they will match a lot of the shoes I have. I don't know if there is a fashion law either of us are breaking, but I think the way we go about our purses is how people go about worksheets. Sometimes you might think it's best to have many worksheets, other times you might want to have only a few multi-purpose worksheets. Keep in mind, it's all based on how you think and what makes the most sense to you. I don't love shoes all that much and I think a few purses fit the need, but my friend always has amazing shoes that perfectly coordinate with everything she wears. Both of us look great—we just have different styles. Now it's time for you to find your own worksheet style and begin by experimenting.

Inserting and Deleting Worksheets

When you begin adding worksheets it is just like adding little purses inside of the big purse. We love that. Think about it, they all have their uses right? The makeup purse has to go into our purse, otherwise it would be hard to find our makeup and we would risk damaging our purse. As you know, the more purses and items you add into a purse, the more you have to move everything around when you are looking for your keys. Well, the same is true with Excel 2007. You don't have to look for your keys inside Excel 2007 but you do have to look for the worksheets, so just keep in mind the more you add in a workbook, the more you have to scroll over and back to see them. If that is okay with you, then keep adding. I like to keep only 6 to 8 worksheets in a workbook and if I need more, then I start a new Excel workbook and rename my file as part 2. Each workbook begins with three worksheets. You can change their names and you can add more worksheets as you deem necessary. If you are going to add and remove worksheets as you work, there is a great little secret that makes it really easy.

As I mentioned, each workbook starts with three worksheets titled Sheet1, Sheet2, and Sheet3, as well as an icon that stands for Insert Worksheet (Figure 4-21). So if you were to add a worksheet you would see the next one as Sheet4, Sheet5, and so on. However, if you were to remove Sheet3 and then add a new worksheet, you would still see Sheet6. So Excel doesn't keep track of the last sheet deleted and add that sheet number back in, it just keeps moving forward in sheet numbers.

Once you have added another worksheet, what if you want to move the worksheets around or rename them? Microsoft Excel 2007 makes it really easy. You can right-click on any worksheet at the bottom (Figure 4-21) and rename the worksheet, or delete it completely.

If at any point you feel the order of your worksheets has been lost because you added another sheet, just left-click and hold the left mouse button down on the sheet name and drag it between the sheets where you want to place it as seen in Figure 4-22. You will see a little white rectangular sheet pop up with a black arrow, and then you can begin moving the sheet. You can only see the little black arrow in my figure, because when I take screen captures the white little sheet goes away. Keep in mind that you can only move the worksheet order in this workbook. You cannot drag this worksheet into a new or another Excel workbook.

Juicy Morsel

To add a new worksheet without accessing any menus or clicking on any icons, just hold down the Shift key and press F11. A new worksheet is added by the name of "Sheet" followed by the next number to the left side of the sheet tab you are on to your current workbook. You can see if you look to the bottom left of your screen.

24	Vacation	$ (79)	$ (79)	$ (79)	$ (79)
25	House/Investmet Expenses	$ (100)	$ (100)	$ (100)	$ (100)
26			EXTRAS		
27	Gifts	$ (44)	$ (44)	$ (44)	$ (44)

2006 / 2007 / 2008 / Sheet3 / Sheet1 / **Sheet2**

Ready — Insert Worksheet (Shift+F11)

Figure 4-21

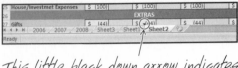

This little black down arrow indicates that Excel will now allow you to move that worksheet.

Figure 4-22

You can select all and copy to move and paste into another worksheet or into other Microsoft documents. In order to do this, go to the worksheet you want to copy from, press Ctrl+A to select all, then press Ctrl+C to copy. Then go to the new worksheet and click anywhere in the new worksheet and press Ctrl+V.

For those of you who prefer to use the menu to rearrange your worksheets within a workbook, here's how:

1. Right-click on the sheet you want to move and a menu similar to that in Figure 4-23 appears.

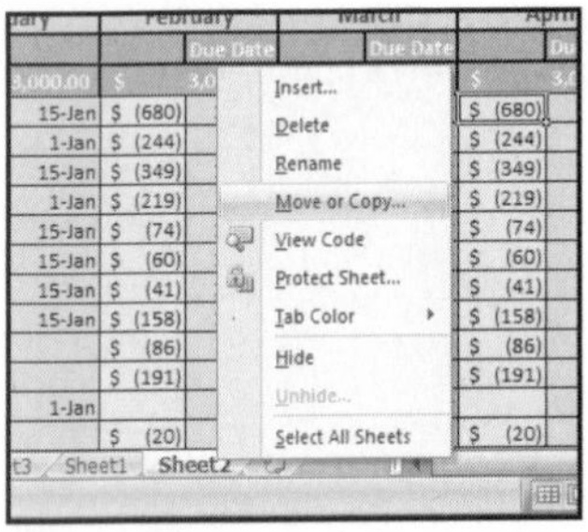

Figure 4-23

2. From the menu in Figure 4-23, select the Move and Copy option, which opens a window much like what you see in Figure 4-24.

A new workbook you can move your worksheet to...

...allows you to select which worksheet you want to put your worksheet in front of.

Figure 4-24

3. From the window shown in Figure 4-24 you can create a copy of this specific sheet you have, or move this sheet to another workbook as shown by the top arrow. You can also move the worksheet before all the other sheets in the workbook by selecting which worksheet to put your worksheet in front of, as shown by the second arrow in Figure 4-24.

Finally, my favorite for all of us who love color—you can select a tab color. The tab color gives your worksheet a sleek new look and enables you to find what you are looking for quickly. It's like color-coordinating our closet contents. It's a little strange to wear tulip pink blouses in the middle of fall or winter, but we know a nice tulip pink would be great for the spring. The same goes for our worksheets. You can color-coordinate them so you know exactly what you are matching them up to. I tend to pick the nicer brighter colors for people I like, or topics I like (like shopping and Christmas presents), and I pick the yuckier colors for taxes. Of course, it's up to your taste.

Rename Your Worksheets

So once you color-coordinate and pretty up your worksheet, you also have to pretty up the tab, it doesn't make sense to leave it as Sheet1 does it? It would be like getting a pedicure and leaving your hands looking like you just got done gardening; that would be dreadful. It's really easy to give your worksheet a nifty name (Figure 4-25) and really come across as the Excel 2007 Diva you are.

Renaming your worksheet is very simple:

1. Double-click on the worksheet name (it might look like Sheet1, Sheet2, and so on). A black highlight will appear on the sheet name, indicating you have selected the sheet name.

2. Begin typing the new name. Done!

3. For those of you who like using menus, you can also right-click on the sheet name you want to rename and a menu from which you can pick the Rename option appears (this is the same menu as that shown in Figure 4-23). Once you select the Rename option the name of the sheet will be highlighted in black much like you see in Figure 4-25 and you can begin typing the new name for your worksheet.

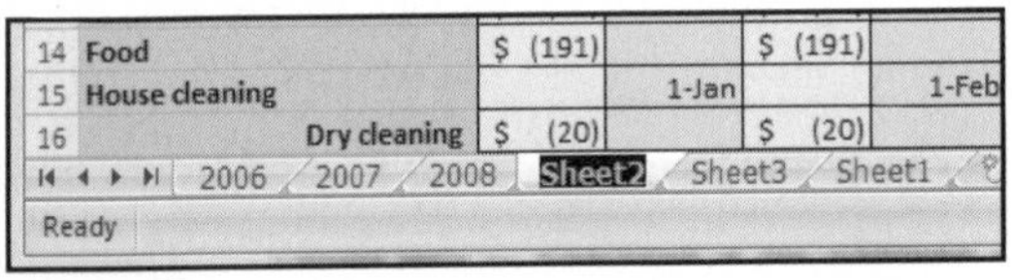

14	Food		$ (191)		$ (191)	
15	House cleaning			1-Jan		1-Feb
16		Dry cleaning	$ (20)		$ (20)	

⏮ ◀ ▶ ⏭ 2006 / 2007 / 2008 / **Sheet2** / Sheet3 / Sheet1 /

Ready

Figure 4-25

Some of you paying attention may have noticed I have covered something similar to Figure 4-25 in Chapter 2; however knowing how I would use a book as a reference I wanted to give you the option of having the information right here where you might also need it.

Copy and Move Your Worksheets

What if you wanted to create a copy of your masterpieces once you're done to make yet another masterpiece? A great example of this would be to keep a monthly expense budget (therefore you would have 12 worksheets in one workbook named after each month), or if you are working on monthly or weekly reports at work, inside which the same type of data or text appears, except each month is a little different in the values that are reported.

Well you know the shortcut from the Office 2007 Ribbon on the Home tab, but there is yet another quick way to create a copy. Follow these steps to do it yourself:

1. Just right-click on the worksheet name area such as in Figure 4-23.

2. Select the Move or Copy option as highlighted in Figure 4-23. Once you select the option a window will come up much like Figure 4-24, in which you can check the Create a Copy option as shown in Figure 4-26.

Figure 4-26

3. From the window you can select the check box to Create a Copy of your worksheet. Notice that once you create the copy the same worksheet is created with the same name; it is put in front of all worksheets (on the farthest left side) and a number, such as (2), comes up in front of it (Figure 4-27).

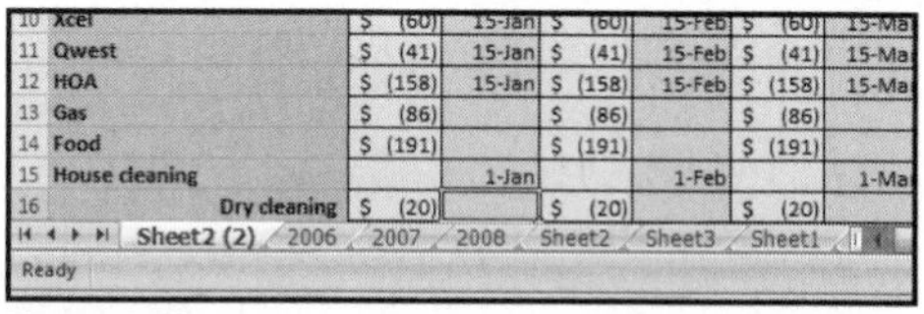

10	Xcel		$ (60)	15-Jan	$ (60)	15-Feb	$ (60)	15-Ma
11	Qwest		$ (41)	15-Jan	$ (41)	15-Feb	$ (41)	15-Ma
12	HOA		$ (158)	15-Jan	$ (158)	15-Feb	$ (158)	15-Ma
13	Gas		$ (86)		$ (86)		$ (86)	
14	Food		$ (191)		$ (191)		$ (191)	
15	House cleaning			1-Jan		1-Feb		1-Ma
16		Dry cleaning	$ (20)		$ (20)		$ (20)	

Sheet2 (2) / 2006 / 2007 / 2008 / Sheet2 / Sheet3 / Sheet1
Ready

Figure 4-27

I don't like the number appearing in front of my worksheet because every worksheet I create is a masterpiece. And I like to organize it properly and give it its own tab color. It's completely okay to reuse work; just change the outlook so it seems personalized. Plus it makes it feel as if the worksheet you created for this new person was a work of art and not just a copy and paste job. I know then you wonder, but what if I can just copy and get it over with? Well that's fine; you can take the afternoon and get your manicure, but don't just make it *look* as if you copied work.

It's All In How You Look At It: Worksheet Presentation

The day before you got a facial and gave yourself the 24 hours to heal. You spent all morning doing your hair; you got your mani and pedi done. Above all you picked out the most perfect dress. You are in all sense of the word PERFECT for that date. Then the doorbell rings and your date shows up dressed in jeans and a t-shirt. You think to yourself: "WHAT THE HECK?" Did someone forget to forward me the "Don't care, be casual and look like a cheapskate" email? I mean your jaw nearly hits the floor when you see this person looking at you as if they have seen an angel and you look at them as if you have seen the garbage man. I mean the nerve to come over in jeans and a t-shirt, without the courtesy to even let you know so you wouldn't go through that much pain and trouble to look your best. I mean what garbage truck did they fall off of?

You might not have had that experience. But that is exactly what could happen to you, if you spend all that time creating the perfect worksheet, then you display it in basic Excel 2007. It's all about presentation, and ladies we are good at that!

We've been serving tea at our tea parties since we received our first tea set. And now we create amazing tables of food for the holidays and decorate our homes. We know all about presentation. After all, if we didn't we would show up for a date looking like we fell off that garbage truck!

A previous chapter covered some of the ways to style up your workbook, and future chapters will take you further down that road (Chapter 7). Here, we're going to focus on making the data accessible, particularly with a large worksheet.

As you create worksheets and add data, your worksheet might grow both horizontally and vertically. How can you present this in a fashion that people can appreciate your work of art? Well there are a number of ways.

Splitting into Panes

What are panes? Think of them as undergarments. No one really sees the undergarments you wear every day; however, they hide certain parts of you and give your dress the smooth feel it needs to look great on you. They don't hide you, but just the certain parts of you that might not be necessary for most people to see. The same is true for worksheets; the panes are there to hide the part of the data or your worksheet that is just not important for you or everyone to see every minute as you work with the worksheet.

Figure 4-28 demonstrates the panes that are ready to be used on the right side of your Excel 2007 worksheet near the scrollbar. By grabbing hold of the areas shown in Figure 4-28 you can drag open the panes so that only a certain part of your data can be seen, while other parts stay stationary and do not change. The most common use of panes is to preserve column heads (and/or row titles, if you have them) when there are more than 30 rows of data. That way, when someone scrolls down to the fiftieth row, they can still see the column head so they know what data they are looking at.

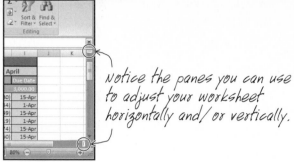

Notice the panes you can use to adjust your worksheet horizontally and/or vertically.

Figure 4-28

These worksheet panes let you see various parts of your worksheet at the same time while keeping other parts stationary. There are two ways to split your worksheet into panes:

1. There are vertical and horizontal Split bars (Figure 4-28) on the worksheet that you can use. By clicking and dragging them you can take them to where you want them to be (Figure 4-29).

2. You can always go back to the handy Office 2007 Ribbon. Go to the View tab. There you will find the Split icon in the Window box, which you can use to create an even split of your worksheet as shown in Figure 4-30.

Figure 4-29

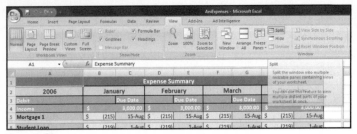

Figure 4-30

3. Once you split the window you now have four scrollbars you can use to show off the masterpiece you created. This way you don't have to worry about scrolling all the way over and losing parts of your row headings or scrolling all the way down and losing your column headings. This is not as good as freezing panes, which is covered next.

Freezing Panes (and Thawing Them Too)

You now know how to split your worksheet and view your great work. But what if you have a lot of data and you want to keep the row and column headings in place while you scroll over and back as well as up and down? You can Freeze Top Row, which is the same as your freezing your column headings. You can Freeze First Column, which is the same as freezing your row headings, or you can Freeze Panes. By utilizing the View tab of the the Office 2007 Ribbon (Figure 4-31) you can freeze what is necessary for the best presentation of your data. This comes in really handy when your boss or a coworker is looking over your shoulder to see what you have worked on, or if you want to show off your Excel 2007 Diva talents to a friend. Keep in mind there are a few other options such as Unfreeze Panes, which only become available after you Freeze Panes.

Figure 4-31

Freeze Panes enables you to keep headings of your worksheet intact while you move the rest of the columns and rows of your worksheet. There are three options (Figure 4-32) when using the Freeze Panes button. You can: Freeze Top Row (useful for preserving column titles as you scroll down), Freeze First Column (useful for preserving the first column from the left which might include row markers as you scroll to the right), and Freeze Panes, which basically allows you to freeze both top rows and left columns as necessary.

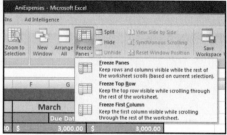

Figure 4-32

Freezing the top row and the first column are pretty self-explanatory. These steps show you how to use the Freeze Panes option:

1. Be sure you're in the worksheet in which you want to freeze panes.

2. Determine how many rows on top and columns to the left you want to freeze. Then, select the cell immediately below and to the right of the row/columns you want frozen.

3. Go to the Office 2007 Ribbon. Select the View tab and go to the Window section.

4. Select the Freeze Panes option from the drop-down menu shown in Figure 4-32. If you were just freezing the top row or first column, you would choose the appropriate option without first selecting a cell. Figure 4-33 demonstrates the frozen panes.

These are the columns that have been frozen.   *These are the top rows that are frozen.*

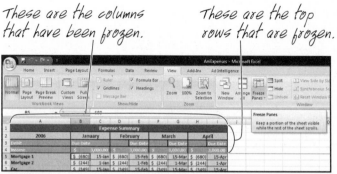

Figure 4-33

Zooming

One of the best features in Microsoft's Excel 2007 is the ability to zoom in and out on a worksheet to view data. If you are working with people who don't like the smaller fonts, this is heaven-sent. There is a new Zoom bar at the bottom-right corner (Figure 4-34) of your worksheet.

Figure 4-34

Some of you might think, well when I installed Excel 2007 and opened it up for the first time I didn't see that Zoom bar. If that is the case it's really easy to add it in. Just right-click on the bottom-right corner and a menu comes up much like Figure 4-35, which has Zoom Slider as the last option, and you can then select to add it by clicking once on the item as shown in Figure 4-35.

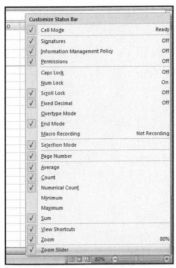

Figure 4-35

Now that you've located (or added) the Zoom bar, here's how to use it. You can either right-click on the slider part and drag the middle arrow to the plus side, which will zoom in and make the contents of the sheet larger, or move it close to the minus sign and make the contents of the sheet smaller. You can also click on the + and – signs to zoom in and out.

Relax, Refresh, Reward

For this chapter's reward, I want you to focus on someone who inspires you; someone you might call your hero. It's very easy to be negative about how things happen in your life and even easier to blame and ask the detrimental question: "Why?" We have a circle of friends who we count on to share our feelings with and we enroll ourselves in various activities. Women tend to spend a lot of time and money on self-help books and psychology. We try the best we can to help ourselves, our loved ones, and others. But there are those special cases where we just don't seem to be able to overcome what is going on in our life.

I, too, have those situations, and I have a hero to help me overcome them. My hero is my Mom. She's had a long journey, involving moving around three continents, taking care of two children, including a developmentally disabled child for 25 years, and surviving a severe depression. Now she has taken the job of a teacher in the public school system and teaches developmentally disabled children in the same high school her disabled son attended. She comes home with ample sad stories of neglected children who have been abused and beaten. She now teaches them to write, read, and play, and shares the many joys of helping these children. She helped me realize life will always be difficult and at times unbearable, so bad that it would be easy to turn to negative things such as alcohol and drugs, but (this is a BIG BUT) it is in the small choices we make every day to see the positive in life: to see the good in life, the happy things, the love. My mother has always, with tears and laughter, been my steady rock. My hero enables me to think out of the box and, no matter what happens, to keep a smile on my face, my goals in front of me, and look for the next challenge to overcome. My hero always says: "We are survivors." Yes English is her fourth language but that doesn't stop her from being great and setting an amazing example. By sharing this I wish to impress upon you to continue with your goals and dreams. Find a hero who, by doing little things every day, makes a great change.

You can find your hero by:

- Identifying people you have always looked up to, admired, or wanted to be like.
- Identifying people you have heard about in movies or history books. Learn more about them on Wikipedia or go to your local library and read more about them.
- Define what exactly it is you liked about them and what made them so great.

Voilà! You have yourself a hero, and you know why you look up to them. When difficult things arise you can always ask yourself how would (fill in the blank with your hero's name) have handled this?

Maybe you already know who you're hero is. If that person is still around, then your task is to make contact: send a letter, give them a call, shoot them a quick email. Let them know how much they mean to you and why.

5

To Do List

Get Excel to do the math for me!

Learn and avoid common errors

Copy and paste to make the most of formulas

Cross reference to get the most of worksheets

Take a stretch break

Using Formulas

When I walk into a shopping mall I want all the stores I need next to each other so I can buy what I came for and walk out. Sometimes I enjoy strolling the mall, but wouldn't it be so much more functional if Nordstrom's, Victoria's Secret, Banana Republic, and Bath & Body Works were all in the same corner of the mall?

Well I see data on a worksheet very much the same way. The scattered data on a worksheet is very much like a mall with all the stores scattered all over.

Your data looks just like that scattered mall on a worksheet, until you apply styles to it (which will be covered in later chapters) and you use formulas to clarify what information the data is supposed to convey. After all, there is nothing attractive about a bunch of numbers on a page floating around without being beautified. By applying formulas and finding what hidden message the numbers hold, you can better share the data and help others understand the data.

Persuading Data with Formulas

Formulas are mathematical equations used to calculate the value of a set of numbers. In Excel 2007, a *formula* is a mathematical equation that is used to calculate a value using your data. Every formula in Excel 2007 begins with an equal sign (=) followed by numbers or text and signs, which are the instructions for the mathematical process you want the program to perform. A *function* is a predefined formula inside Excel 2007. A function also starts with an equal sign (=); however, it is followed by the name of the function, an open parenthesis, the values the function needs to do the work, and then a closed parenthesis (see Chapter 6 for further details on how to use functions).

(What do the parentheses mean?)

Parentheses on a dollar amount signify that a number is negative. That is a common accounting term, which means you are spending money. If you look in the Income section of the spreadsheet (Figure 5-2) you will not see parentheses around the number, whereas the Mortgage 2 amount does have parentheses around it, which means that is an outgoing payment.

So far you have seen the monthly budget you can keep on Excel 2007 as a sample. If you wanted to find out how much you spent on food on average over the four months in the worksheet you would create a formula that adds up the cells that have food expenditures in them, and divide that total by 4. You will learn how to create formulas that will enable you to accomplish more with less time. You will learn more about building formulas in the following sections, starting with "Inserting Formulas into a Worksheet." This will give you the average money spent for food in four months (Figure 5-1).

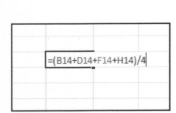

Figure 5-1

Expenses   Income

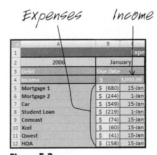

Figure 5-2

All formulas in Excel 2007 begin with an equal (=) sign. That is how Excel understands that whatever comes after the equal sign is a formula. Formulas work in a variety of ways. You can select a cell and begin typing **=200+3**, and once you hit the Enter key you will see that 203 appears in the cell and all other characters are invisible. However, if you return to the cell and double-click or want to edit the cell you will see the formula, not the value calculated by the formula. Therefore you will see something like =200+3, this same formula will show up when you click on the cell once and look at the formula bar.

Cell Referencing

Sometimes you might need to add or subtract the cell values. In that case it would be too hard to type all the values again. Think of when you're people watching in a coffee shop with a girlfriend. You lean over and say, "Look at that guy with that tall girl." Well, you know what you are talking about but they don't—they just see the calm smiling faces you and your girlfriend put on as they walk by. It's the same thing with cell referencing. When you put formulas to use by cell reference you are able to create a third cell that only shows the calm representation of the result and all the work is behind the scenes.

Cell referencing works like this: Excel uses the value of a given cell if you use cell addresses instead of actual numbers in the formula itself. For instance, if you wanted to total up every amount in Rows 2 through 10 in Column C, you could type =C1+C2+C3 ... and so on. The cell address (C2) is the reference. That way, if the data entered in cell C2 ever changes, the formula that references C2 would still be correct.

The Order of Operations

The operations that you can use in Excel are very similar to a calculator. You can add (+), subtract (–), multiply (*), and divide (/). Very similar to math from elementary school, Excel 2007 has certain rules it follows:

1. Always process the items inside parentheses first.

2. Always do multiplication and division before addition and subtraction.

3. If all else is the same, Excel begins calculations from left to right.

Now, ladies, get your plaid skirts and white oxfords on, because we're going to math class! Okay, not really. In fact, the point of inserting formulas into your worksheets is so that your readers don't have to do any math. So, we're not going to do any actual math; instead, the following sections are going to walk you through inserting formulas into a worksheet.

Mnemonic Device

If you forget the order of operations in an Excel equation, just remember this handy mnemonic device that you probably first heard in grade school: Please Excuse My Dear Aunt Sally. This means that Parenthesis, Exponents, Multiplication, Division, Addition, Subtraction is the order you follow.

Inserting Formulas into a Worksheet

For the sake of practice, look at the example monthly expense worksheet (Figure 5-3) to try and calculate how much the monthly expenses are. This will allow you to know how much there is left over after all expenses are added up. Based on what you have learned so far you can type up a formula that adds all the cells that have expenses in them (Figure 5-4) starting with an equal sign.

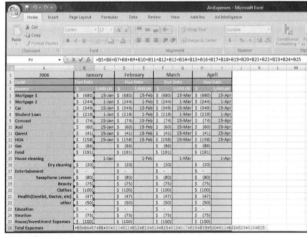

Figure 5-3

This Is Where the Formula Bar Gets Its Name

Remember, you'll be able to see the formula in the formula bar at the top of the Excel screen, and you'll see the value–the answer– displayed in the cell itself.

Figure 5-4

When creating a formula, here are the steps you need to follow:

1. First, figure out where you want the answer to appear. This cell is the cell to which you'll assign your formula and where the answer will appear. It must be a blank cell. Go to that cell and activate it by clicking within it.

2. Decide what mathematical function you need to accomplish. Are you adding? Figure out which cells you need to add and determine their location (X1 through X4, for instance).

3. Start typing into the formula bar. Remember that all formulas must start with an equal sign.

4. If you're adding cells X1 through X4, you would type =X1+X2+X3+X4. If you were multiplying those cells, you would type =X1*X2*X3*X4. If you were subtracting two cells, you would type =X1–X2. If you were dividing two cells, you would type =X1/X2.

5. Now try a more complicated equation. Say you want to multiply two cells, and then subtract the answer of those two cells from 1,000. Here's what you would type: =1000–(X1*X2).

6. When you're sure your formula is accurate, hit the Enter key and view the answer in the cell.

Figure 5-4 shows the formula needed to calculate all the monthly expense cells. What you notice here is that I did not type in the dollar amounts; rather, I typed in the cell addresses, such as B5+B6+etc. (this is called cell referencing, which was covered a few pages back). This is done on purpose; if the value in the cell changes I do not have to rewrite the formula. Excel 2007 will automatically update the value in cell B26 where I keep my total expense. Figure 5-5 shows the answer displayed. You can see how much my January expenses are (that is, $–2,648, as shown in cell B26).

Adding words . . .

If you want to add words rather than numbers, then instead of using =X1+X2 to get the sum of two numbers you will use =X1&X2 to get the two words put together without spaces.

This is the formula.

	A	B	C	D	E	F	G	H	I	J	K	L	M
2	2006		January		February		March		April				
3	Debit		Due Date		Due Date		Due Date		Due Date				
4	Income		5,000.00		5,000.00		5,000.00		5,000.00				
5	Mortgage 1	$ (680)	15-Jan	$ (680)	15-Feb	$ (680)	15-Mar	$ (680)	15-Apr				
6	Mortgage 2	$ (244)	1-Jan	$ (244)	1-Feb	$ (244)	1-Mar	$ (244)	1-Apr				
7	Car	$ (349)	15-Jan	$ (349)	15-Feb	$ (349)	15-Mar	$ (349)	15-Apr				
8	Student Loan	$ (219)	1-Jan	$ (219)	1-Feb	$ (219)	1-Mar	$ (219)	1-Apr				
9	Comcast	$ (74)	15-Jan	$ (74)	15-Feb	$ (74)	1-Mar	$ (74)	15-Apr				
10	Xcel	$ (60)	15-Jan	$ (60)	15-Feb	$ (60)	15-Mar	$ (60)	15-Apr				
11	Qwest	$ (41)	15-Jan	$ (41)		$ (41)	15-Mar	$ (41)	15-Apr				
12	HOA	$ (158)	15-Jan	$ (158)	15-Feb	$ (158)	15-Mar	$ (158)	15-Apr				
13	Gas	$ (86)		$ (86)		$ (86)		$ (86)					
14	Food	$ (191)		$ (191)		$ (191)		$ (191)					
15	House cleaning		1-Jan		1-Feb		1-Mar		1-Apr				
16	Dry cleaning	$ (20)		$ (20)		$ (20)		$ (20)					
17	Entertainment	$ -		$ -		$ -		$ -					
18	Saxaphone Lesson	$ (80)		$ (80)		$ (80)		$ (80)					
19	Beauty	$ (75)		$ (75)		$ (75)		$ (75)					
20	Clothes	$ (100)		$ (100)		$ (100)		$ (100)					
21	Health(Dentist, Doctor, etc)	$ (47)		$ (47)		$ (47)		$ (47)					
22	other	$ (50)		$ (50)		$ (50)		$ (50)					
23	Education	$ -		$ -		$ -		$ -					
24	Vacation	$ (75)		$ (75)		$ (75)		$ (75)					
25	House/Investment Expenses	$ (100)		$ (100)		$ (100)		$ (100)					
26	Total Expenses	$ (2,648)											
27			EXTRAS										

Formula bar: B26 — =B5+B6+B7+B8+B9+B10+B11+B12+B13+B14+B15+B16+B17+B18+B19+B20+B21+B22+B23+B24+B25

This is the answer.

Figure 5-5

Another way to use a formula is to find out how much money is left over after all our expenses are paid every month. Now that you have the total expenses in cell B26, that will be easy. To find out how much money is left over, you subtract expenses from income. In the case of the example worksheet, that means the formula must take cell B4 and subtract B26 from it (that is, =B4+B26). See Figure 5-6.

You might wonder why I chose the plus "+" sign instead of the minus "–" sign. The reason requires you to dust off the high school algebra: the value for my B26 cell is negative, and you don't want to subtract a negative or it will become positive, and the value would be $5,648. In order to calculate what is left over, using the laws of algebra I have to take B4 and add B26 to it to get the remainder of my income, which is $352.

Summing It Up

There is an easier way to add the value of cells together by using a built-in formula (you might recall this is known as a function) in Excel 2007 called SUM, which is covered in Chapter 6.

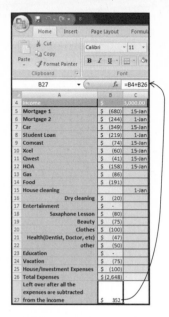

Mind your Parentheses

If you do use parentheses for your equation and forget to close a parenthesis, Excel will warn you with a pop-up window (Figure 5-7). In most cases what the box suggests matches what you need to do; however, if it doesn't just click No and return to fix the formula yourself. There is a pretty nifty thing with Excel where when you type the closing parenthesis for a function it matches it quickly with the open parenthesis in bold () so you know for sure you have closed the opened parenthesis.

Adding expenses to income, because the expense number is negative

Figure 5-6

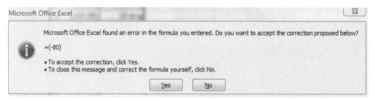

Figure 5-7

You can also click to add the cell into the formula you are building. In order to add the cell rather than type the column header and row number, you can start by typing the "=" in the formula bar, then click once on the cell you want to add, then follow it up with the symbol (+, −, *, /) that best matches what you need, and follow it up with the next cell. When you click each cell a certain color surrounds the cell (Figure 5-8) and you can see which cells have been selected. You can scroll up and down the sheet or go to other sheets. The cell you are adding to the outcome cell does not have to be in view or close range of the final outcome cell (where the answer will reside after you are done with your calculation). If you ever get lost you can always use Ctrl+Backspace to get back.

Notice that the cell addresses (such as B4) appearing in the bottom of Figure 5-8 match the color of the rectangle surrounding the cell they represent. It's a bit stylish (I guess women designed it). It was also done on purpose so it's easier to see which cells are being referenced.

	A	B	C	D	E	F	G	H	I	J	K
4	Income	$	3,000.00	$	3,000.00	$	3,000.00	$	3,000.00		
5	Mortgage 1	$ (680)	15-Jan	$ (680)	15-Feb	$ (680)	15-Mar	$ (680)	15-Apr		
6	Mortgage 2	$ (244)	1-Jan	$ (244)	1-Feb	$ (244)	1-Mar	$ (244)	1-Apr		
7	Car	$ (349)	15-Jan	$ (349)	15-Feb	$ (349)	15-Mar	$ (349)	15-Apr		
8	Student Loan	$ (219)	1-Jan	$ (219)	1-Feb	$ (219)	1-Mar	$ (219)	1-Apr		
9	Comcast	$ (74)	15-Jan	$ (74)	15-Feb	$ (74)	15-Mar	$ (74)	15-Apr		
10	Xcel	$ (60)	15-Jan	$ (60)	15-Feb	$ (60)	15-Mar	$ (60)	15-Apr		
11	Qwest	$ (41)	15-Jan	$ (41)	15-Feb	$ (41)	15-Mar	$ (41)	15-Apr		
12	HOA	$ (158)	15-Jan	$ (158)	15-Feb	$ (158)	15-Mar	$ (158)	15-Apr		
13	Gas	$ (86)		$ (86)		$ (86)		$ (86)			
14	Food	$ (191)		$ (191)		$ (191)		$ (191)			
15	House cleaning		1-Jan		1-Feb		1-Mar		1-Apr		
16	Dry cleaning	$ (20)		$ (20)		$ (20)		$ (20)			
17	Entertainment	$ -		$ -		$ -		$ -			
18	Saxaphone Lesson	$ (80)		$ (80)		$ (80)		$ (80)			
19	Beauty	$ (75)		$ (75)		$ (75)		$ (75)			
20	Clothes	$ (100)		$ (100)		$ (100)		$ (100)			
21	Health(Dentist, Doctor, etc)	$ (47)		$ (47)		$ (47)		$ (47)			
22	other	$ (50)		$ (50)		$ (50)		$ (50)			
23	Education	$ -		$ -		$ -		$ -			
24	Vacation	$ (75)		$ (75)		$ (75)		$ (75)			
25	House/Investment Expenses	$ (100)		$ (100)		$ (100)		$ (100)			
26	Total Expenses	=B5+B6+B7+B8+B9+B10+B11+B12+B13+B14+B15+B16+B17+B18+B19+B20+B21+B22+B23+B24+B25									

Figure 5-8

Copy and Paste Meet Formulas

Once you figure out what you want in a cell and get all the right parts of your formula in, the next step is for you to be able to reuse the same formula, right? Well if you have created your formula by telling Excel 2007 not the value but where the value lives (a.k.a. by reference), then you can't exactly just copy and paste the formula in the cell over to the next column or row.

This is where our mall story can help. The food court in every mall is located in approximately the same place, somewhere near or in the center. The department stores are typically split as far apart from each

other as possible. This is true for most malls. So in the case of our data if you copy the equation and paste it to the next column or cell, the value will change based on the column or row you are pasting it to (Figure 5-9).

Notice this is pointing to =D4+D26 rather than =B4+B26 as shown in Figure 5-6.

Figure 5-9

To paste a formula without having to change all the cell addresses, execute the following steps:

1. Select the cell you want to copy the formula from (you'll know you've successfully selected a cell by the dark black rectangle around the cell you want to copy).

2. With a right-click, open the menu and select the Copy option.

3. Once you select Copy, a dotted line appears around the cell (Figure 5-10), which means you are ready to paste this formula to the new place.

Don't Forget the Shortcut

You can also go to the cell you want to copy to and press Ctrl + V.

22	Education	$	-
23	Vacation	$	(75)
24	House/Investment Expenses	$	(100)
25	Total Expenses	$	(2,648)
26	Left over after all the expenses are subtracted from the income	$	352

Figure 5-10

4. Now select the new cell you want to paste the copied formula into, right-click, and choose the Paste option. Once this step is complete, magic occurs. The formula from the previous cell is copied to this new cell, but the values of this cell have changed because the reference cells are now the reference cells for this column.

To show this to you I have changed the car payment amount from –$349 per month to -$149 for February (let's assume I had overpaid and don't need to send the $200 this month). Look what happens to the "Total Expenses" and the "Left over ..." fields after I copy the formula over (Figure 5-11).

You'll immediately notice the value is $200 less in expense than the month of January. If you open up the formula you will notice all the values in cell D26 have changed to show =D5+D6+etc. (Figure 5-12). You can also do this with multiple cells that contain formulas. In this case, if you wanted to copy the "Total Expenses" and "Total money left over" you can follow the same steps as above for copying the "Total Expenses" formula and highlight both, and copy both and paste both and get to have both "Total Expenses" and "Total money left over" appear for the D column (that is, month of February).

Car payment reduced to $149.

Debit	Due Date		Due Date	
Income	$ 3,000.00		$ 3,000.00	
Mortgage 1	$ (680)	15-Jan	$ (680)	15-Feb
Mortgage 2	$ (244)	1-Jan	$ (244)	1-Feb
Car	$ (349)	15-Jan	$ (149)	15-Feb
Student Loan	$ (219)	1-Jan	$ (219)	1-Feb
Comcast	$ (74)	15-Jan	$ (74)	15-Feb
Xcel	$ (60)	15-Jan	$ (60)	15-Feb
Qwest	$ (41)	15-Jan	$ (41)	15-Feb
HOA	$ (158)	15-Jan	$ (158)	15-Feb
Gas	$ (86)		$ (86)	
Food	$ (191)		$ (191)	
House cleaning		1-Jan		1-Feb
Dry cleaning	$ (20)		$ (20)	
Entertainment	$ -		$ -	
Saxaphone Lesson	$ (80)		$ (80)	
Beauty	$ (75)		$ (75)	
Clothes	$ (100)		$ (100)	
Health(Dentist, Doctor, etc)	$ (47)		$ (47)	
other	$ (50)		$ (50)	
Education	$ -		$ -	
Vacation	$ (75)		$ (75)	
House/Investment Expenses	$ (100)		$ (100)	
Total Expenses	$ (2,648)		$ (2,448)	
Left over after all the expenses are subtracted from the income	$ 352		$ 552	

Total expenses are reduced to $2,448.

Amount of money left after expenses has gone up to $552, which is $200 more than January.

Figure 5-11

The formula where all the cell addresses have changed to D instead of B, which is what they were for Figure 5-5.

Clipboard | Font | Alignment | Number | Style

D26 =D5+D6+D7+D8+D9+D10+D11+D12+D13+D14+D15+D16+D17+D18+D19+D20+D21+D22+D23+D24+D25

	A	B	C	D	E	F	G	H	I
3	Debit	Due Date		Due Date		Due Date		Due Date	
4	Income	$ 3,000.00		$ 3,000.00		$ 3,000.00		$ 3,000.00	
5	Mortgage 1	$ (680)	15-Jan	$ (680)	15-Feb	$ (680)	15-Mar	$ (680)	15-Apr
6	Mortgage 2	$ (244)	1-Jan	$ (244)	1-Feb	$ (244)	1-Mar	$ (244)	1-Apr
7	Car	$ (349)	15-Jan	$ (149)	15-Feb	$ (349)	15-Mar	$ (349)	15-Apr
8	Student Loan	$ (219)	1-Jan	$ (219)	1-Feb	$ (219)	1-Mar	$ (219)	1-Apr
9	Comcast	$ (74)	15-Jan	$ (74)	15-Feb	$ (74)	15-Mar	$ (74)	15-Apr
10	Xcel	$ (60)	15-Jan	$ (60)	15-Feb	$ (60)	15-Mar	$ (60)	15-Apr
11	Qwest	$ (41)	15-Jan	$ (41)	15-Feb	$ (41)	15-Mar	$ (41)	15-Apr
12	HOA	$ (158)	15-Jan	$ (158)	15-Feb	$ (158)	15-Mar	$ (158)	15-Apr
13	Gas	$ (86)		$ (86)		$ (86)		$ (86)	
14	Food	$ (191)		$ (191)		$ (191)		$ (191)	
15	House cleaning		1-Jan		1-Feb		1-Mar		1-Apr
16	Dry cleaning	$ (20)		$ (20)		$ (20)		$ (20)	
17	Entertainment	$ -		$ -		$ -		$ -	
18	Saxaphone Lesson	$ (80)		$ (80)		$ (80)		$ (80)	
19	Beauty	$ (75)		$ (75)		$ (75)		$ (75)	
20	Clothes	$ (100)		$ (100)		$ (100)		$ (100)	
21	Health(Dentist, Doctor, etc)	$ (47)		$ (47)		$ (47)		$ (47)	
22	other	$ (50)		$ (50)		$ (50)		$ (50)	
23	Education	$ -		$ -		$ -		$ -	
24	Vacation	$ (75)		$ (75)		$ (75)		$ (75)	
25	House/Investment Expenses	$ (100)		$ (100)		$ (100)		$ (100)	
26	Total Expenses	$ (2,648)		$ (2,448)		$ (2,648)		$ (2,648)	

Figure 5-12

Now you're practically a formula Diva. You've got a firm grasp on what formulas are, what you use them for, how to use them, and how to copy them. It's time for something a little more complicated: how to employ formulas that use cells from another worksheet than the one in which you are entering the formula.

Cross Referencing Cells Across Worksheets

For those of you who were paying attention earlier, you might have caught what I said about referencing cells in other worksheets in the same workbook. That means you can use the value of a cell from a different worksheet than the one in which you are working in a formula.

Here is how you can cross reference cells across worksheets:

1. Begin by having at least two worksheets with data. Click on the worksheet cell you want the outcome to appear in.

2. Then enter an equal (=) sign and, using the mouse, click on the next sheet where the data lives that you want to add in your cell (worksheet 2 for this example).

3. Now click on the cell you want from worksheet 2.

4. When you return to the worksheet you started with you will see the cell has been populated with the cell address from worksheet 2 for you.

5. You can also type it manually, in which case it will look like =Sheet2!B3 (in this case you chose the B3 cell from Sheet2 worksheet). The exclamation means you are pulling cell B3 data from worksheet 2; it is what Excel 2007 uses to identify that the value is coming from another worksheet. If you were to rename your worksheet to "Expense," the formula would look like =Expense!B3. For a better example look at Figure 5-13.

A Colon Represents a Series

If you were using a series of cells in a column for your formula you would see something like this: B4:B6, meaning select the data from cells B4 thru B6 (B4, B5, B6 is another way to say it; this is further explained in Chapter 6).

The total expenses in the formula bar is =J5+J6+J7+...+'ChristmasExpenses'!J26.

The formula bar shows: =J5+J6+J7+J8+J9+J10+J11+J12+J13+J14+J15+J16+J17+J18+J19+J20+J21+J22+J23+J24+J25+'Christmas Expenses'!J26

	A	B		C	D		E	F		G	H		I	J		K	L	M	N
11	Qwest	$ (41)	15-Jan	$ (41)	15-Feb	$ (41)	15-Mar	$ (41)	15-Apr	$ (41)	15-Dec								
12	HOA	$ (158)	15-Jan	$ (158)	15-Feb	$ (158)	15-Mar	$ (158)	15-Apr	$ (158)	15-Dec								
13	Gas	$ (86)		$ (86)		$ (86)		$ (86)		$ (86)									
14	Food	$ (191)		$ (191)		$ (191)		$ (191)		$ (191)									
15	House cleaning		1-Jan		1-Feb		1-Mar		1-Apr		1-Dec								
16	Dry cleaning	$ (20)		$ (20)		$ (20)		$ (20)		$ (20)									
17	Entertainment	$ -		$ -		$ -		$ -		$ -									
18	Sexaphone Lesson	$ (80)		$ (80)		$ (80)		$ (80)		$ (80)									
19	Beauty	$ (75)		$ (75)		$ (75)		$ (75)		$ (75)									
20	Clothes	$ (100)		$ (100)		$ (100)		$ (100)		$ (100)									
21	Health(Dentist, Doctor, etc)	$ (47)		$ (47)		$ (47)		$ (47)		$ (47)									
22	other	$ (50)		$ (50)		$ (50)		$ (50)		$ (50)									
23	Education	$ -		$ -		$ -		$ -		$ -									
24	Vacation	$ (75)		$ (75)		$ (75)		$ (75)		$ (75)									
25	House/Investment Expenses	$ (100)		$ (100)		$ (100)		$ (100)		$ (100)									
26	Total Expenses	$ (2,648)		$ (2,448)		$ (2,648)		$ (2,648)		$ (2,948)									
	Left over after all the expenses are subtracted																		
27	from the income	$ 352		$ 552		$ 352		$ 352		$ 52									

2006 / 2007 / 2008 / Sheet2 / Christmas Expenses

Expenses have gone up by $300, so my savings for December is only $52 after expenses.

Figure 5-13

The best way to explain this is with an example. Let's think about keeping a separate budget for Christmas in another worksheet in the Excel 2007 workbook you currently might have. You still need to add the expense from the Christmas worksheet to the month of December expense column to calculate how much you have spent in the month of December. Notice what has been added to the end of the equation in column J is 'Christmas Expenses'!J26 (which is the location of the cell that contains my Christmas expense of –$300), which adds to –$2,648 to make a total of –$2,948.

Where does the data come from?

You can use Trace Precedents in the Formula Auditing section of the Formulas tab on the Office 2007 Ribbon to find out where all your data for a cell comes from (Figure 5-14). If you have references to other worksheets a little table will appear along with all the references the cell contains.

If you custom name your worksheets, then rather than "Sheet1!J26" it would have been 'name'!J26, which is the case here (that is, 'Christmas Expenses'!J26) where name is the name you gave to your worksheet as shown in Figure 5.13. If you reorder your worksheets or move your worksheets around Excel 2007 will automatically adjust. Even if you rename the worksheet you chose the cell from, Excel 2007 will automatically adjust to show the new worksheet name in the result box, and the result will stay consistent with what it was before you renamed it.

However, if you do delete the value you were using from a referenced cell (that is, if you were to delete the "Sheet1!J26" value based on the formula you are using) you might get an error. For more information about errors refer to the "Common Errors" section later in the chapter.

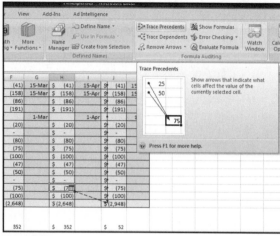

Figure 5-14

In order to remove the trace and go back to working on your worksheet you can use Remove Arrows in the Formula Auditing section of the Formulas tab on the Office 2007 Ribbon (Figure 5-15).

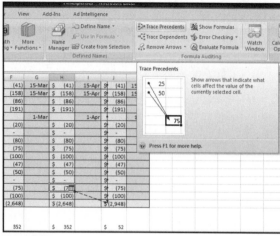

Figure 5-15

Paste Special

For most users Paste Special is just like Paste. But for the Excel Diva like you Paste Special is your secret sauce. With Paste Special you can choose to just copy the value, or the format, the comments, everything but the borders, or All (for everything). Paste Special also allows you to paste the link to a cell, in which case if the value of that cell changes, then so will the cell you copied the value into.

For instance, when the value of the cells changing doesn't matter but you do need the value of the cell that is there right now, you can use the Paste Special option from the pop-up menu when you right-click on a cell you want to copy to (Figure 5-16). After selecting Paste Special from the pop-up menu a new pop-up window appears where you can select what you want to paste over to a new cell (Figure 5-17).

The Paste Special option from the pop-up menu when you right-click on a cell.

Copied cell

This is where you're pasting into.

Figure 5-16

Notice in Figure 5-18 in the bottom right-hand corner there is a little globe with a red circle with an "x" inside and the word "Offline" next to it. This means I am not using the online help. If I were online, the globe would not have the red circle with the x on it and my search would also include results from http://office.microsoft.com.

Figure 5-17

 HELP!

What if you are working along and you don't know which formula to use? There is a great way to get help and understand best what is needed for each function to work. There is online help with Excel 2007. At anytime you can press the F1 key and the help window will come up. You can then type any formula name and click Search (Figure 5-18).

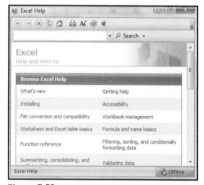

Figure 5-18

Common Errors

As you enter formulas you might see some of the most common errors show up in the cell you are working in rather than the value you are expecting to get. See Table 5-1.

Table 5-1   Common Formula Errors

How the Error Looks in the Cell	What Causes the Error	How to Fix the Error
####	The column is not wide enough for the value in the cell.	Drag the column size wider with the mouse or merge the contents of this cell into two cells.
#DIV/0!	You may have attempted to divide by 0, which is bad math.	Look over the formula and avoid dividing by 0.
#NAME?	You may have mistyped a formula name or typed the name of a formula that doesn't exit.	Check the formula name and try again.
#VALUE	You entered a formula without numbers, it only refers to text.	Check your formula to ensure all cells or numbers have been entered correctly.
#REF!	You removed a range of cells that were part of a formula.	Look through to ensure the formula cell is updated with current cells.
#N/A	There is no information available for the calculation you want to perform.	Look over the function and make sure you are using the right function.
#NUM!	You provided the wrong kind of value, cells or function.	Look over the function and make sure you are using the right function, correct cells and provide the right value.
#NULL!	You selected two ranges of cells to show an intersection, but there is no intersecting (common) cell.	Select two ranges that have at least one intersecting (common) cell.

Relax, Refresh, Reward

Taking 5- to 10-minute breaks every hour or two ensures you'll stay focused. During the break, you can stretch muscles that would otherwise grow tighter and shorter as back muscles grow longer and looser, which causes shoulders to move forward and give the hunchback look to most people who work with computers. My chest muscles tighten up from sitting and typing on a keyboard. For this chapter's self-reward, I'm asking you to try one of my favorite exercises.

Most of you have seen or most likely used a fitness ball. Lay down on the ball and put your feet at a 90-degree angle on the floor. Then open your arms and fall backwards over the ball. If you are very flexible you can use a book in each hand to get a deeper stretch. If you have a fitness ball, or belong to a gym where you have access to a ball, give this a try and just see how it makes you feel.

Fitness balls are also good for posture. Here's another exercise to try: while sitting on the ball, rotate from one side to another with your legs bent at 90 degrees and your feet flat on the floor. This activity engages your core muscles, which help when you stand up, balance, and would help you balance far better on a snowboard. You can also do this by sitting on the tip of your chair putting your feet at 90 degrees on the ground and following the steps above, if you don't have a fitness ball. You can typically pick up a fitness ball for around $20 at most gyms or sporting good stores.

For those of you who might not have a fitness ball, find the corner of a wall and grab it while you stretch the opposite way. Alternatively, you can interlock your hands behind your back and pull both hands down while they are interlocked. This will open your chest muscles and stretch your shoulders.

6

Put Excel Functions

To Do List

- Learn the most common functions
- Sum it up
- Find the median and standard deviation
- Define the minimum and the maximum
- Display things with decimal values
- Function well by doing less

to Work for You

After recently moving, I found the need to visit Bed Bath & Beyond frequently. I was helping a newfound friend pick out presents as well, and he kept asking why I was intrigued by certain items. As he said it: "I'm a guy, I'm simple." He is a software developer, so I asked him: "When you write code, do you use Notepad or Visual Studio?" He said: "Visual Studio. I love how I can do things really fast with Visual Studio and it has code complete, different colors, and all starter projects."

I told him Bed Bath & Beyond is like Visual Studio for a home. We could do things his way by just putting sheets on a bed, but then it would be like writing code in Notepad, without Visual Studio to enable you to accomplish more with less time and effort. He has now found a new sense of liking cabinet liners, rubber sink pads, and mattress covers.

Most of the data you look at in Excel means nothing unless you apply mathematical analysis. Looking at numbers is like looking at the whole Bed Bath & Beyond store. The number of items is overwhelming and you don't know for sure what each item's purpose is. The same thing can be said about math functions: You know there are a lot of math functions, but what are they for and why should you use them? Read this chapter and find out.

What Is a Function?

In Excel 2007, a function is a predefined mathematical process that performs a specific computation, such as adding all the cells in a column. The difference between a formula and a function is that you don't have to tell Excel which mathematical process to apply; you merely indicate which cells or values to use when performing the function. There are many functions in Excel 2007. What do the functions mean, where should they be used, and how can you get what you need to make a great analysis of numbers? Numbers are just characters on a page; it is up to you to assign value and give the numbers meaning. By using the right functions you can evaluate data and explain what the lines on the page are trying to say.

Equal Rights for Functions

Just like formulas, when you want to employ a function in your Excel worksheet, you must start with an equal sign.

Did you know?

Visual Studio is a product from Microsoft much like Office 2007, but it is used by developers to help them write code in their favorite language to create applications. Currently Visual Studio contains Visual Basic, Visual C# (aka C Sharp), ASP.NET, and Visual J#. Visual Studio has been around since 1996.

So to put this in terms of Bed Bath & Beyond, when you leave you have to pay a certain amount for the items that you have chosen based on your needs. Therefore Bed Bath & Beyond's function is to sell you items. The amount you pay is based on what you pick out from the store. Functions work in the same way: depending on what you plug in, the value you get may change but if you plug in multiple values you will get a single value at the end. It doesn't matter how many items I pick up at Bed Bath & Beyond, I have to pay a single final dollar amount at the end. If you bring something back to Bed Bath & Beyond there is still a single dollar amount, only this time the amount is paid back to you rather than you having to pay the amount to Bed Bath & Beyond. In either case it comes down to a single dollar value from one or multiple dollar values.

The rest of this chapter focuses on teaching you the most popular of the 60 different functions available in Excel 2007. You can find information on the other functions by using help in Excel 2007. Try the F1 key, which brings up the online help, but do make sure the computer you are on is online.

The SUM Function

Chapter 5 demonstrated how you can add several cells together and if those cells' values changed, the added value would change to reflect the new total. Figure 6-1 shows the results to jog your memory.

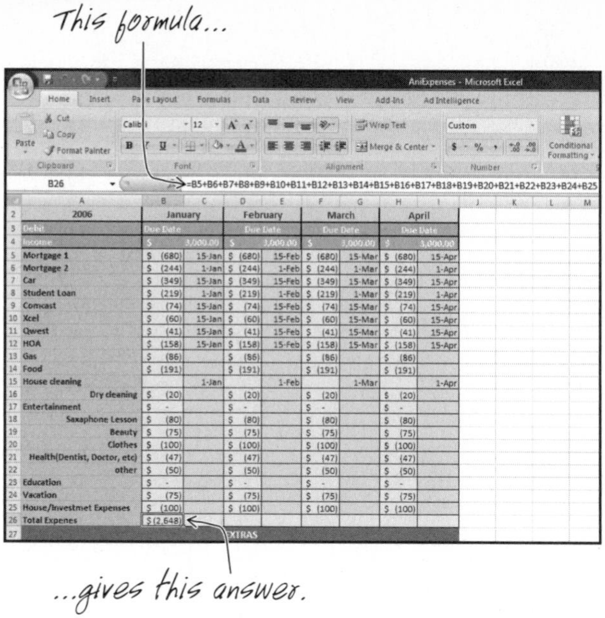

This formula...

...gives this answer.

Figure 6-1

Perhaps one of the most commonly used functions in Excel 2007 is the SUM function, which basically adds all the cells you select and you don't have to type all the =D5+D6+D7+... . When you use the SUM function it will look like =SUM(A1,A2,A3). Why would you care about the SUM function? Let's say you are adding up how many square feet of cabinet lining you need—wouldn't it be easier to just put them into Excel 2007 and then use the SUM function to add them up? So then you can take a drive to your nearest Bed Bath & Beyond (or other favorite home accessory store) and purchase exactly the square feet that you need to line all your cabinets rather than guessing. Okay, I know that sounds a bit geeky. But what about balancing your checkbook? It makes sense to list all the items you have to pay out every month, summarize how much you are spending, and then by a simple subtraction from your income you know exactly how much you can spend at the mall.

The nice thing about Excel 2007 is, because the SUM function is one of the most commonly used functions, Excel 2007 provides a special button just for SUM (Figure 6-2). It looks like a Greek letter.

Numbers Only Please

The SUM function only accepts numbers. If you include a cell that is either blank or filled with text, the SUM function won't work.

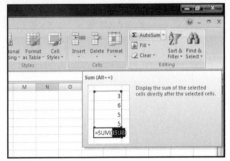

Figure 6-2

To use the SUM function, just follow these steps:

1. Decide which rows or columns of data you want to add.

2. Pick the cell where you want the sum value to show up and activate it. Then you have two options for completing the SUM function.

3. Begin by typing **=SUM** (as shown in Figure 6-3), or you can use the AutoSum button.

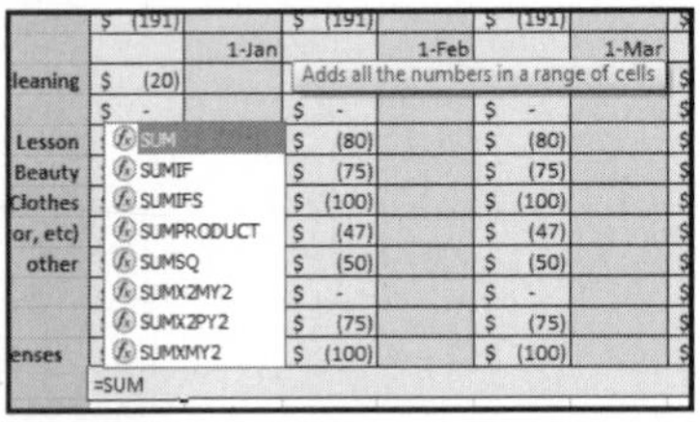

Figure 6-3

3a. If you do want to use the AutoSum button just go to the cell in which you want the value to appear, then click the AutoSum button. The cell will be populated with **=SUM()**, at which point you can use your mouse to select which column or row of data you want to put into the SUM parentheses.

3b. If you want to select cells from various places, just left-click on the first cell, type a "," (comma), then click on the next cell and so on until you are done selecting all the cells you want to add together.

4. Once you are done selecting the rows or columns of data you can then end the =SUM function by putting a closing parenthesis at the end.

5. Press the Enter key, which tells Excel 2007 that you are done selecting numbers and Excel 2007 shows you the outcome (Figure 6-4).

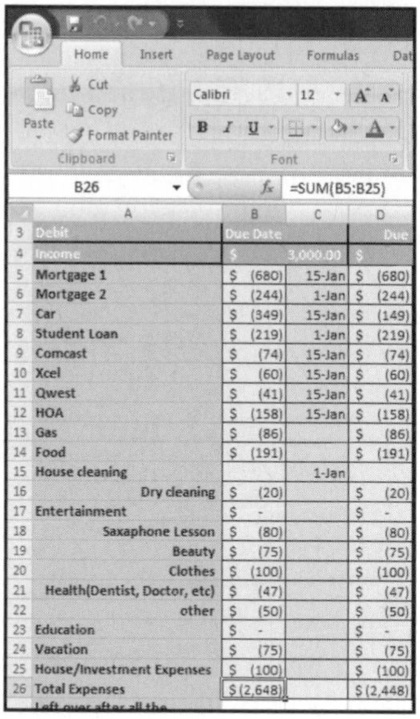

Figure 6-4

So if you want to select a range of numbers to add together, such as the sum of all B5 to B25 cells as well as, for example B27 and B28 in Figure 6-5, you can very easily use =SUM(B5: B25,B27:B28). You probably noticed (how astute you are!) that I skipped cell B26. Cell B26 contains no number and would break the SUM function.

When filling in a series of cell addresses for the SUM function (or any function, really) and you want to skip a certain cell, here's how: Use the mouse to select from B5 and drag your mouse down to B25, place a comma, and then hold down the Ctrl button while you click on B27 and drag to B28 as shown in Figure 6-5.

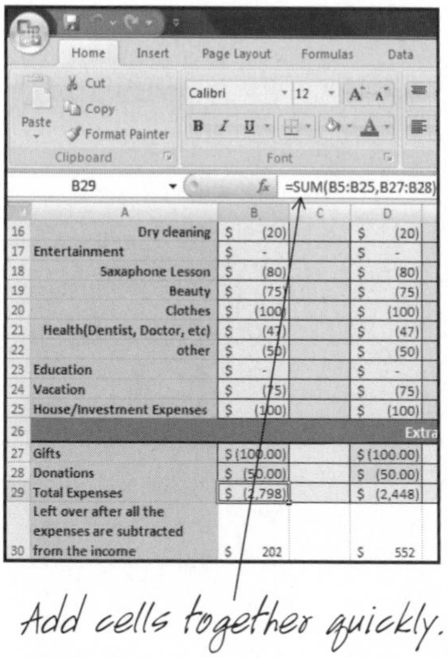

Add cells together quickly.

Figure 6-5

There's More Than One Way to Skin a Cat (or Type a Sum, as the Case May Be)

When typing a series of cells in a sum, you can use commas, plus signs, or colons to separate the cells. A colon indicates a range of cells, meaning all the cells between (and including) those two cell addresses. What you'll notice in Figure 6-4 is rather than there being plus signs (+) between the numbers or even a comma (,), there is now a colon symbol (:). The colon symbol is Excel 2007 shorthand for a range of numbers. So rather than having a (+) or (,) there is now a (:). The formula shown in Figure 6-4 in the formula bar shows you the following formula: (=SUM(B5:B25)), which translated can be written as =B5+B6+B7+...+B25 or =SUM(B5,B6,B7,...,B25).

All of the preceding examples will give the same result as =SUM(B5:B25). However, the following =SUM(B5:B25) to a trained eye, which you are learning to be, is much easier to read.

You'll notice that Excel 2007 color-codes the regions for you so you can easily see which ranges are added to your SUM function, as demonstrated in Figure 6-6. You might not see the colors in your book, but if you do walk through the steps with me you will be able to see the colors in your Excel 2007 worksheet. This should help you as you begin creating more complex functions to know where the errors might occur.

Excel 2007 has 60 built-in math and trigonometry functions (Figure 6-7). I think that is too many, but then again people use Excel 2007 in a variety of ways.

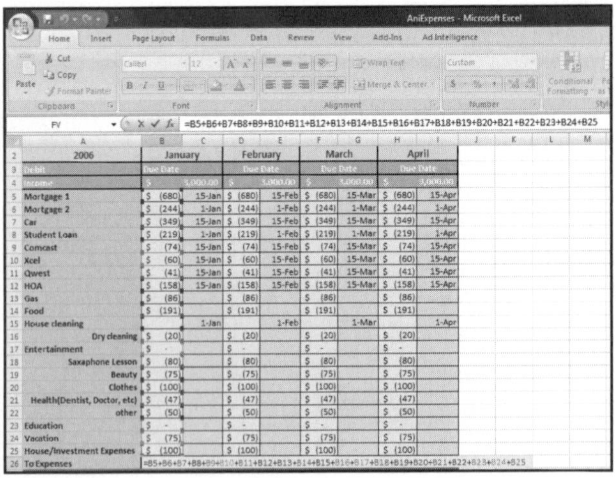

Figure 6-6

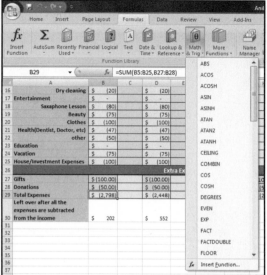

Figure 6-7

Time for a factoid ...

Excel 2007 has 60 built-in math and trigonom-etry functions. You ask what trigonometry is ... well never fear! Trigonometry (also known to mathematicians as "trig") is the branch of mathematics that deals with the relationships between the sides and the angles of triangles and the calculations based on them; therefore they are called the trigonometric functions. Some of the most common functions are shown in Figure 6-7.

In Figure 6-8 you can see where =SUM is typed. This then opens a drop-down menu that shows all functions that start with =SUM in their name. As you hover over each function with your mouse you can see another hover box pop up (also shown in Figure 6-8 to the right, which shows a small explanation of what each function does).

Figure 6-8

The AVERAGE Function

For those of us who want to know how much we spend on average per month so we can see if we can afford something new there is a built-in AVERAGE function. If you do not want to use the AVERAGE function you can always add all the numbers and then divide the sum of all numbers by the number of values you have. So what that would look like for figuring out the monthly expense average would be to add the values in B29, D29, F29, H29, and J29 (as seen in Figure 6.9), and then divide the sum by 5.

=SUM(B29,D29,F29,H29,J29)/5

C	D	E	F	G	H	I	J	K	L	M
(20)	$ (20)		$ (20)		$ (20)		$ (20)			
-	$ -		$ -		$ -		$ -			
(80)	$ (80)		$ (80)		$ (80)		$ (80)			
(75)	$ (75)		$ (75)		$ (75)		$ (75)			
(100)	$ (100)		$ (100)		$ (100)		$ (100)			
(47)	$ (47)		$ (47)		$ (47)		$ (47)			
(50)	$ (50)		$ (50)		$ (50)		$ (50)			
	$ -		$ -		$ -		$ -			
(75)	$ (75)		$ (75)		$ (75)		$ (75)			
(100)	$ (100)		$ (100)		$ (100)		$ (100)			
			Extra Expenses							
0.00)	$ (100.00)		$ (100.00)		$ (100.00)		$ (100.00)			
0.00)	$ (50.00)		$ (50.00)		$ (50.00)		$ (50.00)			
								Average Monthly Expense	$ (2,727.91)	
798)	$ (2,598)		$ (2,648)		$ (2,648)		$ (2,948)			

Figure 6-9

Therefore, you can write an equation in cell K41 that would look like one of the following:

$$=(B29+D29+F29+H29+J29)/5 = SUM(B29,D29,F29,H29,J29)/5$$

However, writing these functions takes too much time and if you need to make changes it would take a long time too. We are all about saving time! So we can write something very simple such as =AVERAGE(B29,D29,F29,H29,J29) and get the average value for the average expense per month.

In order to use the AVERAGE function, execute the following steps:

1. You can begin by selecting the cell in which you want to display the average value.

2. Type **=AVE** in the formula bar and the rest will pop up in a window for you as shown in Figure 6-10. You will notice the drop-down box shows AVERAGE as a function. When you hover over it (Figure 6-10) you will see the explanation of what the AVERAGE function does. You will see the explanation talks about returning the mathematical average of numbers, arrays, and references to numbers. Just think of that as a set of numbers.

3. Then once you have double-clicked on the AVERAGE function or just typed the whole word into your cell, make sure there is an open parenthesis.

4. Begin inserting cell addresses into your AVERAGE function much like the SUM function by right-clicking on the cells you want to add and separating them with a comma.

5. After entering all the cell addresses you want to average, enter the close parenthesis and press the Enter key to lock the value into this cell.

Figure 6-10

Once you finalize which method you want to use to calculate the average monthly expense, whether it's by adding all the cells then dividing by number of cells or by using the =AVERAGE function, you will see the value of AVERAGE is $ (2,727.91), which is the same as –2,727.91 (as you can see in Figure 6-11). In Excel 2007 much like in accounting the parentheses around a number means it's a negative value or expense amount.

> **An array is only ...**
>
> Most places you will read on the web will tell you arrays are essential components of computer science and make it sound really scary! In reality, it's not scary at all ... an array is just a collection of numbers arranged in rows and columns. Easy!

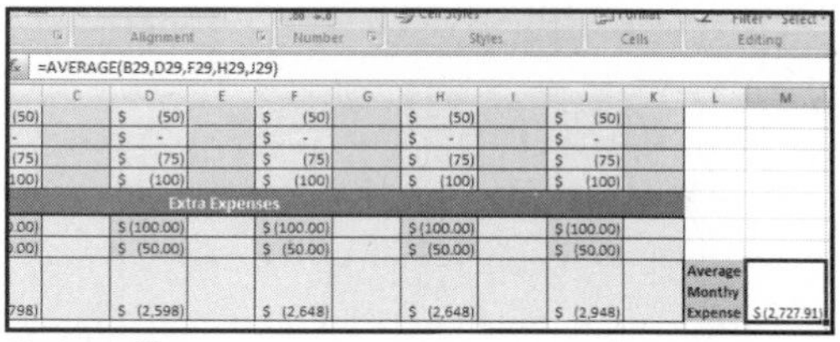

Figure 6-11

If perchance you mistype or are tempted to abbreviate and use =AVG, you will see the #NAME? error appear in the cell in which you are working (as seen in Figure 6-12).

I know it's just a name, so why put such an emphasis on a name? It's all about precision. Just like a decorator knows the difference between a duvet, a blanket, and a comforter, Excel knows the difference between a real function and a made-up one. What's nice about the error message in Figure 6-12 is that all you have to do is look to see if Excel 2007 found what you meant, and if you meant to type AVERAGE you would then just click the Yes button and you would get the average. Don't we wish we could have these error windows in life?

Figure 6-12

Case Sensitivity

You don't have to type the function name in all UPPERCASE, although that is preferred. Excel 2007 is smart to recognize what you mean and shows you the best possible match for the function you are typing. Whether you use the right case of letters or not, Excel 2007 is not case sensitive when it comes to functions.

Statistically for you ...

The median is the middle value in a set of statistical values that are arranged in ascending or descending order. In a nutshell, median means middle.

The MEDIAN Function

Let's start with the definition of a median. The median is the middle in set of ordered values. So why would that matter to you? Well, what if the average just doesn't matter? Because, after all, the average value is rarely the exact amount you spend per month. So from our =AVERAGE function we know the average we spend per month is $ (2,727.91), but if you look at the values in the cells you never see that amount. So if I want to find out what is the middle amount that I would spend per month I would use the MEDIAN function, in which case the value would be $ (2,648) as seen in Figure 6-13.

				Alignment		Number		Styles			Cells		Editing	
fx		=MEDIAN(B29,D29,F29,H29,J29)												
B	C	D	E	F	G	H	I	J	K	L	M			
$ -		$ -		$ -		$ -		$ -						
$ (75)		$ (75)		$ (75)		$ (75)		$ (75)						
$ (100)		$ (100)		$ (100)		$ (100)		$ (100)						
				Extra Expenses										
$ (100.00)		$ (100.00)		$ (100.00)		$ (100.00)		$ (100.00)						
$ (50.00)		$ (50.00)		$ (50.00)		$ (50.00)		$ (50.00)						
$ (2,798)		$ (2,598)		$ (2,648)		$ (2,648)		$ (2,948)		Average Monthy Expense	$ (2,727.91)			
$ 202		$ 402		$ 352		$ 352		$ 52		Middle amount	$ (2,648)			

Figure 6-13

In order to get the median value, execute the following steps:

1. Select the cell in which you want to display the median value.

2. Type **=MED** and the rest will pop up in a window for you as shown in Figure 6-14. You will notice the drop-down box shows MEDIAN as a function

and when you hover over it (Figure 6-14) you will see the explanation of what the MEDIAN function does. You will see the explanation talks about returning the middle number in a set of numbers.

3. Once you have double-clicked on the MEDIAN function or just typed the whole word into your cell, make sure there is an open parenthesis.

4. Insert cell addresses into your MEDIAN function much like the AVERAGE and SUM functions by right-clicking on the cells you want to add and separating them with a comma.

5. Once you are done make sure to close the parenthesis and press the Enter key to lock the value into this cell.

This way you will know the real middle value that was spent from the five months of expenses we have tracked.

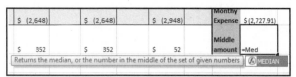

Figure 6-14

The DOLLAR ($) Function or Monetary Display Format

The DOLLAR function converts the numbers in a chosen cell from just a number amount to a dollar amount. Notice the cell in Figure 6-15 that is created by just typing 123. The dollar sign is not there. You can either use the DOLLAR function for one cell at a time or select a set of cells and apply the DOLLAR function to make all the values in the selected cells display as a dollar amount.

Figure 6-15

In order to use the DOLLAR function, follow these steps:

1. Select the cell in which you want to display the value as a dollar amount.

2. Type **=Dol** into the formula bar, and the rest will pop up in a window for you as shown in Figure 6-16. You will notice the drop-down box shows DOLLAR as a function and when you hover over it (Figure 6.16) you will see the explanation of what the DOLLAR function does. You will see the explanation talks about converting a number or text into currency format.

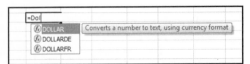

Figure 6-16

3. Once you have double-clicked on the DOLLAR function (or typed =DOLLAR in) make sure there is an open parenthesis.

4. Insert one (and only one) number into this function followed by a comma followed by the number of decimal points you want to see. If you leave the number of decimal points blank you will get two by default, because two decimal places are used for cents on a dollar.

5. Make sure to close the parenthesis and press the Enter key to lock the value into this cell. Your final outcome will display a dollar value in the cell, much like in Figure 6-17.

Font			
fx	=DOLLAR(123,2)		
B	C	D	E
$ -		$ -	$
$ (75)		$ (75)	$
$ (100)		$ (100)	$
		Extra Expenses	
$ (100.00)		$ (100.00)	$
$ (50.00)		$ (50.00)	$
$ (2,798)		$ (2,598)	$
$ 202		$ 402	$
		$123.00	

Figure 6-17

Adding Denominations

In order to add the $ or other denominations you can select the Office Ribbon from the Number section on the Home tab. You can always look for more options by selecting the More Accounting Formats option from the drop-down menu in Figure 6-18.

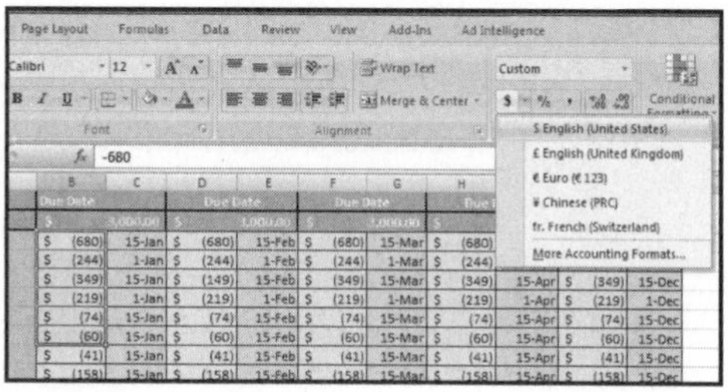

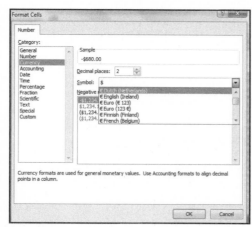

Figure 6-18

Selecting More Accounting Formats will bring up the window in Figure 6-19. In the Format Cells window the Numbers tab opens where you can see the category on the left side is set to Accounting. You can then change the selections on the right side. On the very top of the window you will see the sample area where you can preview how the number will display. Once you are done just click the OK button to return to the Excel 2007 spreadsheet and apply the changes.

Figure 6-19

Note that the denomination button does not convert the $ value to the denomination selected, but it does add the appropriate symbol for the denomination for you in Excel 2007. You must check the value for conversion from other sources. You can begin by going to http://www.live.com and typing the following keywords into the search box: "currency exchange rate".

Adding Decimals

Once you are done formatting the numbers you will then see all the cells with the $ sign as shown in Figure 6-20. Notice in the blue area in Figure 6-20 the $ symbol appears with two decimal places following the number as well. That's because if you look back at Figure 6-19 you will notice the decimal place was set to 2.

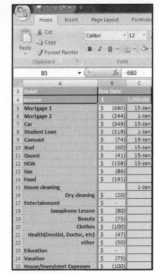

Figure 6-20

In order to add decimals to your cells containing dollar values, follow these steps:

1. Select the cells where there is a value you want to change as shown in Figure 6-20.

2. Go to the Number section of the Home tab of the Office 2007 Ribbon and click on the increase decimal button as shown in Figure 6-21.

Figure 6-21

3. Continue to click as many times as necessary to add two decimal points (for two decimal points two clicks should work).

4. Once you are done make sure to click on the disk icon on top of the worksheet next to the Office Button to save your work.

5. If you want the $ sign to appear and no decimal places, you can simply use the Number area on the Home tab of the Office 2007 Ribbon to make the decimals go away by using the decrease decimal button next to the increase decimal button (which you saw in Figure 6-21). You will see two decimal buttons on the Home tab's Number section as shown in Figure 6-21. The button to the left increases the decimal places, whereas the button to the right decreases the decimal places. The decrease decimal button also explains in a small pop-up window what it does.

Once you have completed the steps your data will look very much like Figure 6-22 with the dollar denomination and two decimals.

Figure 6-22

The Count Numbers, MAX, and MIN Functions

For those of you curious about some other common functions you can find them in the Editing section of the Home tab on the Office 2007 Ribbon as shown in Figure 6-23. The functions are pretty self-explanatory. You can use the Count Numbers function (i.e. COUNT) to count numbers in a row or column of numbers and find out how many numbers are in a selected set of cells.

Figure 6-23

Notice in Figure 6-24 the selected cells have a dotted line around them and the window that came up explains how to use the Count Numbers function. The use of this function is very similar to the SUM, AVERAGE, and other functions. However, once you hit the Enter key when you are done selecting the cells you want the count for you will see a warning message pop up near the cell as shown in Figure 6-25.

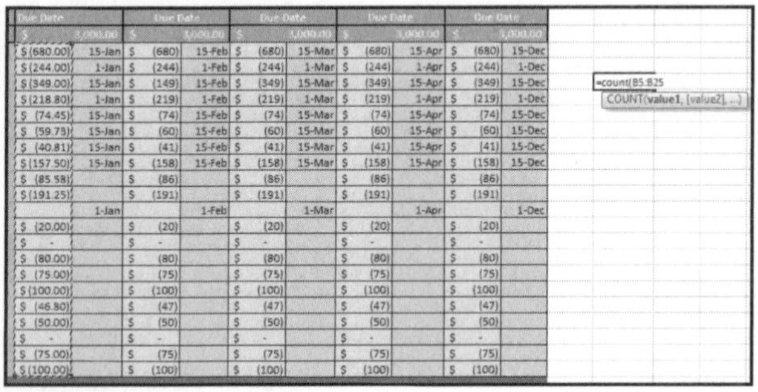

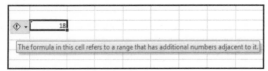

Figure 6-24

Figure 6-25

When hovered over, this warning symbol lets you know that there are other cells with number values around in case you forgot to include them in the range you wanted to count. The MAX and MIN functions work very much the same way except they will return the maximum and minimum value, respectively, for the set of selected cells.

The Standard Deviation (STDV) Function

What is the standard deviation and why is it important? It sounds so complicated but in reality it is not. The best way I can explain it is that we girls like to have our skinny jeans, our regular jeans, and our relax jeans. I have my skinny jeans, which I wear when I am at my ideal size; my everyday jeans, which is one size larger than my skinny jeans; and finally my relax jeans, which are two sizes larger than my skinny jeans to feel more relaxed and just be comfortable. Given I have three pairs of jeans—one skinny, one everyday size, and the other comfortable size—I can say my standard deviation from my everyday jean size is one size. So my skinny jeans are one size smaller than my everyday jeans and my comfortable jeans are one size larger than my everyday jeans. Keep in mind that one size doesn't correlate to a number, it is whatever size you wear, but one size larger or smaller. Standard deviation is calculated the same way and the standard deviation value is always plus or minus the same value (in my case +1 size or −1 size; size can be whatever the next number up and down is from your current size).

Statistically chic ...

Standard deviation is also known as STDV for short. Coming from a heavy background in statistics I will be honest–this is a pretty difficult concept, but it really means the average difference from the middle number. So if there are many numbers farther away from the average value, then the standard deviation is large, but if there are many numbers close to the average value, then the standard deviation is small. The number of times a number appears does not matter.

Other Functions

Are you already so well on your way to becoming an Excel 2007 Diva that you need more functions? You can always select More Functions from the drop-down menu of Figure 6-23, which brings up the window in Figure 6-26, where you can select from other functions.

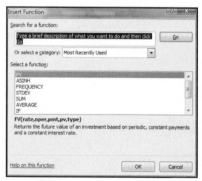

Figure 6-26

In Figure 6-26 you can either search for a function or select from the category and then select from the Select a Function window below. The nice part about this window in Figure 6-26 is that on the bottom of the Select a Function window you can see how the function should be used and what it does. If you want to use other functions that might not be present in Figure 6-26, take a look on the Formulas tab on the Office 2007 Ribbon as shown in Figure 6-7.

This is a fantastic place to play around and learn about more functions. There is one more little hint I will leave you with and that is the Show Formulas button on the Formula Auditing section of the Formulas tab on the Office 2007 Ribbon (Figure 6-27).

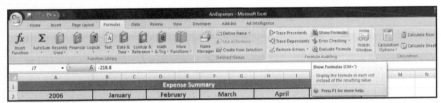

Figure 6-27

The Show Formulas button helps in showing the formulas that are being used in each cell. This way if you are looking at someone else's spreadsheet and want to copy their masterpiece you can use a little secret to see what's under the cover, rather than having to go to each cell at a time. When you are done you can click on the same button to undo and just see the values like before.

Relax, Refresh, Reward

With all this learning you are doing how can we apply it to life? I am all about biting off more than I can chew. If you're like that too, you know that it leaves you with more to do (more roles you must play, and more functions you must fulfill) and less time for you. For this chapter's reward, it's time to take stock of the various functions you perform in life and how much time you spend doing them—and then, spend time doing something you like. As you go about your day, keep track of how much time it takes you to perform those various functions, like cooking, cleaning, doing laundry, ironing clothes, going to the gym, and so on. Once you have an idea of how much time you are spending on tasks you can log them inside an Excel worksheet and you will be better aware of what you can cut out and what you can leave in. The other thing to keep in mind is which tasks do you love? Which ones can you delegate or hire out?

After going through this exercise you will be surprised to find how many of these tasks you can take out and make more time for things you are good at and you love. I am not saying you have to absolutely love everything you do (wouldn't that be nice?), but you can delegate more than you are currently doing, I am certain.

I tracked the following functions and the times I was putting toward them, and found a pattern:

- Laundry—2 hours per week
- Ironing—4 hours per week
- House cleaning—5 hours per week
- Cooking—7 hours per week
- My own manicure—3 hours per week
- Working out—7 hours per week

It turns out it is much more expensive and takes more of my time if I do my own ironing and house cleaning. This got me thinking that I should perhaps find other alternatives such as hiring help, or asking the teens in my family for help. This gave me more time to do the things I love, like cooking, working out, and spending time with friends and family.

So how about you? What are some tasks you do that take a lot of time and you really dislike? Is it possible to perform a shortcut in your life so there's more time for the functions you enjoy?

Excel Fashion and

To Do List

Give your data a makeover

Apply conditional formatting

Change the number format

Apply themes to tables

Use the format painter

Show off your data

Find the music that moves you

Color Coordinating

Ladies, life is about a ride . . . a journey and a process of sorts. Through it you come into situations that help you become better than you were. Recently, I've experienced some bumps in the ride, involving heartbreak and disillusionment. I've spent my life viewing the world in a very black-or-white, good-or-bad, right-or-wrong context, and viewing it from behind plain glasses. Well, after this most recent part of my journey, I've come to appreciate the value of shades of gray, of color. When I went for my regular haircut, my stylist recommended red highlights. I had to consider because it was a scary step for me and my never-been-dyed brown hair, but I decided to go with it. Later, I went to get some new sunglasses, and I fell in love with a pink pair. I didn't think I could do it, but thanks to some new contacts I walked out of there with regular glasses and sunglasses in pink frames. Those changes weren't noticed just by me! I went to lunch and got lots of compliments on both.

By adding a hint of color to my life I have a newfound sense of fun, excitement, and beautiful energy, which is electrifying. I have been able to take an unhappy situation to a new pink rosy finish all with color. This chapter shows you how to use color to do the same thing with spreadsheets. Spreadsheets don't have to be all about boring numbers. It's also about how you present those numbers. We are not all perfect looking but, with color and minor touches, we can bring out our best features and use them to show our perfection.

Make Over Your Data

Once you pick out the data you are working with, the next step is to modify the layout and organize it in a way that makes sense to the person who will be viewing it. If we don't spend the time to format the data (or as we call it, "pretty it up"), then it would be like a girl who shows up for her wedding day in jeans, an old t-shirt, and bad hair. It just wouldn't be right.

Audience Is Key

Whenever you begin to pretty up your data, be sure you keep your audience in mind. What you find easy to understand, people who have spent less time with the data might find difficult.

The Basics of Data Makeover

With Excel 2007 this part is really easy and fun! You can use the Office 2007 Ribbon to format the data and add color and style to your otherwise simple-looking data. In most cases you wouldn't think much of data when you look at it, but when you spend the time to make it look nice, you get the same feeling you did when you ran into an old friend who wore glasses the whole time you knew them, but are in contacts now and you can see a whole new beauty. After all, looking at data (Figure 7-1) is just not much fun unless it looks great and tells a story (Figure 7-2).

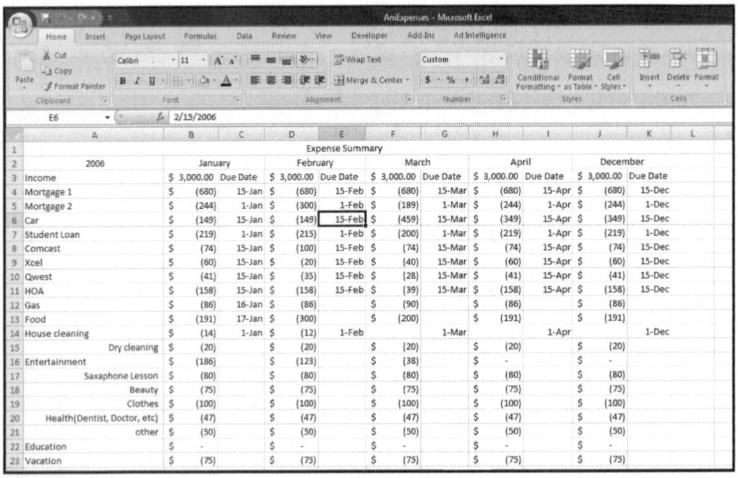

	A	B	C	D	E	F	G	H	I	J	K
1					Expense Summary						
2	2006	January		February		March		April		December	
3	Income	$ 3,000.00	Due Date	$ 3,000.00	Due Date	$ 3,000.00	Due Date	$ 3,000.00	Due Date	$ 3,000.00	Due Date
4	Mortgage 1	$ (680)	15-Jan	$ (680)	15-Feb	$ (680)	15-Mar	$ (680)	15-Apr	$ (680)	15-Dec
5	Mortgage 2	$ (244)	1-Jan	$ (300)	1-Feb	$ (189)	1-Mar	$ (244)	1-Apr	$ (244)	1-Dec
6	Car	$ (149)	15-Jan	$ (149)	15-Feb	$ (459)	15-Mar	$ (349)	15-Apr	$ (349)	15-Dec
7	Student Loan	$ (219)	1-Jan	$ (215)	1-Feb	$ (200)	1-Mar	$ (219)	1-Apr	$ (219)	1-Dec
8	Comcast	$ (74)	15-Jan	$ (100)	15-Feb	$ (74)	15-Mar	$ (74)	15-Apr	$ (74)	15-Dec
9	Xcel	$ (60)	15-Jan	$ (20)	15-Feb	$ (40)	15-Mar	$ (60)	15-Apr	$ (60)	15-Dec
10	Qwest	$ (41)	15-Jan	$ (35)	15-Feb	$ (28)	15-Mar	$ (41)	15-Apr	$ (41)	15-Dec
11	HOA	$ (158)	15-Jan	$ (158)	15-Feb	$ (39)	15-Mar	$ (158)	15-Apr	$ (158)	15-Dec
12	Gas	$ (86)	16-Jan	$ (86)		$ (90)		$ (86)		$ (86)	
13	Food	$ (191)	17-Jan	$ (300)		$ (200)		$ (191)		$ (191)	
14	House cleaning	$ (14)	1-Jan	$ (12)	1-Feb		1-Mar		1-Apr		1-Dec
15	Dry cleaning	$ (20)		$ (20)		$ (20)		$ (20)		$ (20)	
16	Entertainment	$ (186)		$ (123)		$ (38)		$ -		$ -	
17	Saxaphone Lesson	$ (80)		$ (80)		$ (80)		$ (80)		$ (80)	
18	Beauty	$ (75)		$ (75)		$ (75)		$ (75)		$ (75)	
19	Clothes	$ (100)		$ (100)		$ (100)		$ (100)		$ (100)	
20	Health(Dentist, Doctor, etc)	$ (47)		$ (47)		$ (47)		$ (47)		$ (47)	
21	other	$ (50)		$ (50)		$ (50)		$ (50)		$ (50)	
22	Education	$ -		$ -		$ -		$ -		$ -	
23	Vacation	$ (75)		$ (75)		$ (75)		$ (75)		$ (75)	

Figure 7-1

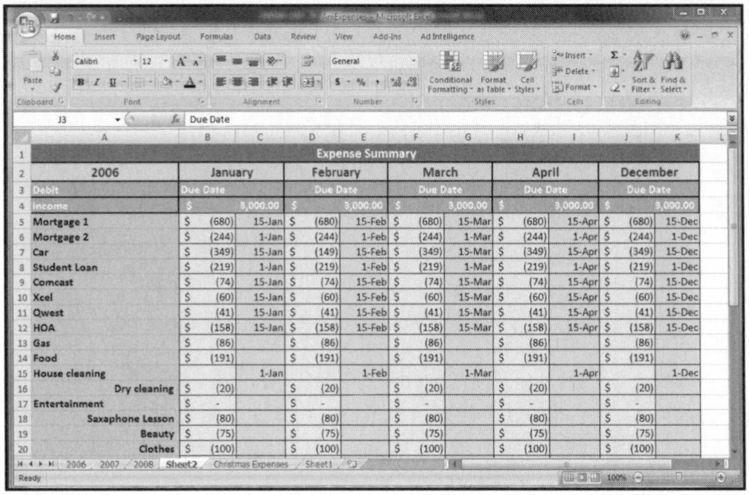

Figure 7-2

How hard is it to do this to your data? Not very. All it takes is a few mouse clicks and a few minutes. The black lines can be done by using the border box in the Font section of the Home tab on the Office 2007 Ribbon (Figure 7-3). Just select the cells you want to put borders around and click the border box shown in Figure 7-3 to select the type of borders you want to add.

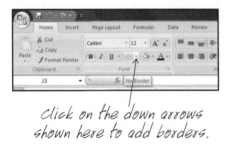

Click on the down arrows shown here to add borders.

Figure 7-3

All the **Bold,** *Italics,* and <u>Underlining</u> can be done using the Font section of the Home tab on the Office 2007 Ribbon. As well as the alignment, merging cells and the styles for the numbers can be done using the Alignment and Number sections of the Home tab on the Office 2007 Ribbon. You can see all of these sections in Figure 7-4.

Did you know ...

The Office 2007 Ribbon was mainly due to the work and research initiated by the End User Engineers (Microsoft employs more than 200 of these). The End User Engineer's job is to find out how most people use a product and how people prefer to use it, so they can build the best and most user-friendly product.

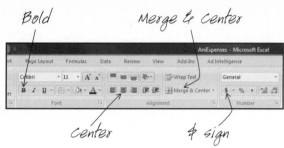

Bold

Merge & Center

Center

$ sign

Figure 7-4

The colors can be added by using the Styles section of the Home tab on the Office 2007 Ribbon (Figure 7-5). You can change the color of the text in the cells or you can fill the cells with color from this area. You can also select the font style and size from this same section as well.

change font here

change font size here

Change the color of the text here

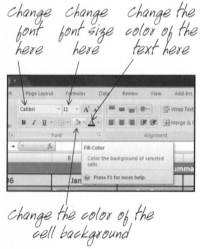

change the color of the cell background

Figure 7-5

What if you wanted to give your text a little bit of attitude by tilting it a bit so it stands out? Well, that can also be done from the Alignment section of the Home tab on the Office 2007 Ribbon as shown in Figure 7-6. There are many other options as well, but if you do put text on a diagonal a lot of attention goes to it. So select where you place the diagonal text carefully, otherwise you might give your reader a pain in the neck (literally).

Make your text tilt like this...

...by using this button on the Alignment section of the Home tab. Note the other options available.

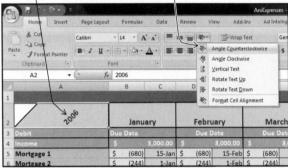

Figure 7-6

Pretty Up the Data Like an Excel Diva

So far I have shown you only one way, the harder way in my opinion, to format your data. But it is important to understand the basics of what is going on before you move forward and use some of the advanced features to help you save time and effort to beautify your data. It's like looking at the women who have learned the art of makeup. They have applied makeup for so long that they can make every stroke count and reduce the time it takes to put it on. As a beginner it probably took them an hour, but after many years and ample practice they can now put on their full makeup, from cleanser to blush, in less than 20 minutes.

The same is true for you, dear Diva. You are now ready to see the shortcuts of making your data look great. Let's begin with the Styles section of the Home tab on the Office 2007 Ribbon as shown in Figure 7-7. You will notice Conditional Formatting, Format as Table, and Cell Styles as options. Let's quickly cover each section.

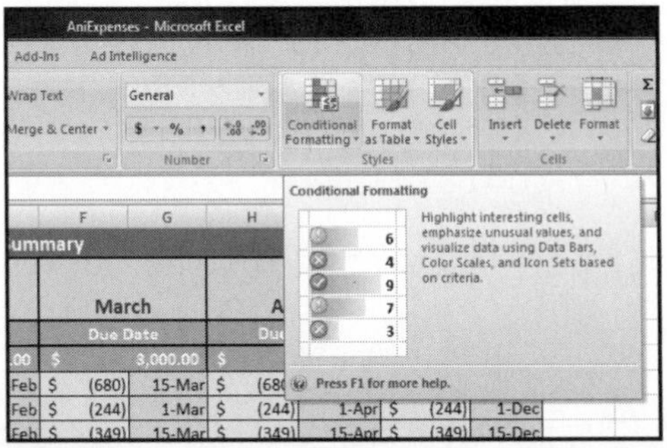

Figure 7-7

Conditional Formatting

When you look at a sea of shoes at your favorite department or shoe store, what helps you identify which shoe you want to try on and then which one you want to buy? Nordstrom's ladies shoe department is laid out in the following manner: the known brands are separate from the seasonal shoes, which are separate from the late season shoes and the bargain aisle. The dress gown shoes are separate from the office shoes, which are separate from the casual, comfortable shoes. Excel 2007 conditional formatting gives you the power to separate your data much like Nordstrom's does with their ladies shoe department, so when different people look at your data, in a quick glance they will know what they are looking at and where to find the pieces of data that they need. You also will be able to tell important things such as how much money are you spending on certain things a month and where to cut from if your expenses are getting a bit high.

A conditional statement is sometimes called an "if/then" statement. If it is sunny, then we'll go to the beach. If it is raining, then we'll go to the mall. Conditional formatting is the same idea. If the data in a certain cell meets certain criteria, then it is represented a certain way (with color, icons, or a bar).

The Conditional Formatting button helps by quickly pointing out the unusual values, and using data bars or colors gives you a quick visual of the story behind the data you are looking at. This button also helps you see color scale of the data you are looking at to see where the largest to smallest data appear. Figure 7-8 shows what is possible with the Conditional Formatting button. I will focus on the three main conditional formatting options:

- Data Bars
- Color Scales
- Icon Sets

Figure 7-8

Data Bars

If you want to see a quick graph-like picture of what is going on with your monthly expenses and where you are spending the most money, this is a great way to do it. The little bars fill the cell your data is in and show you which cell has the largest positive value. Notice that with your data, since we did write our numbers as negative, the largest negative number appears with the smallest bar. Figure 7-9 shows how using data bars looks.

Flash from the past ...

In mathematics a very big negative number like –1,200 is also known as a very small number, because when you compare –1,200 to 2, –1,200 is much smaller than 2.

Figure 7-9

To use the Conditional Formatting data bars, just follow these steps:

1. Select the rows or columns of data you want to use in conditional formatting.

2. Then click the Conditional Formatting button located on the Styles section of the Home tab on the Office 2007 Ribbon.

3. From the drop-down menu select Data Bars, and six samples of colors open in a second menu.

4. From the second menu, select the color you want.

Your final outcome will look like Figure 7-9. Keep in mind that the conditional formatting takes effect immediately, so as you hover over the colors you will see your selected data with bars changing colors.

Color Scales

If you want to see a quick color scale of what is going on with your monthly expenses over several months and where you are spending the most money, this is a great way to do it. The various colors pop up inside the cells and the red colors tell you where the higher concentration of expense is. Figure 7-10 shows how you can quickly see what your data is telling you using color scales.

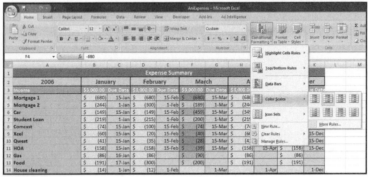

Figure 7-10

To use the Conditional Formatting color scales, just follow these steps:

1. Select the rows or columns of data you want to use in conditional formatting.

2. Then click the Conditional Formatting button located on the Styles section of the Home tab.

3. From the drop-down menu select Color Scales and eight samples of colors scales open in a second menu.

4. From the second menu select the color scale you want.

Your final outcome will look like Figure 7-10. Keep in mind that the conditional formatting takes effect immediately, so as you hover over the colors you will see your selected data with color scales changing colors.

Icon Sets

If you want to see a quick set of icons to help explain what is going on with your monthly expenses over several months and where you are spending the most money, this is a great way to do it. The various icons and colors pop up inside the cells, and the red colors or specific icons will tell you where the higher concentration of expense is. Figure 7-11 demonstrates how icon sets and colors work.

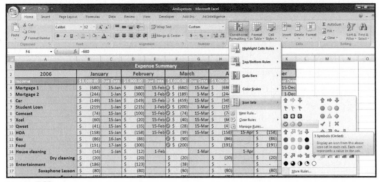

Figure 7-11

To use the Conditional Formatting icon sets, just follow these steps:

1. Select the rows or columns of data you want to use in conditional formatting.

2. Then click the Conditional Formatting button located on the Styles section of the Home tab on the Office 2007 Ribbon.

3. From the drop-down menu select Icon Sets and 17 samples of icons with colors open in a second menu.

4. From the second menu select the icons you want. Notice that you can also have little bar graphs appear in your cell before the data.

Your final outcome will look like Figure 7-11. Keep in mind that the conditional formatting takes effect immediately, so as you hover over the icons you will see your selected data with icons changing.

Format as Table

To follow the analogy from before, when it comes to shoes how can you pick the one that's right for you when they come in many colors and styles? Well, some people would say just get all black, because black will go with anything. True, but not always. It's nice to have a set of shoes with different colors for men and women; it gives your wardrobe a good sense of balance. But depending on the occasion, the clothes you are wearing and the style for that particular year will vary in color and style.

The same is true when you are considering building tables, which will showcase your data. Depending on your audience, and whether or not they might be color blind, prefer specific colors, or just like to see more data than color, your table style will vary. For those specific times you can use New Table Style to change the formatting of your table.

For formatting tables quickly there is the formatting table button located next to the Conditional Formatting button in the Styles section of the Home tab on the Office 2007 Ribbon. This button shows you many choices of table formats. You can also create your own by clicking on the bottom option of New Table Style. Figure 7-12 shows further what options come with the Format as Table button.

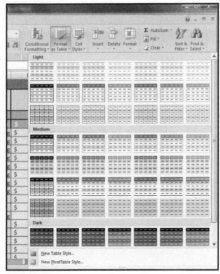

Figure 7-12

Cell Styles

To enhance the look of the cells on your spreadsheet, there is the Cell Styles button next to the Format as Table button on the Styles section of the Home tab on the Office 2007 Ribbon. You can select the header, bold styles, color, and format for the pre-selected cells. You can see some of the pre-created choices available in Figure 7-13. You can also create your own cell style by selecting the last option to create a New Cell Style.

Figure 7-13

To use the Cell Styles, just follow these steps:

1. Select the cell of data you want to use in styling up the cells.

2. Then click the Cell Styles button located on the Styles section of the Home tab on the Office 2007 Ribbon.

3. From the drop-down menu select which section (see the option for sections below) you need. Keep in mind you can only select one item at a time:

   • Good, Bad, and Neutral—for background colors and style.

   • Data and Model—for data and modeling.

   • Titles and Headings—for headings and font for headings.

   • Number Format—for formatting numbers such as %, $, comma, and so on.

   • Or create your own cell style by clicking on New Cell Style on the bottom of the drop-down menu.

Keep in mind that the cell style takes effect immediately, so as you hover over the choices in the drop-down menu you will see your selected data cells changing.

Cell Formatting the Easy Way

Although with Excel 2007 you can use the Font section of the Home tab on the Ribbon, there is a faster way.

Here's a faster, easier way to format cells:

1. Select the cell of data you want to customize.

2. Then right-click and a window much like Figure 7-14 will come up, from which you can select formatting options.

Figure 7-14

3. If the formatting options you need are not available, select the Format Cells option, shown in Figure 7-15. Doing so brings up another window much like Figure 7-16, which will help you with further formatting.

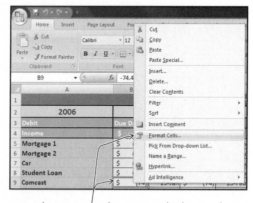

Right-click on the selected cell to see the menu where you can pick the Format Cells option.

Figure 7-15

Figure 7-16

Now for That Perfect Dress: Applying Themes

So now that you have done the formatting of your data, the makeover is partially done. A makeover is not complete with just redoing the hair and face; you also have to pick the right dress and theme to help your data come alive. When helping a girl-friend get ready for that great date you wouldn't just help do her hair and makeup and walk away, would you?

To pick the right dress for your Excel 2007 data, it's time to add a theme. A theme in Excel 2007 is a pre-defined universal design that unifies all of the styles we have been talking about. You can find themes on the Page Layout tab, in the first section titled Themes on the Office 2007 Ribbon (Figure 7-17). When you apply these themes it replaces the formatting you've already applied individually, so make sure you have made a copy of your work before you proceed, or copy and paste to a new sheet and save the document before you continue.

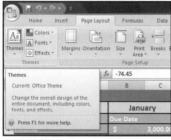

Figure 7-17

By clicking the Themes button you can select a theme that works best with your data (Figure 7-18). Once you select a theme you can see it immediately applied to your data. You can always change the colors or customize your theme. The colors have been picked by graphic designers based on which accent colors go best with the major colors.

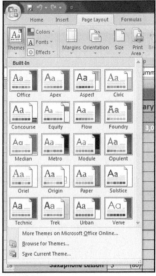

Figure 7-18

There are 20 ready-to-use themes when you click on the Themes button. You can also currently download 19 more from Microsoft Office Online as shown in Figure 7-19. There are more being added every day. Note: You must be connected to the Internet for this to work. Some of the most popular ones you might want to consider are:

- **Office:** Keeps most colors the same as is with the look and feel of Office 2007.
- **Concourse:** Adds a bit larger font and feel.
- **Aspect:** Adds larger font with different colors.
- **Equity:** Adds a very similar feel to an equity statement.

Are you a true Diva? A little too Diva? You're just so picky and none of these pre-defined themes will work, you'll just have to make up your *own* theme? Well, okay. You can do that too.

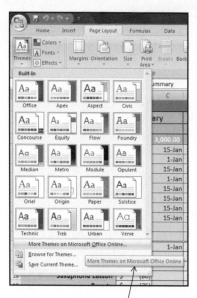

You can download more themes online.

Figure 7-19

Here's how to create your own theme:

1. Spend the time you need to customize the look and feel of your worksheet.

2. Then click the Themes button on the Themes section of the Page Layout tab on the Office 2007 Ribbon.

3. When the menu comes up much like Figure 7-18 go to the bottom and select the Save Current Theme option.

4. A Save Current Theme window will come up, where you can just name and save your current theme, much like you have been saving your workbooks (refer back to Chapter 2).

Dazzle the Numbers

In Excel 2007 the General format is what you see in every cell when you begin typing numbers. However, if you want to see different number formats you have to change the format to suit your need, just like a woman cannot be feminine in everything she does. Let's say if a woman was hunting it would be difficult to show off her manicure and a cute pink skirt while chasing a bear. I'm not saying it's impossible, it would just be difficult. So for those cases where the pink skirt and the perfect manicure don't make sense and the General format just won't do, the Number section of the Home tab on the Office 2007 Ribbon is there to the rescue. You can select the data and make changes to the number formats that are displayed by using the Number section of the Home tab (Figure 7-20).

Click on the drop-down menu to see all the number formats.

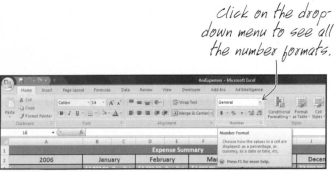

Figure 7-20

Chapter 6 discussed using the =DOLLAR() function to convert a number from its current format to a $ format. However, there are a number of ways to do things in Excel 2007; you can just as easily use the drop-down box from Figure 7-20 to accomplish the same.

There are 11 available formats for a given number in a cell when you click on the drop-down box in Figure 7-20, which is located on the Number section of the Home tab on the Office 2007 Ribbon. You will see the first nine when you open the drop-down and can see another two when you use the scrollbar of the drop-down menu. You can also select the More Number Formats option from the drop-down menu, which brings up the window titled "Format Cells" shown in Figure 7-21, where you can make a specific selection from hundreds of formats.

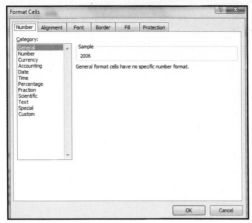

Figure 7-21

Some of the most popular ones you might want to consider are:

- **General:** This format is what Excel 2007 uses by default. It is not a specific format, which gives you plenty of flexibility to pick your format when you are ready.

- **Currency:** This format looks very much like what you might see on your bank statement; it has the $ dollar sign followed by dollars and cents.

- **Short Date:** Shows a short date much like 08/25/2008. Excel 2007 also offers a long date format, which would be day of the week, name of month, then day, then year. An example might look like Monday, August 25, 2008.

- **Percentage:** Displays the value in the cell as a percentage. So if you have 100 in the cell you will see 100.00%. Keep in mind this is different than selecting a cell and clicking the % button in the Number section of the Home tab on the Office 2007 Ribbon.

If the options in the drop-down box just do not offer the format you need you can always select More Number Formats and the window in Figure 7-21 will come up, where you can select the format you want.

Changing number formats is very easy. Follow these steps:

1. Select the cells of data you want to change the format for.

2. Then click the drop-down box in the Number section of the Home Tab on the Office 2007 Ribbon as shown in Figure 7-20.

3. Scroll all the way down to More Number Formats and click on it.

4. Then a window will come up much like in Figure 7-21.

Notice by default the window goes to the General category of the Number tab in this window. This is because the current format of the cell you are working with is General. However, if you had already applied a format, then Excel 2007 would take you to the specific format you had already applied.

As an example, I have picked a cell where I had previously applied the Custom Date format, which is day followed by month (dd-mm). So when I click on More Number Formats the window in Figure 7-21 comes up with the format that I already have highlighted, as seen in Figure 7-22.

Notice the cell I have picked has a date on it, therefore the Format Cells window automatically takes me to Custom dd-mm option, showing me which format I currently have. I can always change this.

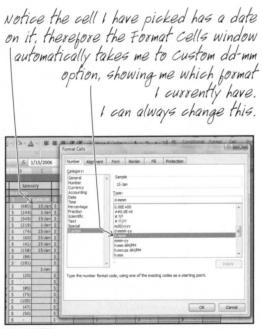

Figure 7-22

The Swingin' Single Quote

There is a little known secret among those who have been using Excel before the 2007 version: it is the single quote. By default when you type a number value into Excel 2007 the value adjusts itself from right to left (so the numbers are right-aligned) after you hit the Enter key, even though when you are typing you are typing from left to right. However, with text values such as words it aligns from the left to right. If you type number values and want to have them line up from left to right as well just put a single quote (') in front of the number and type the number value in the cell. The number then will align from the left to the right and the single quote will not even show up.

You can also always utilize the Number section of the Home tab to make changes to the style of numbers you want to appear in the cell you are working on. Once you settle on a format for your number and now want to copy that format to the cells around it, you don't have to go through the same steps again. You can if you want to, but as Excel 2007 Divas we love to cut down the work and get things done fast.

There is a great little button called the Format Painter located on the Clipboard section of the Home tab on the Office 2007 Ribbon.

Here's how to use the Format Painter:

1. Go to the cell that contains the format you want to mimic in other cells.

2. Select the cell and click the Format Painter button (Figure 7-23). You will see a dotted line appear around the cell you had previously selected.

3. Now go to the cell you want to copy the format to and click on the cell or cells. You see that the format copies over and the cells that were not formatted are now formatted the same as the cell you started from. Once you do this, or click anywhere, the Format Painter will turn off automatically. It is only good for the first click after you click on Format Painter. If you double-click on the Format Painter it will stay on until you click on it again to turn it off.

I love this great little shortcut, plus a little paint brush appears with a thick white cross symbol that indicates to you that Excel 2007 is ready to apply the format you selected to your next selection.

Figure 7-23

Relax, Refresh, Reward

Whether it's classical or modern, or just plain old country, music is the rhythm of life. I grew up with music; it was always a part of our life. In my family when we got together for holidays or any special event we all took turns singing. I know that sounds a bit strange, but after a while when you got used to some people who really didn't want to sing, and others who really sounded bad, the overall experience was fun. For this chapter's reward, I want you to get your groove on and start jamming to some good music. Spend 10 minutes, and follow where the music takes you. http://www.zune.net/en-US/ is a great place to start. This is the Zune community where you can do anything from listen to music, to purchase songs, join a community of others who enjoy the same type of music as you and even buy a Zune. Listening to music has other benefits. You just might feel like getting up and dancing by yourself, which is a great feeling. I find I dance with my broom most every time I am cleaning and I feel much better afterward. It's a great feeling when you are cleaning your house and end up clearing your mind at the same time. Whatever your favorite beat, make a habit of listening to it at least once a day. I love waking up to a great Techno beat; I can dance in the shower, as I get dressed, and as I walk out of the house on my way to work. Plus it guarantees I rarely have a bad day.

Feeling a little self-conscious about dancing? For inspiration, consider going to this blog and reading what Jen Lemen has to say about dancing! "I left that party last night thinking that there is no problem in this world that dancing cannot cure. I mean seriously, what would happen if someone rang a bell everyday at three and you had to stop whatever you were doing and shake what your mama gave you for three whole minutes? What kind of shift would happen in the Universe? If every day we had a chance to dance?" (See her blog at http://jenlemen.com/blog/?p=348).

If you're having a hard time with the idea of traditional music, consider some music that has a strong beat but no words. That's how I found Paul Oakenfold. I really enjoy Paul as a DJ, he just mixes music really well. Although I have not yet found the DJ who has mixed the classics with Techno, I think Paul comes pretty close with some great hits. Check him out at http://www.Zune.net (search for Greatest Hits & Remixes by Paul Oakenfold).

If you do spend some time every day dancing, the next time you go out to the clubs with your friends you might surprise yourself.

8 Dazzle Your Next Meeting

To Do List

Pick your paper size

Mind your headers and footers

Preview your work before you print

Make time for a facial

with a Print

When all is said and done, what you wear, how you prepare and present yourself to others matters. You know it, or you wouldn't dress appropriately for interviews, dates, and important life events. How you present yourself says a lot about how you see yourself. It can also have a positive effect on how you feel about yourself. Dressing nice doesn't have to be expensive–just smart–just like presenting data doesn't have to take hours, it just has to be smart and make sense. This chapter covers how you prepare your data to present it to others in the form of a print-out.

Prints are always simple and in most cases black and white, but in that case everyone knows the data speaks for itself and it's boring. It also shows no extra attention went into the work, and overall it's just not an enjoyable thing to look at. You've noticed that if you feel great and look great people tend to help you faster, things move along better, and the quality of life overall just improves all by itself. Well it's because of how you are interacting with life. The same principle applies here; if you put a little bit of effort here to make a better print, add color, and present data in a more fun fashion, you'll be amazed at how many people pay more attention, enjoy your presentations, and overall how much better you feel about yourself. Plus it will help you get noticed when that next raise evaluation comes around.

What's Your Worksheet Size?

I love the Office 2007 Ribbon, because once again we can go back to the Ribbon for all of our printing needs as well. But before we start talking about printing we need to find out how tall and wide our worksheet is and how it will show up in a print. For that we can take a look at the Page Setup section of the Page Layout tab on the Office 2007 Ribbon and then select the Size option as shown in Figure 8-1.

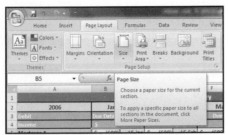

Figure 8-1

Pear Shape or Just Tall

Most of us have heard about the various shapes our bodies come in. There is the bell-shaped figure, the pear-shaped figure, the tall, and so on. The two most common print orientations are:

- **Portrait** (which is often how you hold a paper in your hand)—the taller, skinnier layout with the long way down and short way horizontal on an 8.5 by 11 sheet of paper.

- **Landscape**—The wider, shorter layout with the longer side on the horizontal on an 8.5 by 11 sheet of paper. The Orientation button on the Page Setup area in the Page Layout tab on the Office 2007 Ribbon can help you select (Figure 8-2).

Figure 8-2

If you have more columns than rows it would work best to have the Landscape layout so you have room to show off all your columns. Otherwise, for more rows and fewer columns, Portrait layout works better.

Paper Size

It would make sense for Excel 2007 to only let you pick the paper size your printer can handle. Well Excel 2007 is much smarter than that; it will let you pick a variety of sizes of paper, just in case you do want to make your beautiful worksheet available on a large paper or a smaller one. By clicking on the Size button on the Page Setup area of the Page Layout tab in Figure 8-1 you can see the most common page sizes drop down as shown in Figure 8-3.

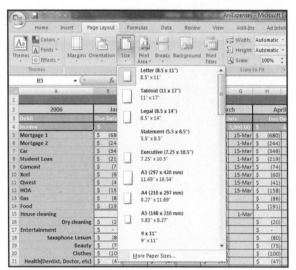

Figure 8-3

By scrolling down to the More Paper Sizes option on the bottom of the menu you can get to More Paper Sizes as shown in Figure 8-4, where you can select more paper sizes, print quality, margins, Header/Footer, and more. The most common sizes that most printers carry are Letter (8.5 × 11 inches) and Legal (8.5 × 14 inches). If your worksheet is wider than it is tall and it's too wide to fit as a Portrait on a Letter size paper, it might make sense to go to a Legal size paper. You can select which paper size makes the most sense before you print.

Figure 8-4

If you do go outside of the bounds of the recommended paper size, just keep in mind that your prints might look a bit awkward. You will have the cutoff where Excel 2007 thinks it should cut off. Therefore, those might be columns that will appear on another page or rows.

Margins

What if your worksheet would fit onto a page if only you were able to fix the margins? Well you can. On the Page Layout tab where you found the Size button on the Page Setup section on the Office 2007 Ribbon, you will see a button titled Margins, much like shown in Figure 8-5.

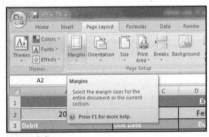

Figure 8-5

When you click on the Margins button a window much like Figure 8-5 will come up, where you can see the three most commonly used settings and a place to customize your own margins in Custom Margins, which is the last option on the drop-down menu in Figure 8-6.

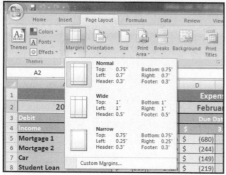

Figure 8-6

Here's how to use the Custom Margins:

1. Open the worksheet to which you're going to apply custom margins.

2. Select Custom Margins from the drop-down menu in Figure 8-6 and a window will come up titled Page Setup, with the Margins tab open, as seen in Figure 8-7. You can also get to this window by clicking on the Margins button in the Page Setup section of the Page Layout tab on the Office 2007 Ribbon.

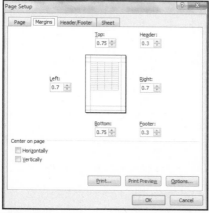

Figure 8-7

3. While in the Page Setup window you can select the width, height, and the side lengths in inches for margins.

4. Once you are done, just click the OK button on the bottom-right corner of the Page Setup window (Figure 8-7) and the margins you have selected will take effect.

Also, keep in mind most of the same options we have looked at so far can also be found when you click the bottom-right corner of the Page Setup section of the Page Layout tab on the Office 2007 Ribbon as shown in Figure 8-8.

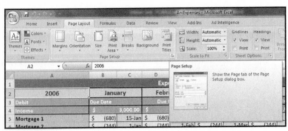

Figure 8-8

Page Break

Page break is a great way to end a page where you want and begin a new page. It specifies where a new page will begin and can be inserted to the bottom and left of the selection. You can find the page break button titled Breaks on the Page Setup section of the Page Layout tab of the Office 2007 Ribbon as shown in Figure 8-9.

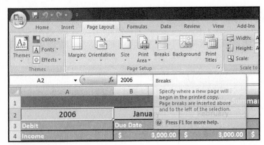

Figure 8-9

Headers and Footers

The things you place in the header or footer of a worksheet will appear on every page of the printed document. A header appears at the top of each page of a document; a footer appears at the bottom of each page. This is a fantastic place for page numbers, your name, listing the file location, listing the date it was last updated, or making a document confidential. You can find the Header & Footer button located on the Office 2007 Ribbon on the Insert tab in the Text section as shown in Figure 8-10. You can also find it when you click the bottom-right corner of the Page Setup section of the Page Layout tab on the Office 2007 Ribbon as shown in Figure 8-8.

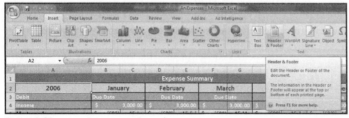

Figure 8-10

To add a header or footer you can do the following:

1. Go to the worksheet you want to apply the header or footer to.

2. Click the Header & Footer button located on the Text section of the Insert tab on the Office 2007 Ribbon and a window much like Figure 8-11 will come up.

You can begin typing text into the header here.

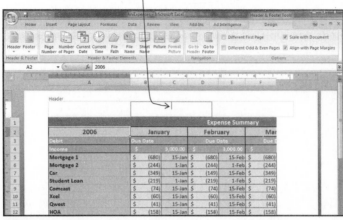

Figure 8-11

Shortcut

Keep in mind that most of the same options we have looked at so far can also be accessed by clicking the bottom-right corner of the Page Setup section of the Page Layout tab on the Office 2007 Ribbon shown in Figure 8-8.

3. Take a moment to look at all the options displayed for you on the Office 2007 Ribbon. This is a new tab called Header & Footer Tools. From the left to right on the menu, you can select to work on the header or footer, add certain elements from the Header & Footer Elements, Navigation, and Options.

4. Once you are done, just hit the Esc key and then select the Normal view from the bottom-right corner of the Excel 2007 window as shown in Figure 8-12.

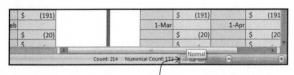

Click the Normal view button to get back to your worksheet.

Figure 8-12

The Magic Mirror: Print Preview with Enabled Changes

Remember how nice we said it would be to know exactly how you'd look in a dress without having to actually put it on? Well you can with your prints from Excel. Before you print a page you can see exactly what your print will look like, which is a great way to save yourself trips to the printer, and save a few trees. For those of you who think of the trips to the printer as exercise, you might have to sign up at the local gym after this great little feature. This is a great new feature with Excel 2007.

To see what your prints will look like before you print, follow these steps:

1. Go to the worksheet you want to preview before printing.

2. Click on the Page Break Preview button located on the Workbook Views section of the View tab on the Office 2007 Ribbon and a window much like

Figure 8-13 will come up. Notice that although you cannot really read the data, you can pretty much see what the print-out will look like in case you need to make changes.

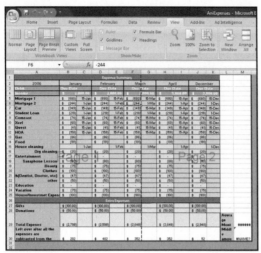

Figure 8-13

3. When you are done, click the Normal button located on the Workbook Views section of the View tab to go back to the style of screen you had before.

In the previous versions of Excel you couldn't see how the changes you made to data would look in a print right away. You had to go to Page Preview where you would see your mistakes and when you returned to the main worksheet you couldn't see the mistake anymore. Well with Excel 2007 you can edit your data even in Page Layout view (Figure 8-13). You can find the Page Layout view on the View tab on the Office 2007 Ribbon (Figure 8-13).

Since Excel 2007 gives us many options to accomplish the same task, we can also preview our print by going to the Office Pearl and clicking once on the button, resulting in a drop-down menu. If you scroll down the menu and stop on the Print option, you will see a secondary drop-down menu from which you can select the Print Preview option as shown in Figure 8-14.

New in 2007

You can now make and see changes in Print Preview! In previous versions of Excel when you went to the Print Preview mode you could not make adjustments to the data on your worksheet. Now, you can!

Figure 8-14

This is one final step to see how your print will look (Figure 8-15) before you actually print. Note inside this Preview window that you cannot make any changes to your worksheet and must hit either the Print button to print or the red button with an x on it to exit and go back to your worksheet.

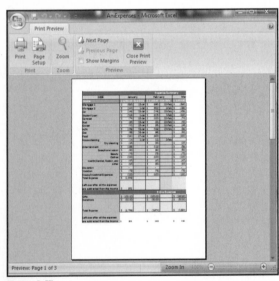

Figure 8-15

What to Print

In Excel 2007, there are various ways to print. But before printing, there are several decisions you'll have to make: which printer to use (if you have more than one in your office or home), how many copies, and whether to print the whole workbook or just certain pages.

The best place to start is the Print window (Figure 8-16) where you can make all the option selections for your print. You can find the Print window by clicking on the Office 2007 Pearl, which results in a drop-down menu that includes the Print option. From there you will see a secondary drop-down menu (Figure 8-14) from which you can select the Print option, which will open a window much like in Figure 8-16.

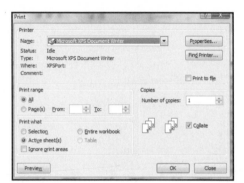

Quick Tip

As a time saver, you can hold and press Ctrl + P to bring up the Print window shown in Figure 8-16.

Figure 8-16

On this window you can also select to print a specific range of pages in the Print Range section, choose to print the whole workbook or active sheets in the Print What section, as well as number of copies in the Copies section.

Select Print Properties

In the Print window you can click on the Properties button, which brings up the properties of the printer you are connected to. As you become an Excel Diva you will be able to use this section to customize how your printer will deliver the print. You can choose stapling, front and back printing, and so on. However, since it is specific to the printer you are attached to, just take a look. In most cases you can just use it as is.

Find a Printer

If you do not already have a printer you have used before, you might have to go looking for a printer, which is when the Find Printer button comes in handy on the Print window as shown in Figure 8-16. Once you click on the Find Printer button, a window much like Figure 8-17 comes up from which you can select a printer. This might also be a time to call someone who has a printer connected to their computer in your office to help you, since printer names and locations vary.

Figure 8-17

How to Print

Okay, you've now defined your page layout and paper orientation, you've defined what you want to print, and how much you want to print on each page. You've found the printer and set the options for the printer. Now, you just have to get those materials to the printer. Excel 2007 offers several options for printing:

- You can click the Office Pearl button, from which you will get a drop-down menu. If you scroll down the menu and stop on the Print option, a second drop-down menu appears. Select the Print option as shown in Figure 8-14.

- You can use the shortcut by pressing Ctrl+P to bring up the Print window as well.

- You can always select the Quick Print option under the Print option in Figure 8-14 if you just want to print the worksheet you are in.

All three of these are fantastic ways to get to print. Once you open the Print window just click the OK button and you can pick up your prints at the printer.

Relax, Refresh, Reward

This chapter has helped you learn how to put a good "face" on your worksheets for printing. Now it's time to put a good face on yourself. For this chapter's reward, I'd like you to give yourself a treat: a facial.

If you take care of your skin, it will take care of you, and if you don't, then it will not last. We spend so much time finding the perfect foods, making the perfect home, and trying to do everything that's right, but we forget to take care of ourselves and relax once in a while. Just like taking care of your hair and drinking plenty of water, you also need to take care of your skin, hydrate it, give it nutrients, and go through daily routines to make sure you take care of it the best you can. Obviously the more time you put into your skin the better it will look, but that doesn't mean you abuse it. So once in a while it's important to get a facial from a professional if possible. The professionals learn a lot about the latest natural ways to take care of skin, which is good to learn. I wouldn't recommend handing your skin completely over to them, because after all it is your skin and they already have their own to worry about.

I find facials a great way to unwind and give back to my skin. It doesn't have to be expensive, just fun and relaxing. You can always read about how to make your own masks and mix your own natural mask on http://beauty.about.com/od/skinflaws/a/facemasks.htm. These are pretty good recipes made from ingredients you can find in your home. Just grab a few friends and have them come over and do a ladies afternoon on a Saturday once every two months or so. This way you have something to look forward to, you can give (and get) attention, and celebrate your skin when you are done.

So simply put, get a few magazines and a few friends and throw yourself a facial party. Or you can go out there and find yourself a licensed professional and get a real one. Make sure the facial esthetician is licensed and, if possible, that there is a dermatologist on staff. This way if there are any questions the doctor can answer them right away.

9

Add Pictures

To Do List

- Add pictures to data
- Create flowcharts
- Add lines to your spreadsheets
- Format shapes and art
- Select from many shapes, stars, and banners
- Enjoy your hobby

to Your Spreadsheet

Just like you put makeup on your face, there is a need to dress up and put makeup on your data. Although our definition of beauty may differ, all of us enjoy beautiful things. And then data is so bland. But if we dress it up, all of a sudden people want to not only look at the data, but also understand the why, how, and when of the data, and then really get excited about it.

Excel 2007 has all the tools you need to create really amazing graphics to better explain your data or ideas you have about your data. Since women can be so very creative, I think the graphic part of Excel 2007 is especially helpful for us ladies. And if you do have graphics from other programs you like, you can most likely import them into Excel 2007 without a problem. This chapter will get you acquainted with the graphics features of Excel.

Using Shapes and Clip Art in Your Worksheets

I was interviewing for my role as the Identity Product Manager with the .NET Framework Product Management group when I realized the power of not only Excel but also Microsoft PowerPoint 2007. I had written a Business Plan Document that included some data about what I was hoping to give to the role I was applying for. I had used Excel 2007 to just write a list of items, which looked okay but not great. Then I started to use the shapes in Excel 2007 and began playing with the shape format and adding shadows and colors. Soon I had something that was not only good quality information but also very pleasant to the eye. I then imported my work into PowerPoint 2007 (which I will talk about more in Chapter 11) and I was set for my interview. After I got the position, everyone told me how impressed they were with the Business Plan Document, and now it has become a standard for the interviewees, where the hiring manager asks the interviewees to present their document before the interview. But also, I got a pat on the back from all the interviewers about how great my document looked and they all asked me if I had used WPF (Windows Presentation Foundation), part of the .NET Framework group of programming languages. They were surprised to find out I did it all in Microsoft Excel 2007 and Microsoft PowerPoint 2007. Ladies, you have the talent, now just make it look good. After all that time you spend preparing yourself physically and mentally for an interview, it's a good idea to have a resume and (if necessary) a portfolio to match. This chapter will walk you through all kinds of the fun things you can do to jazz up your worksheets and make a killer impression.

For all your shapes and clip art needs you can go to the Insert tab on the Office 2007 Ribbon. On this tab, in the Illustrations section you can find the Clip Art and Shapes buttons. You can either use the clip art that is already in Excel 2007 or search online for more in the sections to come. The Shapes button will open a world of shapes for you to use to help better explain the story your data is trying to tell you.

Clip Art

To explain a specific concept or story you are trying to show with your data, clip art (Figure 9-1) is just the thing. These are previously saved little pictures that help you tell your data's story better.

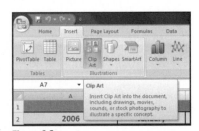

Figure 9-1

Once you are ready to begin searching for just the right clip art to help bring out the best story about your data, just click on the Clip Art button and follow these steps:

1. Once you click on the Clip Art button located on the Insert tab on the Office 2007 Ribbon, a menu will come up on the right side of your Excel 2007 worksheet much like Figure 9-2.

2. Leave the To search For: box blank, and choose All Collections from the Search In: drop down just like shown in Figure 9-3.

3. Then make sure to click the arrow next to the Results Should Be box and select All Media File Types.

4. Click the Go button and a set of results will fill the white space below much like in Figure 9-4.

5. Once you select the clip art you want to use from the menu of clip arts, double-click on it and the clip art will show up on your worksheet. Then you can move the clip art and size it to your liking.

The little green circle that appears on the top of the picture will help you rotate the picture if that is what you want to do; just grab it with your mouse and rotate it to your liking.

Figure 9-2

Figure 9-3

Figure 9-4

More Clip Art Options

What if the clip art you want is not showing up in the search? Well you can search on Office Online by selecting the link shown on the bottom of the Clip Arts Search window in Figure 9-5. You must make sure you are connected to the Internet when you click this link. When the web page loads you will find several sections about clip arts: a daily clip art and a section on the bottom of the web page where you can search by categories (and there are many).

Figure 9-5

Shape it Up

Excel 2007 graphics tools have a lot of great shapes you can choose from, or you can create your own. You can go to the Insert tab on Office 2007 Ribbon where you'll see a variety of graphic options. You can select the Shapes button (Figure 9-6) in the Illustrations box.

Figure 9-6

In most cases people have not used other graphics programs, so Excel 2007 does a nice job of very easily showing you what to do, and the knowledge you learn with Excel 2007 transfers well to other programs. Let's get started by dragging a shape and working with it (Figure 9-7).

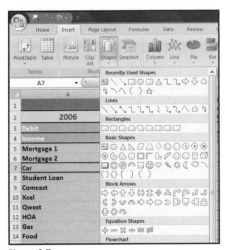

Figure 9-7

To add shapes to your worksheet, follow these steps:

1. Click on the Shapes button on the Illustrations section of the Insert tab.

2. From the drop-down menu you can select the shape you want and click once on it. When you do the mouse pointer will turn from an arrow (or what your default mouse pointer is) to a small thin cross.

3. Now you are ready to go to the location on your worksheet where you want to insert the shape. Start where you want the picture to start and click and drag it to the desired size.

4. If you want to move your shape you can select it and drag it to the desired position.

5. You will also see a rectangular frame appear around the shape as you move it. You can use the frame to move the shape around as well (Figure 9-8) and expand the size. The frame will go away once you click away from the shape.

This green circle helps with rotation.

The frame that helps with sizing the shape.

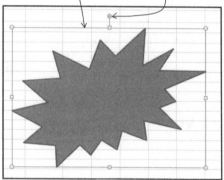

Figure 9-8

Rotate Your Shape

You'll notice that when you select your shape a green circle appears on top of the rectangular box. Once you hover over the green button on top of the shape a circular arrow will become visible and you can begin rotating the image. This is a great way to get a nice effect from the shape. If you rotate the shape too much or change your mind after rotation you can always use the undo button (Figure 9-9).

Figure 9-9

Formatting Shape Effects

Notice a new tab comes up called Format on the Office 2007 Ribbon when you drag a shape to your worksheet as shown in Figure 9-10. This tab helps you format and customize your shape to give the right Diva-like style to your worksheet.

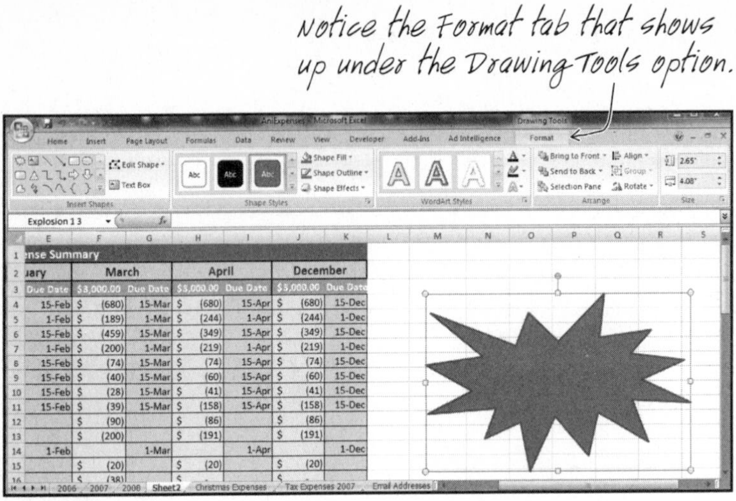

Notice the Format tab that shows up under the Drawing Tools option.

Figure 9-10

You can use the following sections of the Format tab from the Drawing Tools area (which only shows up as an Office 2007 Ribbon tab, when you begin working on a WordArt) for:

- **Shape Styles**—Fill the shape with a different color, change the outline and shape effects to add shadowing.

- **WordArt Styles**—Change the text that might appear inside the shape, change the text color, outline, and effect if you want to add shadowing.

- **Arrange**—Rotation, alignment, bringing the shape to front or sending it to back as a water color are some of what you can find in this section.

- **Size**—Where you can update the size of the shape by selecting specific inches.

Undo! Redo!

The undo button is next to the disk symbol on top of the page next to the Office 2007 Pearl. You can also press Ctrl + Z for undo.

Similarly, if you want to move forward to a change you had made before you clicked undo (Ctrl + Z, or the undo key) you can always use the redo button on top next to the undo button or press Ctrl + Y.

Adding Lines to Your Worksheet

Ever hear the shortest distance between two points is a line? Well you can use a variety of lines from the Shapes button on the Illustrations section of the Insert tab to help showcase your point. Use the straight lines for calling attention to a certain area. The broken lines can go around pictures or callouts as well as the squiggly (like the S shaped) lines. You can also use the free-shaped line at the end of the front row to draw any freestyle line as a shape and rotate it later using the green circle, which pops up after you are done drawing. You can find all the possible lines on Figure 9-11. The steps for inserting lines in your worksheet are the same as those discussed for adding shapes; just go to the Lines section as shown in Figure 9-11.

Figure 9-11

Rectangles

Rectangles are a fantastic way to draw attention to a specific section of data inside Excel 2007. The cells inside Excel 2007 are rectangular, therefore making it easy to use a larger rectangular shape to help you tell the story you found in the data. To use the rectangle shape, go to the Shapes button on the Illustrations section of the Insert tab on the Office 2007 Ribbon. You can use any of the rectangles in Figure 9-12 to enhance your data.

Figure 9-12

Once you pull them and display them in your worksheet, you can use the same green circle on top of the temporary rectangle that comes up and rotate the shape as well as move it using the temporary rectangle. There is also a little yellow diamond that comes up with these shapes that you can use to round the corners of the rectangle (Figure 9-13). The steps for inserting rectangles in your worksheet are the same as those discussed for adding shapes; just go to the Rectangles section shown in Figure 9-12.

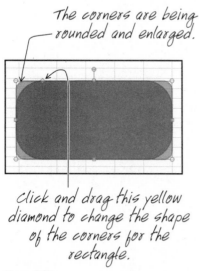

The corners are being rounded and enlarged.

Click and drag this yellow diamond to change the shape of the corners for the rectangle.

Figure 9-13

Adding Common Shapes to Your Worksheet

If you want a set of common shapes you can choose from the section in the Shapes drop-down menu titled Basic Shapes. They can be found when you click on the Shapes button on the Illustrations section of the Insert tab on the Office 2007 Ribbon. Any of the basic shapes in Figure 9-14 can be used to enhance and add to the character of your worksheet. Once you have selected the basic shape you want to add, remember you can use the green circle to rotate the shape and the little yellow diamond to change various parts of the shape, such as turning a smiley face to a regular or sad face. The steps for inserting basic shapes into your worksheet are the same as those discussed for adding shapes.

Figure 9-14

Block Arrow

There are a variety of arrows you can use from the Shapes button on the Illustrations section of the Insert tab. Use any of the block arrows (Figure 9-15) to enhance the style of your data on your worksheet.

Figure 9-15

Also remember you can use the green circle to rotate your block arrows and the little yellow diamonds to change the direction and width and thickness of the arrows (Figure 9-16). Notice on this shape that you have more than one yellow diamond since there are multiple ways you can change this arrow. The steps for inserting block arrows into your worksheet are the same as those discussed for adding shapes.

Figure 9-16

Adding Equation Shapes to Your Worksheet

There are a variety of equation shapes you can use from the Shapes button on the Illustrations section of the Insert tab. By using the equation shapes in Figure 9-17 you can create explanations of what and how you derived the outcome you did.

Figure 9-17

Also, keep in mind you can use the same green circle to rotate the equation shape as well as the little yellow diamond to make the shape thick or thin (Figure 9-18). The steps for inserting equation shapes into your worksheet are the same as those discussed for adding shapes.

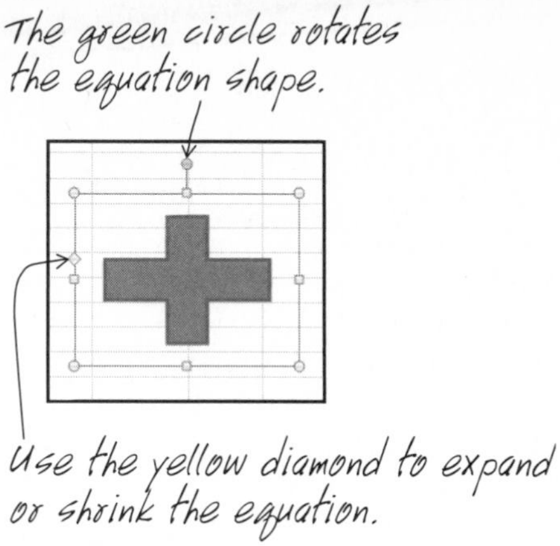

The green circle rotates
the equation shape.

Use the yellow diamond to expand
or shrink the equation.

Figure 9-18

Flowcharts

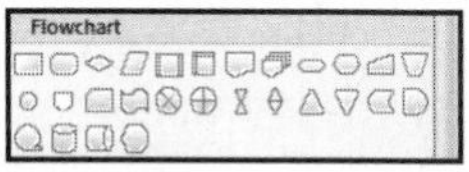

There are a variety of pieces to build a flowchart that you can
use from the Shapes button on the Illustrations section of the
Insert tab on the Office 2007 Ribbon. Also, keep in mind you
can use the same green circle to rotate the equation shape,
and you can also use the block arrows from above and lines
to illustrate how data or the idea you are presenting will flow.

Figure 9-19

By combining the block arrows and lines with the flowchart shapes (Figure 9-19) you
can present a thought very clearly and cleverly. Now that you have the tool, take it
to the next level ladies! The steps for inserting flowchart pieces into your worksheet
are the same as those discussed for adding shapes.

Stars and Banners

There are a variety of stars and banners you can use from the
Shapes button on the Illustrations section of the Insert tab on
the Office 2007 Ribbon. You can use the stars and banners
to display a part of your worksheet, which really stands out.
Also, keep in mind you can use the same green circle to
rotate the stars or banners you pick to display your data with (Figure 9-20). The
steps for inserting stars and banners into your worksheet are the same as those discussed for adding shapes.

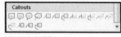

Figure 9-20

Callouts

There are a variety of callouts you can use from the Shapes
button on the Illustrations section of the Insert tab on the
Office 2007 Ribbon. You can use callouts (Figure 9-21) to
explain certain parts of your data or worksheet, especially if
you know your data will be sent around the office to people who don't know the
data as well as you do. Plus it's a fun way to add some character to your otherwise
black-and-white worksheet.

Figure 9-21

Also, keep in mind you can use the same green circle to rotate the callouts you pick to display your data with (Figure 9-22) as well as use the little yellow diamond to move where the callout points and how pointy the callout is. The steps for inserting callouts into your worksheet are the same as those discussed for adding shapes.

Figure 9-22

Easy Access

As you add more and more shapes to your worksheets, you might find that you are using some of the same pieces over and over again. This is particularly true when working on flowcharts. Excel 2007 makes this easier for you by giving you the option of selecting Recently Used Shapes (Figure 9-23), rather than having to look down the full menu (Figure 9-7). This is also a great way to cut down on work when you want to remember which shapes you used on your last worksheet while you're by the water cooler gossiping about the other latest news about your boss.

Figure 9-23

Relax, Refresh, Reward

There is a saying: "People come into your life for a reason, a season, or a lifetime." I think the same applies for hobbies. Most anyone I speak with is always amazed at all the things I am knowledgeable about. Well the trick is, it has all come over time; I didn't get all the knowledge at the same time. Hobbies also come into your life much like friends do. At times new hobbies can serve as a vehicle of making new friends. I would say yoga, reading, volunteering, learning new things, and working out are in my life for a lifetime. Other things in my life come and go based on season or a reason. I love snowboarding. I started out skiing for five seasons before I began snowboarding five seasons ago. So for this month's reward, I want you to dedicate some extra time on your favorite hobby. If you cannot think about a hobby or cannot think what you want to learn, let's begin with answering a few simple questions:

- What do you enjoy doing?

- What do you find yourself doing when you have free time?

- What do you daydream about?

- What would you do if money, time, or any other item in your life was no object or obstacle?

- Who would you do it with?

- What about your hero; do you know what hobbies she has?

You can always read on the web about new hobbies you want to get into or find blog posts about people who are doing what you want to learn. I even learned about a site where people are willing to teach you their language in exchange for learning yours. What a fantastic way to connect across the world, make a new friend, and have a chance to enjoy a new hobby. After that the world seems like a much smaller place, doesn't it?

You can check out the site I go to at http://www.mylanguageexchange.com.

Hobbies don't have to be expensive. There are many volunteer organizations, where you can get free training or lessons as long as you commit to help the youth and the in-need. I have learned basketball and bowling from Special Olympics. I found out anyone can volunteer to be a coach and make these special kids happy. I also found out making these children happy is very, very easy. It just takes a heart and happiness and they become happy. So I learned two new sports and they got to have me coach them and make a fool of myself. I made them happy by being there and I got to be happy by making them happy and learning something.

Add Visual Power:

To Do List

Adding WordArt

Choose the right SmartArt

Use clip art pictures

Have a manicure to feel amazing

Use WordArt and SmartArt

When starting a new phase of my life in Seattle, I found out there was a Yahoo group for Armenians there. I wrote numerous entries suggesting getting together to hang out. After the first meeting, I never heard from the few who responded. I finally met another successful globetrotting woman who was not only smart and strong, but an amazing speaker. We became fast friends one Sunday as we walked around Green Lake. The simplicity and eloquence of her words was inspiring, and I felt a true connection.

I had always wondered why people mistreated, disrespected, and fell short of the high bar they set for themselves at the start of a relationship or friendship. My newfound friend, wise beyond her years, simply said: "People have been hurt in the past and they act out the pain they have experienced, somehow trying to get even—in most cases subconsciously—and you just happen to be the recipient of it. However, there is always a lesson there for both."

My new friend took simple words and put them together to make them amazing! You can do the same thing to your Office documents by adding WordArt and pictures. Office 2007 makes it easy to add the right visual effects to really make your Excel spreadsheets, Word documents, or PowerPoint slides pop.

Using WordArt

On the Office 2007 Ribbon to the left of the Home tab you will find the Insert tab. As you move from left to right on the Insert tab you will find the Text group, which contains the WordArt button (Figure 10-1). By clicking on the button you open the menu (Figure 10-2), which gives you a selection of colors, outlines, shapes, and styles of letters you can use. You can use this to enhance and bring attention to the title or certain areas of your worksheet.

Figure 10-1

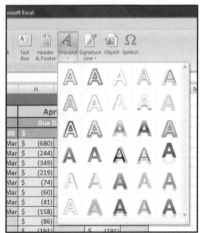

Figure 10-2

Adding Text to Your WordArt

Once you click on the WordArt menu (Figure 10-3) a text box with the words "Your Text Here" comes up. Much like when you insert shapes, which you learned about in Chapter 9, you can use the rectangle that surrounds the text to move it to a different location, and you can also use the little green circle to rotate the text. The rectangle and green circle are both shown in Figure 10-3. Just begin typing and "Your Text Here" will be replaced with what you are typing.

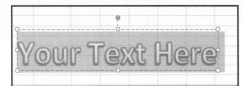

Figure 10-3

Along with the text box that shows up in Figure 10-3 with "Your Text Here" inside, you will also notice a new tab appear next to Add-Ins called Drawing Tools (Format) as shown in Figure 10-4. You can use the new tab shown in Figure 10-4 to customize the look and feel of your WordArt. So now type in the text you want to appear in the box.

Figure 10-4

Once you are done typing your text in the box, you can double-click on the text to open up the Drawing Tools to change the look of your text using the options in the Format tab, shown in Figure 10-5.

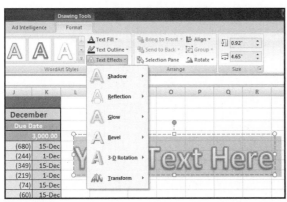

Figure 10-5

Now you see it . . .

The Format tab only comes up if you double-click on a shape or WordArt.

The first two groups on the left of the Format tab are shape-related. The three groups on the right apply to WordArt. You can fill the text with different colors, change the color of the outline, and change the text effects, as well as align, rotate, and change the size.

Special Effects for WordArt

In the Text Effects drop-down menu you will find Shadow, Reflection, Glow, Bevel, 3-D Rotation, and Transform. With Excel 2007 you can immediately see the results as you change the text effects, which makes it easy to get work done and free up more of your time. In the past you would have to select the specifications of what you wanted the text to look like, the color and everything else, and then close out the window to see what your text would look like.

Doing this numerous times became cumbersome and took a lot of time. With Excel 2007 this process is much easier because you can see the changes to the text immediately in plain view. Once you have the text effects picked out, you can align and rotate your text in the worksheet to achieve the stylish look you want.

Be Smart About Your Art

With all the things you have to do in a day, wouldn't it be great if Excel 2007 created its own graphics so you wouldn't have to do that work too? Well Excel 2007 doesn't come with a "this is what I mean" button, but it does give you a great big head start, so you will have that extra time to reward yourself with those cookies you had been planning to bake from scratch (or buy from the really good bakery down the street).

Choose Your Art Wisely

The days of going to your graphic designer friends are over. You can get your ideas together and create your own art that makes sense according to the data you will be including. I mean how many of you really buy designer art anyway? We always get the reprints, which look just as good and don't cost as much. It's the same here, except you don't have to get the cheaper version because you can create the real thing from scratch. What am I talking about? Well, let's go to the Office 2007 Ribbon and go to the Insert tab. You will find a button called SmartArt (Figure 10-6) in the Illustrations group. With SmartArt you can create art that can speak for itself.

What's so smart about SmartArt?

Most of us spend a lot of time pulling together shapes to create graphics that make a statement, because "a picture is worth a thousand words," right? With Office 2007, Microsoft has made it easy for us to create the pictures we need to explain what our data means.

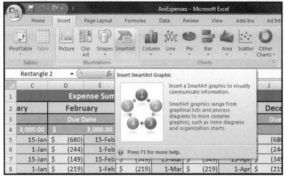

Figure 10-6

Once you click on the SmartArt button you will be able to select from a menu of items (Figure 10-7) you can add to your worksheet. SmartArt will either lay over the cells of data you have, or you can move it to a location without data or to a new worksheet.

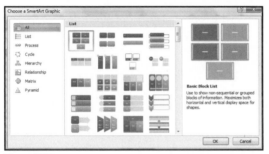

Figure 10-7

Customizing SmartArt

When the Choose a SmartArt Graphic window comes up, the "All" option is chosen by default on the left side of the window, and the Hierarchy Organization Chart is chosen. Do pay close attention to what is picked by default; it might vary for you. It doesn't matter, because you can go through and pick the SmartArt that's right for you.

Once you select the SmartArt you want to work with, just double-click on it and the SmartArt will appear on the worksheet. In this case, since I like the pyramid, go to the Pyramid option on the left side of the Choose a SmartArt Graphic window and then select the Basic Pyramid as shown in Figure 10-8. From there you can begin entering in text into the SmartArt and changing how the SmartArt looks.

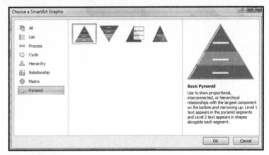

Figure 10-8

Notice in Figure 10-9 that two new tabs (Design and Format) have been added to the Office 2007 Ribbon. You can use these new tabs to better customize how your SmartArt looks.

Figure 10-9

1. Once SmartArt opens on your worksheet you can use the rectangle that surrounds your SmartArt to place it wherever you want.

2. Then you can either double-click on [TEXT] to begin typing your text, or click on the two little arrows on the left side of the SmartArt (Figure 10-10) to open the "Type your text here" box and begin typing your text as shown in Figure 10-11.

3. If you want to add more layers to the pyramid (more than three items in the pyramid, since three is the default), or any other SmartArt you can do that in the "Type your text here" box. Some SmartArts have a limit of how many layers or items you can add.

4. They will show a little red X mark to the left of the text in the "Type your text here" box, to show you, in order to maintain the quality of the SmartArt, that it cannot be expanded more and that you have met the limit of items you can add.

Click on these little arrows to open a text window.

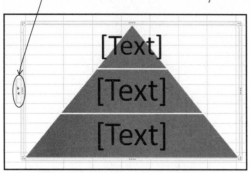

Figure 10-10

Notice the window on the left titled "Type your text here."

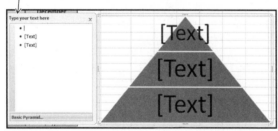

Figure 10-11

5. You can also set the size of the text box, by using the rectangle around the [Text] area.

6. The little green circle on top of your SmartArt is a great place to go to rotate your SmartArt. Rotating your SmartArt will give it a very arty feel and make the figure more attractive to the eye.

To tab or not to tab?

Tabbing through the choices to add text is not possible. You have to do a manual mouse-click. However, you can tab within the "Type your text here" box.

What if you want to change the color and format of your SmartArt and give it that picturesque look? Well, you can select the Change Colors button (Figure 10-12) in the SmartArt Styles group of the Design tab of the SmartArt Tools on the Office 2007 Ribbon. Keep in mind the SmartArt Tools are only visible when you double click on a SmartArt.

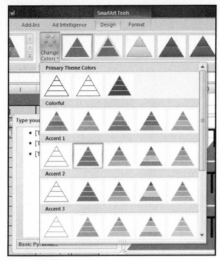

Figure 10-12

From the SmartArt Tools you can use the Change Colors button to change the color of your SmartArt to pre-selected colors or create your own masterpiece. Once you select the color mix you like, then you can begin to play with the SmartArt styles and see which texture you like for your graphic. Once you are done with picking the texture you can then right-click on the SmartArt image and begin to change the format the same way you did with shapes in Chapter 9.

Figure 10-13

You can right-click and go to the Format Shape (Figure 10-13) item on the menu to see how you can change the shadow, transparency, and background of your image for a final, fun SmartArt (Figure 10-14).

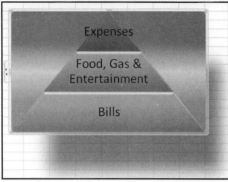

Figure 10-14

Adding Pictures

Just like you added clip art in Chapter 9, you can add pictures.

Adding pictures to your Excel spreadsheet is easy:

1. Go to the Insert tab on the Office 2007 Ribbon just right of the Home tab in the Illustrations section to find the Picture button.

2. By clicking on the Picture button you will open the Insert Picture window (Figure 10-15) where you can browse through your computer files to find the picture you want to enter.

3. In this case we will use the Sample Pictures folder by double-clicking on it and the folder will open up much like in Figure 10-16, from which you can select the picture you want to include.

4. Once you select the picture you want to use, just double-click on it and the picture will be added to your worksheet. It's a nice little touch to give your worksheet a little life as shown in Figure 10-17.

5. Once you import the picture, you can use the rectangle surrounding your picture to expand and shrink the picture as well as to move it.

6. There is also a green circle on top of the picture that you can use to rotate the picture.

7. You can also right-click on the picture and go to Format Picture to set the shadow, transparency, and other formats.

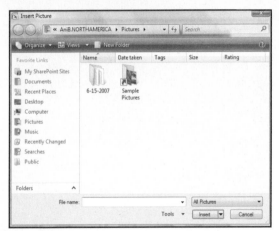

Figure 10-15

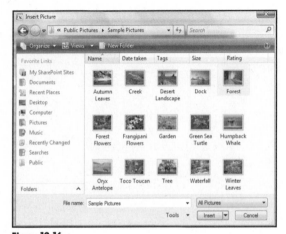

Figure 10-16

Figure 10-17

Relax, Refresh, Reward

Getting a manicure and a pedicure at a salon is a great way to enjoy and reward yourself for all the hard work your fingers have done with Excel 2007; your feet will feel great too. Plus you just might meet someone really great or get an inspiring idea.

Your nails, though at times annoying and brittle, are an extension of you. You spend all that time on your face, your hair, and the clothes you wear, but forget your hands? The first thing after you say hello to people when you meet them is to shake their hand. Most people during a handshake notice your hands and fingers. In warmer weather, depending on the type of shoe you're wearing, people will notice your toes as well. If you're going to make a great impression it is important to take time to pamper one of your most important possessions. You can be more confident about shaking hands with that potential new boss or client, or showing off the Excel presentation you worked so hard on when you aren't worried about how your hands look.

Okay, there are some rules for colors, but you don't have to follow them. It's not as if the nail police will hunt you down if you don't. During the winter the darker, warmer colors like reds, oranges, and browns are usually best, and in the spring and summer months you can wear the paler or brighter shades like pale pink or bright yellow. You don't have to match your toes to your hands. As a matter of fact you can wear pink on your toes and French manicure on your hands; I do it all the time. I love the fact that I can also have the manicurist paint a little flower on my finger or toe for some pizzazz! It's your time, be daring!

If I do decide to get my mani and pedi done at a salon, I always meet new people and enjoy a great conversation. I have met my accountant, lawyer, and several great friends at the nail salon. Plus the nail salon is where I got the great idea to get you inspired about Excel 2007 with this book (and reward yourself for making the effort to learn)!

11

Charting Your Course

To Do List

Explain the data with charts

Create a PivotChart

Create a bar graph

Add some color for a touch
of perfection

What goes on the axis?

Eat asparagus for your health

with Excel

The generalizations about men and women abound, particularly when it comes to numbers (ever hear that men are better at math, women are better with grammar? Men are more physical and data-driven, women are more emotional and artistic?). Well, thanks to studies and to powerful women and men the world over, we know those stereotypes are less true than they are self-fulfilling prophecies. You might have heard, though, that most stereotypes or generalizations have basis in anecdotal truth. Well, we aren't going to solve this debate anytime soon, and thankfully when it comes to Excel 2007 charts, there is something cool for everyone. There are both numbers and ways to display the numbers that allow us to be creative and logical at the same time. You can really create some amazing Excel 2007 charts while having fun and being creative.

Know Your Charts

Basically, a chart is a visual way to represent data by the numbers. This helps others see where the weight of the data is—concentrations and trends become evident when represented visually. Excel 2007 provides you with several different options to display your data visually. Think back to your high school math days and picture a typical line chart that you often see in commercials where a jagged red line moves up and down and more down, showing a downturn in sales or something. You will recall that there are two types of data. The months go across the bottom on the horizontal or X-axis, and the amount of sales in hundreds of dollars is on the vertical Y-axis.

Take some time and get acquainted with the chart options available. Go back to the Office 2007 Ribbon and move right of the Home tab to the Insert tab. Once you click on the Insert tab you will find the third section from the left titled Charts (Figure 11-1).

Figure 11-1

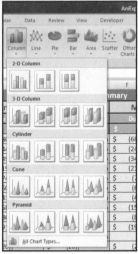

Figure 11-2

This is where you can select the type of chart you want to create. You can choose from several categories of charts, including Column, Line, Pie, Bar, Area, Scatter, and Other Charts. Within each category, there are several to choose from. Let's start with the Column category (see Figure 11-2). There are several choices, such as two- or three-dimensional or pyramid. The Other Charts option has, you guessed it, even more chart options.

After creating your chart, there are some design options that allow you to add your personal touch. The following sections walk you through creating a chart and dressing it up a bit, before moving on to PivotCharts.

Creating a Chart in Excel

First, determine which data you want to include in your chart. For the purposes of this chapter, I'll use data from the worksheet we've been playing with so far. Let's look at all the expense items as things that will end up on the left side (or Y-axis) of our chart and the dollar figure on the bottom of our chart (X-axis). Once you clarify what data will end up on which axis, you are now ready to use the Office 2007 Ribbon to begin creating your masterpiece.

Ch- ch- ch-changes

Keep in mind that any changes you make to your data will automatically be incorporated into your chart courtesy of Excel 2007. What's not to love?

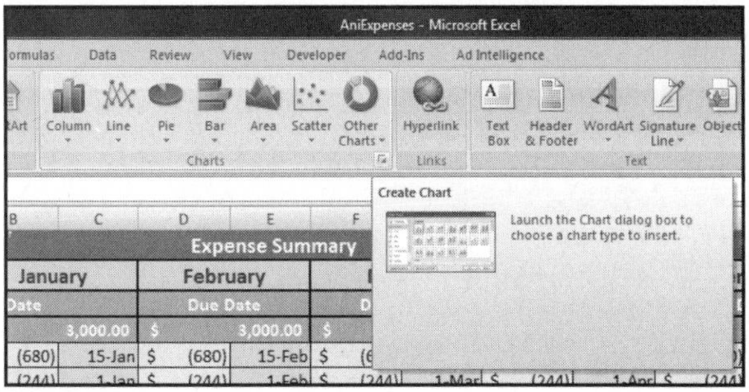

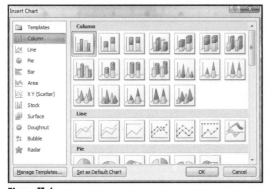

Figure 11-3

If you click on the little arrow at the bottom-right of the Charts section (Figure 11-3), the Insert Chart window (Figure 11-4) comes up. This is the Chart Wizard I mentioned before.

See Your Options

If you are uncertain about what type of chart to pick, you can always click the little arrow on the bottom-right of the Charts section of the Insert tab on the Office 2007 Ribbon to see all the charts (Figure 11-3) and to use the Chart Wizard (Figure 11-4), where you set up the chart step by step.

Figure 11-4

Different Chart Types

You can always hold your mouse over each type of chart listed to read a quick note about what each chart group can do. To see what types of charts are in each category, just click on the down arrow of that category. Let's take a few minutes and talk about the different chart options we have:

- **Column**—Used to compare values across different categories.
- **Line**—Used to show change in trends over time.
- **Pie**—Used to show the contribution of each value to the total amount; note all values must be positive.
- **Bar**—Used to compare multiple values.
- **Area**—Used to emphasize differences between several sets of data over time.
- **Scatter**—Used to compare pairs of values, especially when they represent different measurements.
- **Other Charts**—New to Excel 2007, used here to build a doughnut, surface, stock, bubble, or radar chart:
  - *Doughnut*—Displays the contribution of each value to a total like a pie chart, but it can contain multiple series.
  - *Surface*—Shows trends in values across two dimensions in a continuous curve.
  - *Stock*—Shows stock chart with the Open, High, Low, and Close values.
  - *Bubble*—Resembles a scatter chart, but compares sets of three values instead of two. The third value determines the size of the bubble marker.
  - *Radar*—Displays values relative to a center point. Use this chart when the categories are not directly comparable.

Creating a Chart

The first step in creating a chart is to select the chart type. Then go through the steps in the Chart Wizard. It's as easy as that.

Follow these steps to create a chart:

1. Open your worksheet and go to the Insert tab on the Office 2007 Ribbon.

2. In our case we will be working with a Column chart, so select the data you want to chart and then click on the Column button in the Charts section of the Insert tab.

3. Click on the 3-D Clustered Column shown in Figure 11-5. As you hover over each type of chart inside the Column drop-down window, a small explanation appears to help you better understand each chart.

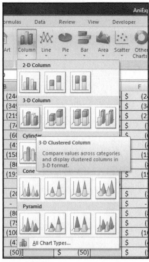

Figure 11-5

4. When you click on the 3-D Clustered Column, two things happen simultaneously. Three new tabs are added to the Office 2007 Ribbon under the Chart Tools title: Design, Layout, and Format. You can see this in Figure 11-6. A chart also appears with 3-D clustered columns on your worksheet. Note that since my values are negative, the chart shows the data going below the value of 0, much like what you see in Figure 11-7.

Figure 11-6

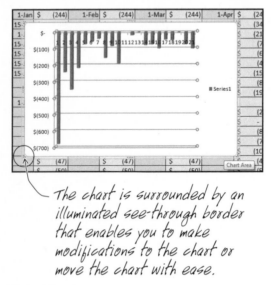

The chart is surrounded by an illuminated see-through border that enables you to make modifications to the chart or move the chart with ease.

Figure 11-7

5. You will notice that the chart came up (Figure 11-7) on top of our worksheet, and perhaps doesn't look that great, but it's a great start. Move it where it will be more visually appealing. The next section shows you how.

Moving Your Chart

If you've finished the previous Do It Herself, you know that the inserted chart comes up in the center of the worksheet. It will be easier to modify the appearance of this chart if you move it to its own worksheet or to a clear section of your current worksheet.

You have two options when it comes to moving the chart. You can use the rectangle surrounding the chart (the see-through border), or you can use the Move Chart button on the farthest right side of the Office 2007 Ribbon.

Here's how to move the chart using the mouse:

1. Click on the chart to illuminate the rectangular surroundings of the chart.

2. Click anywhere in the see-through border, and drag the chart to any location on the current worksheet.

Here's how to move the chart using the shortcut keys:

1. Click on the chart to illuminate the see-through border surrounding the chart.

2. Press Ctrl + C to copy the chart.

3. Move your cursor where you want the chart to appear, either a cell in a blank area of your worksheet or a new worksheet.

4. Press Ctrl + V to paste it into the new location.

Here's how to move the chart using the Move Chart button:

1. Click on the chart to select it and open the Design tab, one of the three new tabs that appear.

2. On the Design tab, locate the new button on the far right side, the Move Chart button shown in Figure 11-8.

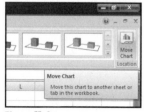

Figure 11-8

3. Clicking the Move Chart button opens the window shown in Figure 11-9. The window shows two options: one to move the chart to a new sheet and one to have the chart become an object in an existing worksheet. For this example, choose the Object In option.

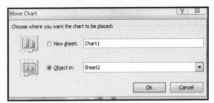

Figure 11-9

4. The Object In option has a drop-down menu, which lists the current worksheets in your current workbook. Select the worksheet in which you'd like to place the chart. Figure 11-10 shows the Sheet2 worksheet selected.

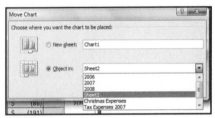

Figure 11-10

Chart Smart

If you try to copy the chart to a new workbook, the chart type will copy, but it will be blank; see Figure 11-11. This happens because the chart can only pull data from the workbook it is in. If you want the whole chart, data included, in the new workbook, you'll also need to copy the data the chart was created from.

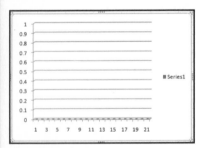

Figure 11-11

Modify the Chart's Appearance

Once a chart is created in Excel, three extra tabs are added to the Office 2007 Ribbon (in order from left to right): Design, Layout, and Format.

Changing Axis Names and Labels

To make a chart truly useful, you need to know what each part means. That means you need to create labels. Follow the Do It Herself steps in order to change the top of your chart to show the expense names from Column A of your worksheet.

Slight Data Modifications Might Be Necessary

You can change the data from negative to positive by multiplying all the cells by –1 (negative 1). You might remember from the chapter on formulas that in Excel negative numbers (such as expenses, in this case) show up in parentheses. That way the chart will not look upside down and will be easier on the eyes.

To change axis names and labels, just follow these simple steps:

1. Right-click on the chart to display the pop-up menu (Figure 11-12). Choose the Select Data option.

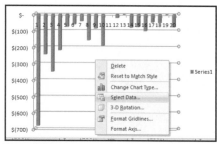

Figure 11-12

2. The Select Data Source window (Figure 11-13) will open. Add the titles of your expenses to the chart here.

The horizontal axis, by default, is labeled with numbers, because we have not entered any horizontal labels yet.

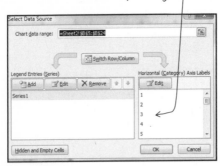

Figure 11-13

3. Now click on the button to the right of the Chart Data Range, which brings up a box like Figure 11-14.

The dashed line shows which data is selected.

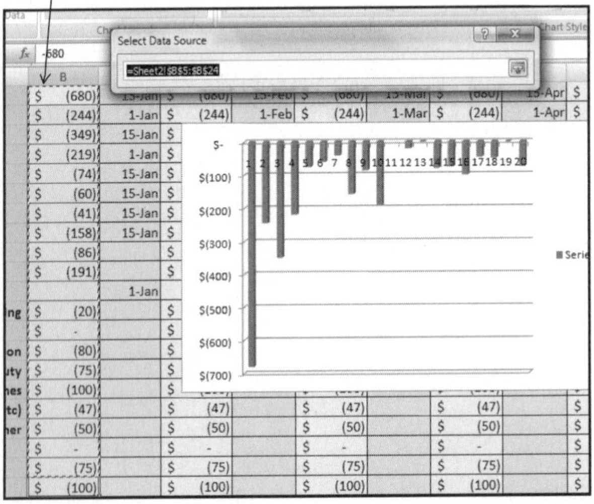

Figure 11-14

4. Select the name and data columns. You will see a dashed line around both columns. Check your screen against Figure 11-15.

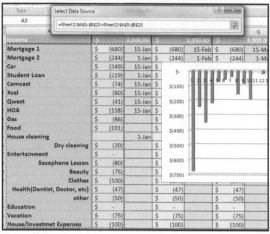

Figure 11-15

5. The text inside the Select Data Source window has changed to show both columns, and should read like this: =Sheet2!$A$5:$B$25+Sheet2!$A$5: $B$25. If you have it right, click the button next to the text, as shown in Figure 11-16.

Click this button to return to the Select Data Source window.

Figure 11-16

6. Back in the Select Data Source window, check that the titles for each expense are in the Horizontal Axis Labels box, as they are in Figure 11-17.

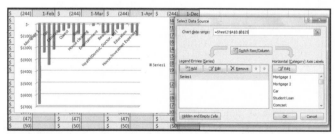

Figure 11-17

7. Click the OK button to exit out of the Select Data Source window. You are now done.

Dress Up Your Chart

Now that you know how to accurately label the chart on the horizontal axis, you need to know how to change the Chart Layouts and Chart Styles to find what looks best with your data. For each chart category you saw in the Charts section of the Insert tab (refer back to Figure 11-1), there are approximately six to eight different chart layouts. The different layouts are not named (each one doesn't have its own specific name), but they are numbered, such as Layout 1, Layout 2, and so on. The biggest difference among the layouts is the placement of the chart title, and the horizontal and vertical axis labels. Here's an example that will help you see these differences.

Now that you know how to select and label the data, it's time to make it fancy. You can pick the color and the style of the chart. Just like you wouldn't wear jeans everywhere without dressing them up or down at times, the same applies here. Charts look good, but depending on the style and layout you select, they can look perfect. Here's how:

1. Select the chart you want to work on by clicking on it. (Remember three tabs will become available on the Office 2007 Ribbon.)

2. Click on the Design tab and go to the Chart Layouts section located next to the Data section as shown in Figure 11-18.

Figure 11-18

3. There are three options shown. Use the up and down arrows next to the options or click on each option to view that layout. Select the layout that looks best to you.

Some Finishing Touches

We know from making that perfect holiday meal, or decorating our room or that little doll house we had growing up as kids, that there is nothing like a finishing touch. Excel 2007 makes the finishing touches really fun and exciting, especially since you can see the final outcome of what your chart will look like as you go. Let's get started with the Layout tab in the Chart Tools section, which is only visible when you have a chart selected. When you click on the Layout tab in the Chart Tools section you now have a set of tools you can use to change the layout of your chart, as shown in Figure 11-19.

Figure 11-19

Modify the Layout of Your Chart

When you click once on a chart, three more tabs appear on the Office 2007 Ribbon. The second from the right is the Layout tab, which contains a variety of ways to change the layout of the chart you clicked on (Figure 11-19).

Format

From the left to the right Figure 11-19 is filled with a variety of ways to change your chart to create a masterpiece or something fun. On the far left of Figure 11-19 you will find the drop-down that says Plot Area. By clicking to the right (where the little arrow is pointing down) you will be able to see all the other areas of your chart you can customize. Once you pick the area you want to customize with this drop-down box, you can click on the button below the drop-down box called Format Selection. By clicking on the Format Selection box you will launch the Format window (Figure 11-20).

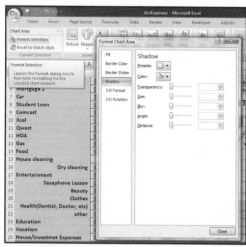

Figure 11-20

In Figure 11-20, you can format the item you selected from the drop-down on far left side of the Layout tab. You can add 3-D format, rotation, and shadowing to give the parts of your chart those finishing touches.

Insert

As you move right on the Layout tab you find the Insert section. You can add shapes and pictures to your chart here. This part works much the same way as was covered in Chapter 9. For more details on inserting pictures and shapes, please look at Chapters 9 and 10.

Labels

The third section on the Layout tab from the left side is the Data Labels section (Figure 11-21). With the Chart Title button you can add titles to your chart, and decide whether you want the title to be overlaid on the chart or placed on top of the chart. In Excel 2007 all titles, legends, and data labels are kept in the same section: the Labels section of the Layout tab of the Chart Tools. Remember the Chart Tools tab only appears when you are working on a chart.

Figure 11-21

To the right of the Chart Title is Axis Titles, which you can use to title what the bottom of your chart and the left side of your chart show (Figure 11-22). The button in the center is the Legend button, which helps add legends to explain what the data is about. You could, if you wanted to, add the same expense category from several months to the chart and see how they show up (the chart in Figure 11-22 only shows the month of January). You could have a different color or style of column and matching legend to represent that new data in your chart.

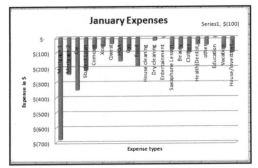
Figure 11-22

To illustrate the exact amount of money being spent for each expense item (each column), click the Data Labels button to the right of the Legend button, and from the drop-down menu, select Show (Figure 11-23). And finally, you can add a data table using the button to the right of the Data Labels button titled Data Table to further enhance your chart.

Figure 11-23

Axes and Background

Using the Axes button in the Axes section of the Layout tab (found in the Chart Tools Layout Tab section) you can change how the bottom and left side of the chart look. Using the Gridlines button as shown in Figure 11-24, you can add that checkerboard look (and you thought plaid was out of style), to give your chart a gridline background.

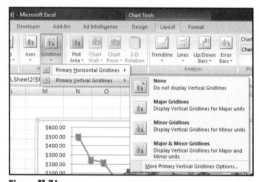

Figure 11-24

Moving to the right of the Axes section on the Layout tab is the Gridlines area, where you can change how the wall and floor of the chart look. You can also rotate the chart to give it that three-dimensional (3-D) look. Also, you can name your chart. This name doesn't appear anywhere visible, but it helps you keep track of the chart. If you have four charts on a worksheet, and they are named Chart 1, Chart 2, Chart 3, and Chart 4, it would be hard for you to figure out which chart was tied to which data. Naming is a way for you to be able to differentiate the charts from one another. If you only have one chart, you probably want to ignore this box.

Creating Tables and PivotCharts in Excel

So far you have learned the basics of how to take data from the spreadsheet and create graphs. But what if you have repetitive data like the expense spreadsheet I have been using so far? I call that repetitive data because it repeats, because I keep track of the same expenses every month. What if I want to see if there are changes in each expense category or how much I spend in each category? For this purpose, I need a PivotTable and then a PivotChart. It is difficult to talk about a PivotChart without first explaining a PivotTable. A PivotTable is an interactive way to quickly summarize large amounts of data. The Excel 2007 Help menu states that a PivotTable is especially designed for:

- Querying large amounts of data in many user-friendly ways.

- Subtotaling and aggregating numeric data, summarizing data by categories and subcategories, and creating custom calculations and formulas.

- Expanding and collapsing levels of data to focus your results, and drilling down to details from the summary data for areas of interest.

- Moving rows to column or columns to rows (or "pivoting") to see different summaries of the source data.

- Filtering, sorting, grouping, and conditionally formatting the most useful and interesting subset of data to enable you to focus on the information that you want.

- Presenting concise, attractive, and annotated online or printed reports.

You often use a PivotTable report when you want to analyze related totals, especially when you have a long list of figures to sum, and you want to compare several facts about each figure.

Now that you know the basics, let's get started.

Creating a PivotChart is easy using the following steps:

1. Begin by selecting the data you want to use in your PivotChart. Then, use the Office 2007 Ribbon and select the Insert tab.

2. Now, select the first button from the left in the Tables section called PivotTable. Figure 11-25 shows this in more detail.

Figure 11-25

3. Once you select the data, click the PivotTable button and a window similar to Figure 11-26 comes up where you can make further selections. The window will already have the Table/Range box pre-filled with the data you have selected.

Figure 11-26

4. Now you choose if you want the final chart to show up in the current worksheet or in a new worksheet. I like to create the chart in a new worksheet since it does take a lot of space and will create a PivotTable for me as well.

5. Click the OK button on the window shown in Figure 11-26. A new worksheet will be created inside of which you will see a window similar to Figure 11-27.

6. At this point, choose what type of a chart you want along with more options.

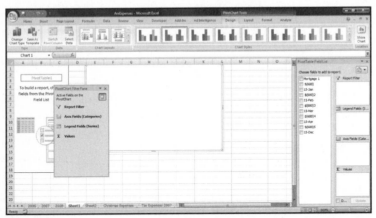

Figure 11-27

Make sure . . .

to select the PivotChart from the drop-down box of the PivotTable, located in the Tables section of the Insert tab on the Office 2007 Ribbon. Otherwise you end up with a PivotTable rather than a PivotChart. The default for the PivotTable button is a PivotTable.

In order to make certain you have selected the right option from the PivotTable button when the window in Figure 11-26 opens, you should select the top of the window for the words PivotChart or PivotTable depending on what you want to create. But always make certain you pick the right option since the PivotTable button is a drop-down button.

Design Your PivotChart

You now have all the data that you have pulled into this PivotTable and PivotChart from your original Excel 2007 Expenses Worksheet. Now you can pick whether you want to display everything in the PivotChart or just show certain items that might be important to you.

On the right side of the screen in Excel 2007 as shown in Figure 11-27, you will see the PivotTable field list, from which you can make your selection to include the fields in your graph. As you hover over each field you will see the color change as shown in Figure 11-28.

Once you click on the field you will have a pop-up menu as shown in Figure 11-29, from which you can select all the fields or just some of them based on what you are trying to show.

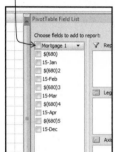

Click here to select the field to include in the PivotChart.

Figure 11-28

Figure 11-29

Once you select the fields you want to include in the PivotChart you will begin to see each field appear on the chart as you select it. Figure 11-30 shows further what the PivotChart will look like once you have selected all the fields from the right side of the screen in Excel 2007.

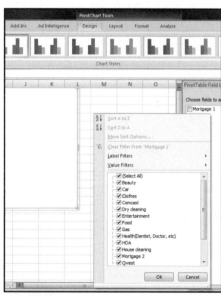

Figure 11-30

Chart is graph . . .

In Excel a chart is the same as a graph, therefore you will see a lot of reference to charts. In Excel there are tables and charts. These are most commonly known as tables and graphs outside of Excel.

Once you have created the PivotChart you can go to the Chart Layouts section of the Office 2007 Ribbon as shown in Figure 11-31 and select the type of PivotChart you want to create. The Chart Layouts section contains anywhere from six to eight types for each chart layout. The types determine where the header, footer, axis label, and legends will show up on your chart.

up and down arrows scroll through all the layouts.

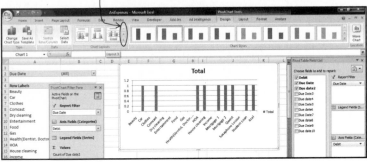

Figure 11-31

If you notice, Excel 2007 is pretty smart. While you were creating your PivotChart Excel 2007 was creating a PivotTable for you, as shown in Figure 11-32.

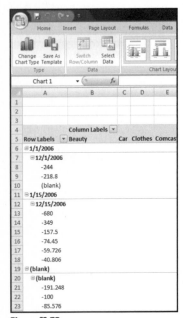

Figure 11-32

Relax, Refresh, Reward

Well, you've now completed the last chapter in Part II, Excel 2007: Live It!. Until now, you've been learning how to perform some of the more common tasks in Excel. Before moving on to Part III, Excel 2007: Love It!, where you'll learn how to put this newfound knowledge to practical use, take a minute and reward yourself by treating yourself right. It's time to eat your vegetables!

I recently read that frozen vegetables are better than fresh ones at times, since it takes time to drive the fresh vegetables to the stores where you buy them. With frozen vegetables, the vegetables are frozen right after they are picked so the nutrients and freshness are locked inside.

Whatever type of vegetable you pick it's best to include a few with every meal, and, no, two slices of tomatoes and some carrots don't count. I always love fresh broccoli; if you find it at a farmers' market, it tastes great by itself. If you want to add something to it, then I would recommend some cheese or dressing based on what you are in the mood for. Asparagus is much the same way. The thinner the asparagus the better it tastes. If you do cook vegetables make sure to use a bamboo steamer and don't overcook, or use very little water. The more you cook vegetables the more nutrients are lost. After all, much like humans, vegetables are made up of mainly water.

I know some of you may not find eating vegetables much of a reward, but anything that honors what your body needs is indeed a reward. Besides, it's all in how you prepare them. Here's one of my favorite recipes for asparagus:

 1 bunch of medium-sized asparagus, about 1 lb

 2 Tbsp of the most exquisite extra virgin olive oil

 2 Tbsp freshly grated Parmesan cheese

 1 teaspoon lemon zest (freshly grated lemon rind)

 Salt and freshly ground black pepper

1. Prepare the asparagus by rinsing them thoroughly, break off any tough, white bottoms and discard. Cut into 1- to 2-inch sections, slicing the asparagus at a slight diagonal.

2. Fill a medium-sized saucepan half way with water; bring to a boil. Add the asparagus and reduce heat slightly to a simmer. Parboil the asparagus for exactly 2 minutes. Drain the hot water. While the asparagus are still hot, toss them in a bowl with the olive oil, Parmesan, and lemon rind. Salt and pepper to taste. Serve warm or room temperature. (Find more fun simple recipes at http://www.elise.com/recipes.)

(III) Love IT!

"You must learn day by day, year by year, to broaden your horizon. The more things you love, the more you are interested in, the more you enjoy, the more you are indignant about, the more you have left when anything happens."

– Ethel Barrymore

12

Build a Shopping Spree

To Do List

Add up expenses

Figure out spending money

Create a budget spreadsheet from scratch

Set spending priorities

Design a daring budget spreadsheet

Shop, Shop, Shop till I drop!

Budget from Scratch

A favorite coach of mine often said: "Good judgment comes from experience; experience comes from a lot of bad judgment and mistakes." Making mistakes is the best way to gain experience. As our experience increases, our judgment becomes better. What does this have to do with Excel? Well, outlining budgets is one really common use of spreadsheets. Chances are, you've probably made some monetary decisions that you might consider a mistake. This chapter will walk you through the process of using a budget in Excel, so you know exactly how much money you can spend on whatever it is that excites you, be it a fancy handbag, a donation to a charitable cause, a good pair of hiking boots, or a road trip.

Budget Basics

A seminar I attended taught me to divide my money into five categories by percentage: to pay the bills, save for the future, obtain education, make donations, and have fun! By understanding exactly how much money you have coming in every month and how much it will cost to pay your bills, how much for food and gas, donations, fun, and education, it makes life a lot easier and your bills more understandable. Separating your expenses into these five categories ensures you are always aware of how you are spending your money, so you will know when it's time to make adjustments. Plus, this is a great way to relax with a cup of tea on a Saturday afternoon. Calculating your monthly budget can also be a good reason to call together a few friends for coffee and adjust your Excel spreadsheets together!

Dollar Divas

One quick note here: I'm an Excel expert, not a financial expert. Any numbers I use here are theoretical and meant to give you practical examples working in Excel.

Now let's go back to what I was saying before; if I had a $100 a month income I would spend it as shown in Figure 12-1.

31	Expense Habits								
32 Total Monthly Income	$ 100.00								
33 Expenses = 60%	$ 60.00								
34 Future Fund = 10%	$ 10.00								
35 Education = 10%	$ 10.00								
36 Fun = 10%	$ 10.00								
37 Donations = 10%	$ 10.00								

Figure 12-1

Based on the previous description of my budget you will see that I spend:

- 60%, or $60 out of my $100 on Expenses (bills, credit cards, all living expenses such as food, gas, phone bills, and so on)

- 10%, or $10 out of my $100 on my Future Fund (savings, 401K, IRA, and so on)

- 10%, or $10 out of my $100 on Education (books, seminars, books on CD, yoga, kickboxing classes, art classes, musical instrument lessons, or anything else that helps me become a better, more well-rounded person)

- 10%, or $10 out of my $100 on Fun (going out to eat with my girlfriends, drinks at a club, shopping at the mall, movies, buying a new board game, and so on)

- 10%, or $10 out of my $100 on Donations (clothes I give to churches, money I donate to causes, museums, gifts, and so on)

It is very important to pick a simple method for dividing your expenses and stick to it. It's not a good idea to borrow from one category to cover costs in another. That doesn't mean you can't adjust your budget, but it does mean you cannot simply change it because you want to overspend at the mall.

In order to have a healthy financial picture and a clear understanding of your finances, some self-discipline and adherence is crucial.

Ladies, to become a Diva you have to know what is going on with your expenses, and Excel 2007 is there to guide you. No matter how difficult it may be to stick to your financial plan at first, you have to use your Diva abilities to encourage yourself to budget wisely. The end result is well worth your trouble! Remember: it's never about how little money you make, but rather about how much more you will make if you have the right habits and if you truly understand the cause of your overspending.

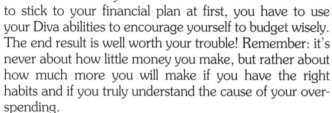

Expense plan ...

You might want to add another area to your budget where you save up for an amazing vacation, day at the spa, or something greater. Whatever it is that you save for, just make sure you stick to your plan.

consider in your expense category include rent/mortgage, car payment, utilities, groceries, transportation/gas, and any special monthly expenses you know that you have (and yes, that little manicure kit counts too). It's only when you count all these little expenses that you can better understand where your income is spent, plus when tax season comes you can just use your Excel 2007 Diva Budget worksheet to help pull all the information about your taxes together faster. Being an Excel Diva is all about making things easier and giving you back as much time as possible. If this is your first detailed worksheet, it may be easier to learn using my exact examples, then make a new one with your actual numbers next.

Create Your Own Diva Budget Worksheet

Now, it's time to put what you've learned in earlier chapters to practical use. Get your fingers warmed up, Divas, because it's time to create your own Diva budget worksheets. Before getting started, it's important to know how much of your income goes to expenses. If you can't or don't want to live off only 60% of your income, you'll need to adjust that up. Things to

To Each Her Own

Now, just because I spend 10% on education and self-improvement doesn't mean you have to. (Hey, you're probably perfect already!) You can set yours up in any configuration you want, so long as all areas total 100%.

Quick Math Refresher

To figure a percentage, remember this from junior-high math: X over 100 is equal to **is** over **of (is/of)**, so you multiply the "is" by 100 and divide that by the "of" and you get X, and X is the percentage. In a fog? Think of it in sentence form: "The total of my monthly expenses **is $1,220** out of a total monthly income **of $2,000**." More simply, you divide monthly expenses ($1,220) by monthly income ($2,000) and move the decimal point two places to the right. Either way, you end up with 61%.

Now let's begin with creating your Diva Budget worksheet:

1. Open a new workbook in Excel 2007 by clicking on Excel 2007 (from either the Start menu, clicking on the Vista Pearl or by clicking on the shortcut).

2. Save it as "Annual Budget," by using the Office Pearl button on the top-left corner of the Excel 2007 window.

3. Rename the first worksheet from "Sheet 1" to **Expenses,** followed by an underscore and the year (if this is an annual expense report) or Expenses followed by an underscore and the month and year (if this is a monthly expense report). For this exercise we will just call our worksheet Expenses_2008.

4. Add a header to the Expenses_2008 worksheet, as well as month names and due date columns. Here's how:

   1. Type **Expense 2008 Summary** in cell A1 and highlight cells A1 through Y1. Use the Merge & Center button in the Alignment section of the Home tab.

   2. In cell A2 type the year, in this case 2008.

   3. In cell B2 type the month name such as "January" for the cell B2, then highlight B2 and C2 and click the Merge & Center button in the Alignment section of the Home tab. Do this for every month in the year.

   4. In cell A3 type the word **Income.**

   5. In cell B3 type your take-home income amount for that each month. The take-home income is the paycheck you take home every month. This is the amount that is deposited into your bank account (most companies do direct deposit if you use it). Once you type this amount, use the $ symbol button in the Number section of the Home tab on the Office 2007 Ribbon to turn this value into a dollar amount.

6. In cell C2 type the words **Due Date.**

7. Once you are done do the same thing for every month for the year. Go through and add take-home income for every month and the words "Due Date."

So far your worksheet should look similar to Figure 12-2. You are free to choose your colors, themes, and text formatting. (For this example I have only placed five months into the worksheet. You should have all 12 if this is an annual expense tracking worksheet).

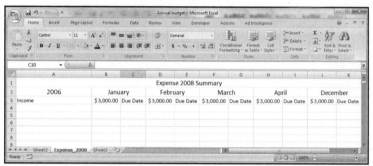

Figure 12-2

5. Now insert the categories of your expenses in the A column starting in cell A4. I have inserted the following for our example: cell A4 is Mortgage 1, A5 is Mortgage 2, A6 is Car, A7 is Student Loan, A8 is Comcast—you can see the pattern. Now you can add the following to the rest of the A column: Xcel, Qwest, HOA, Gas, Food, House cleaning, Dry cleaning, Entertainment, Saxophone Lesson, Beauty, Clothes, Health (Dentist, Doctor, etc.), other, Education, Vacation, House/Investment Expenses.

6. The last line you enter, in this case A25, will be "Total Left After Expenses Paid."

7. Now fill out the expense amount for each item in the A column in the B column, and D column and F column and so on. This will give you all the expense items for each month under your take-home income number. As you enter the $ amount, make sure to start each cell by typing "–123" (so negative sign (–) then the value) and then click on the $ symbol button in the Number section of the Home tab to turn this value into a $ amount. This will put all your expenses in negative, which is what you want (since expense is money out of your account).

8. Next to each expense item place the date the bill is due (hence the column header Due Date). To format the date to look like the date in the example, once you are done typing your date (example: 01/15/2008) click on the down arrow in the Number section of the Home tab on the Office 2007 Ribbon, which opens the drop-down menu as shown in Figure 12-3 from which you can select to go to the More Number Formats option.

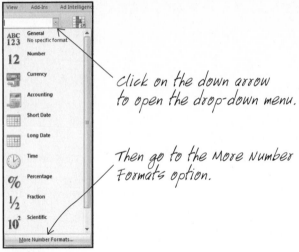

Click on the down arrow to open the drop-down menu.

Then go to the More Number Formats option.

Figure 12-3

9. Once you click on More Number Formats, a window titled Format Cells will come up much like in Figure 12-4 where you can select "Date" from the Category section and "14-Mar" from Type section and then click on the OK button. You can use the Format Painter (the brush button) from the Clipboard section of the Home tab on the Office 2007 Ribbon to apply this format to all the date cells. At this point your worksheet should look something like Figure 12-5.

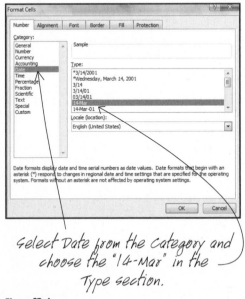

Select Date from the category and choose the "14-Mar" in the Type section.

Figure 12-4

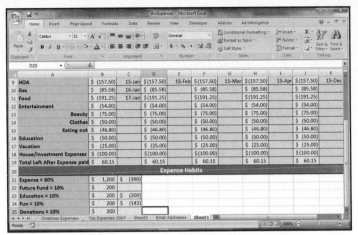

Figure 12-5

10. Insert the following equation into B25, D25, F25, and any other columns where the expenses are at the 25th row: **=B3+SUM(B4:B24)**. Keep in mind B will change to D for the D column, F for the F column, and so on. This equation will help you calculate total expenses (which are kept in negative numbers, that's why we added the minus sign in front of the expense amounts in step 7). We then add that number to our income (from basic algebra that means we subtract it) and we get the total money left over see Figure 12-6.

If this number is a positive number, that will mean we have cash left over after paying expenses. If that number is negative, then we are overspending on our expenses.

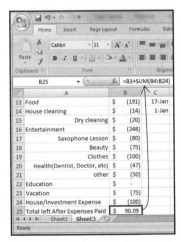

Notice the amount left over is $90.09 and the equation is shown.

Figure 12-6

11. Merge cells A26 through Y26 and type the words **Expense Habits.**

12. Begin typing **Expenses = 60%** in cell A27, **Future Fund = 10%** in cell A28, **Education = 10%** in cell A29, **Fun = 10%** in cell A30, and **Donations = 10%** in cell A31.

13. Fill the cells in the B column in front of A as follows: in B27 type **=.6*B3,** which will give you 60% of your income and help you see how much 60% of your income is. In the cell next to this, which is C27, you can type **=B27+SUM(B4:B15)** to find out how much more or less you are spending on expenses based on how much you should be spending. (Keep in mind this percentage is up to you; you can choose to spend 70% on expenses, but whatever number you choose to spend just stick to it.)

14. Follow the same process as in step 12 for Future Fund, Education, Fun, and Donations. You might notice Future Fund and Donations are not being tracked in your worksheet, so you need to add them in if you want to track them. Education is there and easy to track. Fun is not. Well we can count Entertainment and eating out as fun and add them together to find out how much you spend on fun every month, then add that to the Fun cell A25 to find out if you are within range or not.

15. Once you are done with steps 10 through 13, your outcome should look something like Figure 12-7.

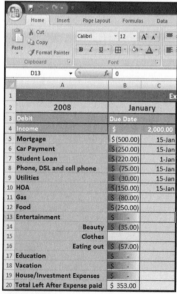

Figure 12-7

16. In row 20 across all cells you can see the money left over (Figure 12-7) after you are done with expenses. This money can be considered your Spending Money if you do not want to contribute to your Future Fund or make donations.

17. Now it's time to find out which expense item is your highest and what, if anything, you can do to change it. Otherwise you might have to find a way to increase your income. At first glance it's hard to tell but when I highlight the column B5-20 and apply conditional formatting as shown in Figure 12-7 from the Home tab, I can quickly pick out the highest expenses: Mortgage, Car Payment, Food, and then Student Loan payment.

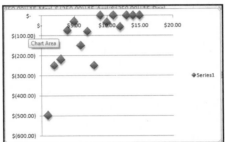

Figure 12-8

Make it Fit

Don't forget, you might need to resize the columns to get your words to fit. This means you use your mouse and double-click on each column or row line and Excel 2007 will automatically make the cell big enough to fit the content inside the cell.

18. Another way to look at this is to chart the expense items and see where the peaks appear as shown in Figure 12-8. You can create a chart by just highlighting the row of data, such as A5 to B20, and then clicking on the Insert tab and selecting the type of chart you want to create, which will then appear in your worksheet. As you notice the same four areas show up again: Mortgage, Car Payment, Food, and then Student Loan payment as shown in Figure 12-8.

19. In this case let's take a look at each expense and find out if we can cut any of them or reduce them in any way. Turns out you cannot really reduce the mortgage, but the student loan might be something you can reduce if you refinance. When it comes to food, let's look and see if we can reduce that a bit, go on more dinner dates perhaps. You definitely must eat and spend your money as you see fit; in this case we are just picking examples.

20. After looking through all the expenses it becomes apparent in our example that if we eat out a little bit more and spend less on food life becomes a little more balanced, because eating out goes under Entertainment and food costs go under Expenses. We also notice that the 60% is not working well, so it would make better sense to perhaps spend 80% on expenses and 10% on fun and 10% on education. That will look something like $1,600 for Expenses, $200 for Fun, and $200 for Education.

Formatting Your Budget Worksheet to Add Pizzazz

If you have not been formatting and adding themes to your worksheet as we went along, I will help you pull that together here. If you want to find out more about colors and themes make sure to go over Chapter 7. For now let's get started pretting up our worksheet:

1. If you have not been formatting your data, then your worksheet probably looks something like Figure 12-9.

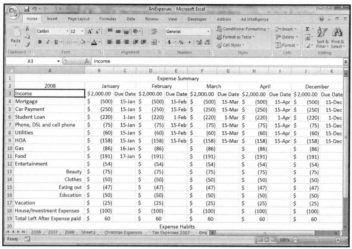

Figure 12-9

2. To add colors and themes let's begin with adding lines around the cells. This is pretty easy; just highlight all the data cells and click on the border dropdown menu in the Font section of the Home tab as shown in Figure 12-10.

Figure 12-10

3. To add color to the "Expense 2008 Summary," let's begin with clicking on the cell that has "Expense 2008 Summary" in it and click on the Cell Styles button in the Styles section of the Home tab. Select the color you like. Then click on the Bold button in the Font section of the Home tab and enlarge the size of the text and style of text in the Font section as well on the Office 2007 Ribbon. Then apply the same format using the Format Painter (the paint brush button) from the Clipboard section of the Home tab on the Office 2007 Ribbon to apply the same format to Row 31 titled "Extra Expenses."

Size to Fit

In Excel if you try to enter numbers that are bigger than the cell size, that is, if the cell can only hold four numbers and you enter five, the cell will display the value you entered as #####. In this case just double-click on the column line, or drag the cell to a bigger size and this problem will go away and you will see your full five numbers. Keep in mind that just because you cannot see the numbers doesn't mean they are not there.

4. Now use the same techniques as in step 3 for rows 2 and 3 for the year, and the month names, the take-home income, and the due date. You are always welcome to use different colors.

5. Highlight cells A5 to A20 and pick a theme, bold, and font size, and apply the same formatting using the Format Painter for cells A27 to A31. And select a different theme and text color for cells B5 to K20 and B27 to K31 (for our example and for your worksheet wherever you have expense amounts and date values).

6. Next, highlight all the expense values and use the Decrease Decimal button to decrease any extra decimal points you do not want as shown in Figure 12-11. By now your worksheet should look something like Figure 12-12.

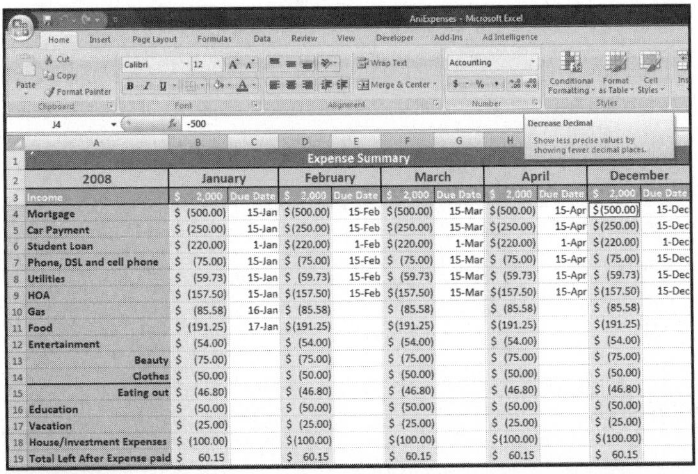

	A	B	C	D	E	F	G	H	I	J	K
1	Expense Summary										
2	2008	January		February		March		April		December	
3	Income	$ 2,000	Due Date	$ 2,000	Due Date	$ 2,000	Due Date	$ 2,000	Due Date	$ 2,000	Due Date
4	Mortgage	$ (500.00)	15-Jan	$(500.00)	15-Feb	$(500.00)	15-Mar	$(500.00)	15-Apr	$(500.00)	15-Dec
5	Car Payment	$ (250.00)	15-Jan	$(250.00)	15-Feb	$(250.00)	15-Mar	$(250.00)	15-Apr	$(250.00)	15-Dec
6	Student Loan	$ (220.00)	1-Jan	$(220.00)	1-Feb	$(220.00)	1-Mar	$(220.00)	1-Apr	$(220.00)	1-Dec
7	Phone, DSL and cell phone	$ (75.00)	15-Jan	$ (75.00)	15-Feb	$ (75.00)	15-Mar	$ (75.00)	15-Apr	$ (75.00)	15-Dec
8	Utilities	$ (59.73)	15-Jan	$ (59.73)	15-Feb	$ (59.73)	15-Mar	$ (59.73)	15-Apr	$ (59.73)	15-Dec
9	HOA	$ (157.50)	15-Jan	$(157.50)	15-Feb	$(157.50)	15-Mar	$(157.50)	15-Apr	$(157.50)	15-Dec
10	Gas	$ (85.58)	16-Jan	$ (85.58)		$ (85.58)		$ (85.58)		$ (85.58)	
11	Food	$ (191.25)	17-Jan	$(191.25)		$(191.25)		$(191.25)		$(191.25)	
12	Entertainment	$ (54.00)		$ (54.00)		$ (54.00)		$ (54.00)		$ (54.00)	
13	Beauty	$ (75.00)		$ (75.00)		$ (75.00)		$ (75.00)		$ (75.00)	
14	Clothes	$ (50.00)		$ (50.00)		$ (50.00)		$ (50.00)		$ (50.00)	
15	Eating out	$ (46.80)		$ (46.80)		$ (46.80)		$ (46.80)		$ (46.80)	
16	Education	$ (50.00)		$ (50.00)		$ (50.00)		$ (50.00)		$ (50.00)	
17	Vacation	$ (25.00)		$ (25.00)		$ (25.00)		$ (25.00)		$ (25.00)	
18	House/Investment Expenses	$ (100.00)		$(100.00)		$(100.00)		$(100.00)		$(100.00)	
19	Total Left After Expense paid	$ 60.15		$ 60.15		$ 60.15		$ 60.15		$ 60.15	

Figure 12-11

Expense Summary

2008	January	Due Date	February	Due Date	March	Due Date	April	Due Date	December	Due Date
Income	$ 2,000	Due Date	$ 2,000	Due Date	$ 2,000	Due Date	$ 2,000	Due Date	$ 2,000	Due Date
Mortgage	$ (500)	15-Jan	$ (500)	15-Feb	$ (500)	15-Mar	$ (500)	15-Apr	$ (500)	15-Dec
Car Payment	$ (250)	15-Jan	$ (250)	15-Feb	$ (250)	15-Mar	$ (250)	15-Apr	$ (250)	15-Dec
Student Loan	$ (220)	1-Jan	$ (220)	1-Feb	$ (220)	1-Mar	$ (220)	1-Apr	$ (220)	1-Dec
Phone, DSL and cell phone	$ (75)	15-Jan	$ (75)	15-Feb	$ (75)	15-Mar	$ (75)	15-Apr	$ (75)	15-Dec
Utilities	$ (60)	15-Jan	$ (60)	15-Feb	$ (60)	15-Mar	$ (60)	15-Apr	$ (60)	15-Dec
HOA	$ (158)	15-Jan	$ (158)	15-Feb	$ (158)	15-Mar	$ (158)	15-Apr	$ (158)	15-Dec
Gas	$ (86)	16-Jan	$ (86)		$ (86)		$ (86)		$ (86)	
Food	$ (191)	17-Jan	$ (191)		$ (191)		$ (191)		$ (191)	
Entertainment	$ (54)		$ (54)		$ (54)		$ (54)		$ (54)	
Beauty	$ (75)		$ (75)		$ (75)		$ (75)		$ (75)	
Clothes	$ (50)		$ (50)		$ (50)		$ (50)		$ (50)	
Eating out	$ (47)		$ (47)		$ (47)		$ (47)		$ (47)	
Education	$ (50)		$ (50)		$ (50)		$ (50)		$ (50)	
Vacation	$ (25)		$ (25)		$ (25)		$ (25)		$ (25)	
House/Investment Expenses	$ (100)		$ (100)		$ (100)		$ (100)		$ (100)	
Total Left After Expense paid	$ 60		$ 60		$ 60		$ 60		$ 60	

Figure 12-12

Displaying Your Budget with Charts

I think it is very important to see how much of my money is being taken up by which expense item. For this, Excel 2007 has the fantastic conditional formatting. There are various ways for me to use the conditional formatting. Or I can always plot a graph quickly to see where my money is being spent. I walked you through creating a quick chart and showed the final outcome in Figure 12-8. Here we will use conditional formatting to find out what happens to our income in real time. So let's begin:

1. To quickly find out where most of your income is being spent, just select a month's worth of expenses and then use the conditional formatting as shown in Figure 12-7 to see where the greatest expenses are. To apply the conditional formatting to other months, you can either use the Format Painter or just select the full column and apply conditional formatting. This has been shown in Figure 12-7.

2. Keep in mind that in Figure 12-7 we are only looking at one quick way to apply conditional formatting. You can use other conditional formatting ways, with pictures and arrows, as we talked more about in Chapter 8. Also, since your numbers are negative (in accounting negative shows expenses, and positive shows income), then keep in mind that you are looking for the smallest bar for the most expensive items and the largest bars are the closest to 0; therefore, they are the least of your expenses.

You are now done creating your expense worksheet and should be able to keep track of how your money is being spent. Next time you want to plan a shopping spree, you will know exactly where to cut and how to save for that big shopping day.

Relax, Refresh, Reward

At the end of a long week, it's pretty fun to go out dancing with friends. Club entry and that cute dress are among some of the most expensive items we spend our money on, not to mention the financial toll we pay for drinking the alcohol. With every drink banking in at a $7 minimum, if you add up at least five cocktails per person (three for yourself and probably two more for a friend) that is a total of close to $40, in addition to the parking and the cover. So you are looking at around $50 at the minimum for every night you go out with friends. This is a great way to reward yourself if that is your fun thing for the month (as we discussed earlier as entertainment), but if you party this way every weekend, as you can see that adds up to nearly $200/month. You can easily come up with other activities with your girlfriends that are as much fun and don't require you to leave the comfort of your home for the clubs at all. Pop open a bottle of wine, relax, and enjoy one of my favorite activities:

1. Agree upon a random Friday or Saturday night and call it Game Night. Then pick a board game like Monopoly or Robert Kiyosaki's Cashflow 101 game (my favorites!). Both of these games teach the rules of money as well as how to work less and make money while you sleep. By searching Robert Kiyosaki on a search engine like www.Live.com you can find the numerous books he and his colleagues have written about money.

2. Get together with your computers and spend some time putting your expenses for the prior week into your expense spreadsheet. This way you will see and understand how you spend your money, where most of your expenses are, and how much money you have left to have fun with. You can also plan what your next educational outing will be with your friends, whether you decide to take a seminar together or read a book about something you all enjoy learning about.

Once you spend time understanding how you spend money, then you can go out and have a great time shopping. With the knowledge you gained from your board games and your understanding of your spending habits, by the time you get to the mall you will know exactly how much money you have to spend. Before you go to the mall it's always a great idea to make a list of all the things you need and all the things you want so that you can practice good spending habits, and make sure to purchase two things you need and one thing you want. There are a lot of programs, books, and seminars out there that help you make a list of things you want in your life. Recently there has been hype around Rhonda Byrne's book *The Secret,* which talks about the laws of attraction and how the universe wants to give you gifts. If you make a list, then you make a clear distinction of what you want and everything else will just fall into place. Some other authors you might turn to for financial guidance are T. Harv Ecker, Anthony Robbins, Donald Trump, and Warren Buffet. When you pass that Borders on your way to Nordstrom's, I would suggest popping in and grabbing one of their books!

13

Save Time with Macros

To Do List

Save time and accomplish more with macros

Record macros for repetitive tasks

Use Excel 2007 for mailing lists

Fill a toolbox

and Mail Merge

Are you a master of squeezing every last minute out of a 24-hour day? You know what I mean: there's always something to be done, and you won't sleep unless everything that needs to be done is done, no matter what. Well, I know one person like that: my mother. Through the years she has managed to work full time, run a side business, take care of the family's needs, take care of my disabled brother, complete all the chores, finish school, and still have time left in the day to always help and show love and kindness to not just us but her extended family, friends, and others.

After all the hard work for just daily life, when the holidays rolled around my parents would sit down with more than 100 cards and begin hand-writing each Christmas card and envelope address. I know if I could travel back in time, at the very least, the Christmas card piece and the birthday cards could have been done by Excel. Unfortunately I cannot travel back in time, but I can share with you how to simplify your life using macros in Excel 2007 so you will have more time for rest, personal chores, and your family and friends.

Automate Excel 2007 with Macros

Don't you just love the meals that come in a box where all you do is add water and set it aside for a few minutes and, voila, you now have a great meal for you and your family? Saves time and saves you the annoying task of having to cook again yet another meal you have already made in the past and do the same ordinary task. Same thing can be said about Christmas cards. Don't you love the photo studios that take a picture of you and your family, write a few kind holiday wishes, and all you are left to do is sign your name? Or some studios will even print your family name on the photo cards for you. Then all you have left to do is address the envelope, place your return address, and take all the stuffed envelopes to the post office where they can be meter stamped and off they go.

Those are some great tricks to cut back on the repetitive tasks we have to do during our lifetime. Well, you can cut back on repetitive actions in Excel 2007 as well with macros. What are macros? They are small programs you record or write to show off your Diva-like skills and help with the repetitive tasks.

Defining a Macro

Do you remember Chapters 6 and 7 and the discussion about formulas and functions? Recall that a function is a kind of shortcut to having Excel perform math calculations for you. Well, macros are a different twist on the same idea. A macro is a little program that a user creates that tells Excel to perform a certain set of tasks (that you define) in a certain order (that you also define) for you. Macros are prerecorded or programmed to help with repetitive tasks.

For instance, let's say that you're making a spreadsheet of recipe ingredients. Every so often, you need to insert a dividing row (one for produce, one for staples, one for baking ingredients, and so on) that's formatted differently than the rest. Instead of having to manually insert a new row, format it with a black fill and white, 14 point, bold text, and insert a blank row beneath it, you could record or write a simple macro that allows you to press a pre-determined shortcut key (Alt+Q, for example), and have Excel do all that for you at once, saving you several keystrokes or mouse clicks many times over. This is just one example, but there are many ways that you can use macros to save you time.

If you're a programming Diva, you can certainly write your own macros from scratch. For most of us Excel Divas, this is a little deeper than we want to go. Instead, we'll focus on using the recorder in Excel to record macros that you can "play back" later as needed.

Zip Your Purse: Enabling Macros

First things first. Before going about creating and running macros, you need to enable your Excel to accept VBA code, which macros are written in.

In the past VBA (Visual Studio for Applications) has been used to pass along viruses to damage code, applications, or documents on computers, so therefore Microsoft no longer allows VBA code to run without asking you to ensure you want to run it. In order to be able to run macros you have a take a few steps for your own safety. If you do get an Excel 2007 workbook from others you might see a box that pops up asking if you want to enable the macros. Make certain the workbook is from a trusted source before enabling the macros.

Let's begin our macro adventure by enabling Excel to accept VBA. Follow these steps:

I. Open Excel 2007 Options by clicking on the Office 2007 Pearl on the top-left corner of Excel 2007 and bring up the full menu. Select Excel Options from the bottom of the menu (Figure 13-1).

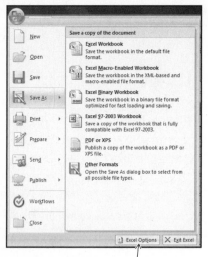

Select Excel Options from the menu to enable the Developer tab to see macro settings.

Figure 13-1

2. From the Excel Options window go to the Popular tab on the left and check the box to "Show Developer tab in the Ribbon" as shown in Figure 13-2.

Check the box to select Show Developer tab in the Ribbon.

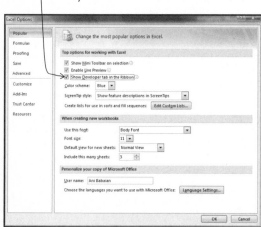

Figure 13-2

3. Once you check the box, click OK. The Developer tab appears on the Office 2007 Ribbon next to the View tab, as shown in Figure 13-3.

Figure 13-3

4. Go back to the Excel Options window and select the Trust Center from the left tabs. This brings up a window like the one in Figure 13-4. You are doing this to change specific macro settings.

Did you know . . .

The Trust Center contains security and privacy settings, which help keep your computer secure. Changing these default settings is not recommended. However, for these macros we will act like Excel Divas and make a small adjustment.

Click on the Trust Center Settings button (found in the Trust Center) to bring up macro settings.

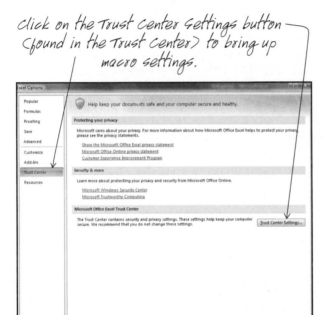

Figure 13-4

5. In the Trust Center, click on the Trust Center Settings button, which brings up the settings window.

6. From here select the Macro Settings tab, on the left. On the Macro Settings screen, you will need to choose the setting you prefer. The options are:

- **Disable All Macros without Notification**—Sets it up so you are not asked whether you want to disable the macro. Excel automatically disables all macros. If you choose this option, be aware that if you do want to run a macro, you will have to visit this screen again and change the setting. This is the option Excel 2007 selects by default for macros.

- **Disable All Macros with Notification**—Excel 2007 disables all macros, such as when someone sends you a macro or if you create one yourself, but in this case it will ask you if you want to enable them. You need to enable each one before you can use it.

- **Disable All Macros Except Digitally Signed Macros**—In this case if a company such as Microsoft, or the company you work with or for creates a macro, they can sign it digitally, so that you know who it is from and that it is secure. Enable this option if you know and trust every company that might have macros inside the workbooks they send you.

- **Enable All Macros (Not Recommended; Potentially Dangerous Code Can Run)**—The most dangerous option is to enable every macro without question. Notice the parentheses next to it saying that it is not recommended. Enabling all macros leaves you open to dangerous macros that may contain viruses. If you are the creator of your workbook, and you know that you didn't write any viral macros into your workbook, this option helps save you a few clicks. But if you are receiving workbooks from other people, I wouldn't suggest this option, because of the risk.

7. Select Disable All Macros with Notification, as shown in Figure 13-5.

Select Macro Settings from the left side to enable the Macro Settings in the main window.

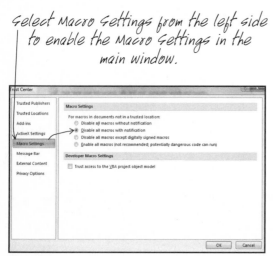

Figure 13-5

Making Your Favorite Moves: Using Macros

There are a variety of macros you can use to buy back time when it comes to Excel 2007. To get started, go to the Office 2007 Ribbon and select the View tab. On the View tab, go all the way over to the right side where you will find the Macros button (Figure 13-6).

Best Practice

By leaving the default setting as is, if macros do come in Excel 2007 worksheets I might get from others, I am given the option to enable them if I want to. I know this section was a bit scary but we want to make sure to address everything, so you can have the Diva-like confidence of knowing what is there and where to get more information.

Selecting the Macros button shows you further macro options.

Figure 13-6

Once you click on the Macros button, you'll see three options from which to choose (Figure 13-7).

- **View Macros**—Allows you to see any macros already written or recorded
- **Record Macro**—Allows you to create a new macro
- **Use Relative References**—Moves your active cell in a pattern you determine

Select from the three macro options.

Figure 13-7

Did you know?

Macros are not just specific to Excel 2007. Macros are available in the entire Office 2007 suite of products, including Word 2007 and PowerPoint 2007.

The Use Relative References option is really fun. The best way to explain it is with an example. Say you meet a new person, a girl who becomes your really good friend; let's call her Jackie. You notice that Jackie always runs 15 minutes late. After a while you adjust to her schedule by running 15 minutes late yourself every time you are supposed to meet her. Then you meet another girl through Jackie; her name is Renee. You can assume that because Renee is friends with Jackie, she will also run 15 minutes late all the time. After all, how else could they be friends? That adjustment is what Use Relative References handles. (OK, there are plenty of punctual people who are friends with tardy people; it is just an example to illustrate the point.)

In this case, though, say you start in cell B3, and you need to jump to E3; if you Use Relative References, the next time you use it, if you are in cell B8, you will go directly to E8. A pretty nifty time-saver.

Record a Macro

Okay now that you've seen the options under Macros, it's time to record your first macro.

Recording a macro is pretty easy:

Input the macro name, the key(s) to press for the shortcut, and the place you want to store the macro.

Figure 13-8

1. Click on the Macros button on the View tab on the Office 2007 Ribbon and select Record Macro to get started. The Record Macro window will open (Figure 13-8).

2. The first blank is the box where you name your macro. A good idea is to give it a descriptive name—something you can remember later and recognize what it does. Otherwise, by default Excel 2007 will name each macro as Macro 1, Macro 2, and so on . . . which makes it hard to remember which did what later.

3. Now it's time to choose a keyboard shortcut, the key(s) you will press to run the macro. Enter it by pressing whichever keys you've chosen as a shortcut (after appropriately placing your cursor as shown in Figure 13-8, of course). If you choose a letter that is already being used for another shortcut, the Shortcut Key area might add the Shift or Alt key, so that Ctrl+S becomes Ctrl+Shift+S, because Ctrl+S is already being used as a shortcut for Save.

What if . . .

The shortcut letter you want to use for your macro is already in use? Excel 2007 (and Office 2007 in general) has some shortcut keys built in, so make sure to select letters that are not in use. A great way to test is to try Ctrl + the key you want to pick before you start working on your macro to see if it does anything.

4. The next option involves determining where you're going to "keep" the macro. This option is known as "Store macro in". In most cases it works best to just keep the macro in the workbook you are in; therefore the default option in this drop-down box is great. Otherwise, if you know you will be using this macro in other workbooks as well, then it would be best to save it to Personal Macro Workbook, so you can have access to it when you need it (via the View Macros option discussed earlier).

5. Now, fill in the Description area. This is not only for you, but for others who might use your macro as well. Type a short description of your macro to explain what it will do.

6. Once you are done entering in all necessary information, click the OK button. Excel will now record your keystrokes until you tell it to stop. Note that sometimes it takes a few tries to get this right because you might have to do things the long way in order for the macro to record. If that's the case, you might need to go back and delete your previous attempts. Deleting macros is discussed in just a bit.

Every Little Thing

Excel will record absolutely everything you do—every move your cursor makes. Be sure you've thought about what precisely you want to record before beginning so you don't end up with unnecessary deletes and whatnot. That means if you start with one cell selected, and then move two cells over and one cell down before entering anything, anytime you run that macro, it will move two cells over and one cell down from where you started when you hit the shortcut keys for that macro.

7. Once you are done doing what you want to record, click on the Macros button of the View section on the Office 2007 Ribbon and click Stop Recording (Figure 13-9).

Select the Stop Recording option when you are done recording your macro.

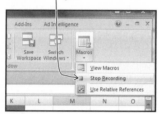

Figure 13-9

Once you click Stop Recording you are now ready to reuse the macro in other parts of your workbook. Once the macro has been recorded, from now on you can just hold down the Ctrl key and hit the shortcut key you chose for that macro to have the same thing occur again. You can use macros to do all sorts of things, like adding your name and address in the same place in any other worksheet, or adding or subtracting a certain value from a series of cells. Any other repetitive task you have to do in Excel 2007 can be done using a macro.

View a Recorded Macro

If you want to view or make changes to your Excel 2007 macro you can use the View Macros option from the drop-down menu, when you click on the Macros button, on the View tab on the Office 2007 Ribbon (Figure 13-10).

Select the View Macros option from the menu to view your macro and make further changes.

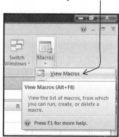

Figure 13-10

Viewing a previously recorded macro is pretty easy:

1. Click on the Macros button on the View tab on the Office 2007 Ribbon and select View Macros (Figure 13-10) to get started.

2. Once you select the View Macros option from the drop-down menu of Macros (shown in Figure 13-9), you will see a window (Figure 13-11) where you can make further changes to your macro or delete it completely.

Make any changes to your macro or just delete it.

Figure 13-11

You'll note a few interesting things on this window. You can see the list of other macros, if you have others, in the white box in the middle of the window. Here is where description becomes important. In case you do create many macros, the description of each macro helps you remember what the macro was created for. Macro options in this window include:

- **Run**—Executes the macro (you can always just use the shortcut instead).

- **Step Into**—Puts you into a software developer window where you can view the code that runs the macro. For further information about this, pick up a book about Visual Basic for Applications (VBA). This section is beyond what we will be covering in this book. Another great place to find information is http://Office.Microsoft.com, where you can find free videos, information, and samples.

- **Edit**—Similar to Step Into, only now any changes you make will not immediately take effect; rather the changes you make will take effect next time you run the macro.

- **Delete**—Completely deletes the currently selected macro from your computer.

- **Options**—Opens a Macro Options window for the selected macro (Figure 13-12), where you see the name of the macro and can make changes to the description and to the shortcut.

Figure 13-12

Again, for further information on how to edit macros or write more complicated ones, you are now ready to pick up a book on VBA (Visual Basic for Applications).

Delete a Macro

Occasionally, you will need to delete a macro. Perhaps you recorded something incorrectly, or perhaps you just don't use that macro anymore and you want to delete it so you can reassign the shortcut keys to a new macro. In any case, here's how you do it:

It's a very simple process to delete a macro:

1. Click on the Macros button on the View tab of the Ribbon and select View Macros (Figure 13-10) to get started.

2. Once you select the View Macros option from the drop-down menu of Macros, you will see a window like Figure 13-11.

3. From this window select the name of the macro you want to delete, and then click on the Delete button.

4. Once you click the Delete button, a window will come up (Figure 13-13).

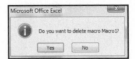

Figure 13-13

5. The window in Figure 13-13 asks you if you really want to delete this macro. This is to keep you from accidentally erasing an important macro. Click Yes and the macro is deleted; click No if you have made a mistake.

Using and recording your own macros makes you a true Excel Diva. By this point, you should have mastered using, recording, and deleting those time-saving friends we call the macro. Now this chapter moves on to cover another major time-saver, this time using Word: a Mail Merge.

A Few Advanced Tips for the Diva in You

In Excel 2007, much like in the rest of Office 2007, there are many ways to do the same task. If you'll remember, the Developer tab was mentioned in Figure 13-3. For those of you wondering what that tab can be used for, you can record, delete, and view macros here as well. You can also insert specific controls and view the software code of how it's being done. This is a fantastic time to look up how to write Visual Basic Applications and learn more about what's possible. As an Excel 2007 Diva you should know what each tab does.

Automate Excel 2007 with Mail Merge

The beginning of this chapter talked about how much time my parents and others have spent on Christmas cards and items in their life that have been repetitive. Excel 2007 is so robust, you can use it to print and keep all the names and addresses of everyone you want to send the Christmas cards to, and then use it to create a Mail Merge in Word 2007. Mail Merges automatically generate address labels, or can print directly on the envelopes. This also works if you don't like online banking and end up writing the address on your bill envelopes every month.

Merge Like a Pro

Simply make a worksheet and label the first row with First Name, Last Name, Title, Address, City, State, and Zip Code on top of the columns. You can actually uses whatever column headings you want, so long as each column name is unique. It will be much simpler if you fill in every row (not leave any blank rows), otherwise you will have to deal with them later in Word 2007.

Before you begin the Mail Merge steps, take time first to type the letter or email in Word that you want to send, organize, and customize, then start the Mail Merge process. Setting up a Mail Merge is not difficult:

1. Open Microsoft Office Word 2007, by going to the Vista Pearl, then selecting All Programs, navigating to the Microsoft Office folder, and then selecting Microsoft Word 2007 (or just click on the Vista Pearl and type into the Start Search box "Word," and Microsoft Word will appear as an option. Then, just click to start Word 2007.

2. Go to the Mailings tab and select the Start Mail Merge section as shown in Figure 13-14. From here you can click on the Start Mail Merge button to see the full drop-down menu as shown in Figure 13-15.

Figure 13-14

Figure 13-15

3. From here you can create letters, emails, print labels, or print envelopes. The best way to do any of those tasks is to walk through the wizard on the bottom of the menu. The wizard is a series of windows that will guide you through six steps to successfully create the labels or printed envelopes that you need to simplify your life and gain more time.

4. Once you start the wizard (which opens to the left of your Word 2007 document by default), the first thing you do is select what type of a Mail Merge it will be. Please pick E-mail Messages for this example (Figure 13-16). Then click Next on the bottom of the screen. Keep in mind the wizard will open to the left of your Word 2007 document by default.

The options for the Mail Merge are:

- **Letters**—Official letters with headers that you will print and mail.

- **E-mail Messages**—Email messages that you have pre-typed and now you want to send a separate email customized with the person's name.

- **Envelopes**—Print specific envelopes with different destination addresses.

- **Labels**—Print labels with different destination addresses.

- **Directory**—To help create a single document containing a catalog or printed list of addresses.

Figure 13-16

5. When you select E-mail Messages, a window like Figure 13-17 comes up from which you can select how you want to set up your letters. By default the "Use the current document" option will be selected. This is what we want. If in the future you want to start from a template or an existing document that is not open yet, you can use the other two options. Click Next.

Figure 13-17

6. Now you can select the recipients of the email from a window that will look much like Figure 13-18. In this case select "Use an existing list." The other options are "Select from Outlook contacts" or "Type a new list."

7. Below the Select Recipients section is the Use an Existing List section (if you had selected one of the other two options in the Select Recipients section, then this section on the lower part of the screen in Figure 13-18 would be different).

Figure 13-18

8. Now you can either click Next, or click Browse in the Use an Existing List section, which brings up a window that looks like Figure 13-19. Use Browse in this example and point to the Excel file where you saved the email addresses.

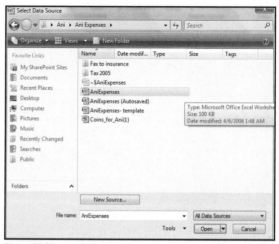

Figure 13-19

9. Once you find that file, double-click on it, and a window comes up (Figure 13-20) where you can see the Excel 2007 worksheets and can select the worksheet that holds the email addresses. By default Excel will think the first row is where the headers are and will discount it. If you want to change this, uncheck the box, seen on the bottom of Figure 13-20, where it reads "First row of data contains column headers."

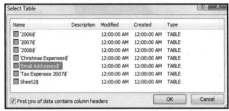

Figure 13-20

10. Now that the Email Addresses worksheet is selected, another window will come up, as shown in Figure 13-21, where you can select which people on the list should receive the email. By default everyone on your list will be selected.

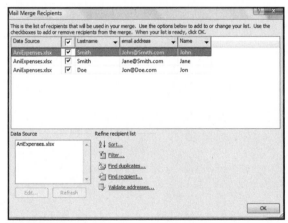

Figure 13-21

11. Select your recipients and click on the OK button. A new window, shown in Figure 13-22, comes up where you can begin typing your email

if you have not done so already. Because you are an Excel 2007 Diva, you have already written the email, so just click Next, which brings up another window, shown in Figure 13-23.

Figure 13-22

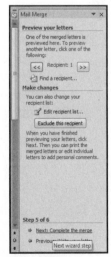

Figure 13-23

12. Now you have a chance to preview your email one last time before it goes out. Keep in mind that you have to be connected to Outlook 2007 for this process to work smoothly; otherwise you will have to spend some time setting up a mail client like Outlook or Outlook Express. Outlook is part of the Office 2007 suite. If you do not have an email client, you may be able to do only manual letters.

13. Once you are done previewing, click Next, which will take you to Step 6 of 6 of the Mail Merge Wizard. This step opens a window similar to Figure 13-24, where you can either print each letter or create each email. You are done!

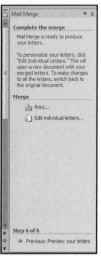

Figure 13-24

Relax, Refresh, Reward

Part of being a true Diva is being a Diva in *every* area of your life. You take risks, you learn from your mistakes, and if all else fails, you move on and do better. But in most cases you will even surprise yourself and do such a great job it will be something you will want to brag to your friends about. In this chapter, you learned how to use tools that Excel and Word offer to simplify your life. For this chapter's reward, I'd like to suggest you take a trip to the tool section of your local home improvement store and stock up your own toolbox.

Even the Spring 2007 issue of *Oprah At Home* highlighted the need for women to have their own tools. They can be pink tools if that's what floats your boat.

There is nothing wrong with pink, as long as it gets the work done. In the article, the author recommends a certain set of tools to keep in your chest, from standard pliers, to needle nose pliers, screwdrivers, wrench, hammer, stud finder, WD-40, measuring tape, and a drill. I would add to that list a saw, a couple of different types of screws, a couple of different types of nails, electrician's tape, make sure you have both Phillips (4 headed) and flat-headed screw drivers as well as number 2 pencils, and finally extra extension cords. It's amazing where they come in handy. At the end of the day you can hang your own blinds, pictures, put up your own shelves, paint your own walls, and even do your own floors (whether tile or wood).

Ladies, doing it yourself for that super-Diva feeling just feels great. After you're done you can have your mimosa, the manicure, and put on your best heels and skirt and feel competent and attractive. I can attest that getting dressed to go out after I have just completed a do-it-myself project feels AMAZINGLY COOL! To me that is what it means to be supersmart Diva!

14

Sharing Your Worksheet

To Do List

Include website links in your worksheet

Share your spreadsheet with care

Email your worksheet to a friend

Choose a career mentor

While recently talking to a friend of mine who had just taken her board exams after having put medical school on hold to care for two family members battling cancer, she said, "It's so great to be surrounded by such strong women, it always motivates me to keep going." I told her I felt the same way about her.

I have another friend who makes a point to call me and keep me positive and focused no matter how my day might go. He tells me the truth and will not sugarcoat it; with him it's about being logical. I check on him as well and make sure he keeps the certain level of integrity he wants in his life.

I have yet another friend who is there to help me pick out the right dress, the right shoe, and the right guy. She is also an immigrant who has gone from working two jobs to holding a steady job and climbing her way up the insurance empire. She is focused and strong when it comes to her career and her beliefs while still holding on to her feminine side.

Staying connected is so important. People who have a strong social circle can endure many things. They not only help people overcome hardships, but also live longer, healthier lives. In this chapter you'll learn about how you can stay connected with Excel 2007 and share information with your family, friends, and coworkers. You might want to link other projects, pictures, or websites to your workbook. You're about to learn how.

Link it Up

Perhaps you are creating a spreadsheet for work where you really need to reference another document or data on the web. Or it could simply be a list of all the items you want to buy for Christmas, or a wish list of the things you want for yourself. You'll probably want everyone to quickly and easily access those documents and websites so they'll know exactly what you're talking about. Excel 2007 allows you to share that information by adding links.

Existing File or Web Page

For the times when you need to add the website address (also known as a Uniform Resource Locator or URL) there are several options. You can just go to the website and click once on the website address bar so that the web address is completely highlighted. In some cases you may have to double-click on the address. If the address bar doesn't fully highlight, press Ctrl+A to select the full address. Once the address is highlighted you can then right-click on it and choose the Copy option to copy the address (Figure 14-1).

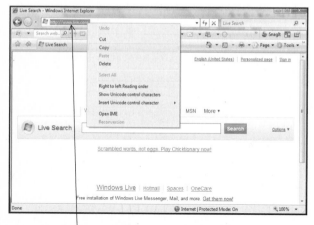

Right-click on the selected address bar to bring up the menu and copy the address.

Figure 14-1

Once you copy the address you can then return to your Excel 2007 worksheet and add the website address to a cell by left-clicking on the cell you want and then right-clicking and selecting the Paste option from the drop-down menu (Figure 14-2).

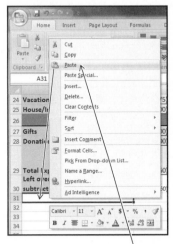

Click on the Paste option from the menu to paste a value into the cell.

Figure 14-2

Once you paste the information in, it will just look like text, which means everyone who sees your worksheet will see what the website address is, but the address will not be active. If your coworker or boss wanted to check out the website, they couldn't just click on the address in the spreadsheet and go to the website.

There are a couple more steps to making the link active, so that when other people view the electronic copy (sometimes also called *soft copy*) of your worksheet they can click on the link and go to the website. First click once on the cell you just copied the address into, then immediately right-click and select the last option from the menu, which is Hyperlink (Figure 14-3). (Of course, you must be connected to the Internet for this to work, as well as for all the upcoming sections.) In the Insert Hyperlink window you will find four options on the left side: Existing File or Web Page, Place in This Document, Create New Document, and E-mail Address. Also, to the right of these options you will find Current Folder, Browsed Pages, and Recent Files.

Figure 14-3

Once you select the cell and the text in the cell you want to add a hyperlink to, you can follow these steps:

1. Right-click on the selected text in the Excel 2007 worksheet cell and a pop-up window will come up much like in Figure 14-3 from which you can choose the Hyperlink option.

2. Once you click on the Hyperlink option a window much like in Figure 14-4 will come up titled Insert Hyperlink.

Paste the website address into the box here.

Figure 14-4

3. In the Insert Hyperlink window, click Existing File or Web Page on the far left side.

4. In the Address section you can right-click and choose to paste the address you copied from Figure 14-1, which will look something like Figure 14-5.

Figure 14-5

5. Now click OK and you are done. You have just created a hyperlink to the selected text in the Excel 2007 worksheet you selected.

6. For adding a link to a file, you follow very much the same steps from 1 to 3, and then select the file name from the bottom of the Look In section, as shown in Figure 14-6.

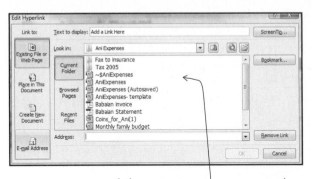

You can select the specific file you want from this section, once you select the folder the file is in.

Figure 14-6

7. If you cannot find the file you want, you can use the drop-down arrow from the Look In section to browse to the folder where the file is you want to connect to. Once you find the file, choose it and you are done.

When you click on each button to the far left side of the Insert Hyperlink window in Figure 14-4, you will find different options to the right of them. The Text to Display bar on top is where you type the text you want everyone to see when they look at the worksheet cell; if you have already selected text before you clicked on the Hyperlink option from the pop-up menu in Figure 14-3, that text will appear here. And on the bottom is the Address drop-down box where you need to copy the file path, web address, or email address as you saw in the preceding Do It Herself Art section. Let's look at what each of the sections are for Existing File or Web Page.

Current Folder

From here you can link to a document in the current folder. The current folder is picked from the Look In section when you click on the down arrow very much like in Figure 14-4. You can add a quick link to your Excel 2007 worksheet.

Browsed Pages

This is a great place to find web addresses to websites you have been to recently as shown in Figure 14-7. If you want to connect your Excel 2007 worksheet cell to a specific address and you do not remember which website it was, you can look here for the past month's worth of websites.

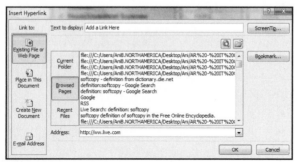

Figure 14-7

Recent Files

The Recent Files section pulls up the most recent files you have worked on for the last week, or a maximum of 40. You can access this area similarly to the Current Folder and Browsed Pages sections by clicking the button titled Recent Files.

Place in This Document

What if you wanted to reference the reader to another worksheet, or a certain place on the worksheet that is outside of the screen they are viewing? Well, you could just type notes all over your Excel 2007 worksheet, but that's messy and looks very unprofessional. It would be like pasting sticky notes about your presentation all over your boss's computer. Since that is not the look you're going for (at least I hope you're not) it makes more sense to add a link to what you are talking about. It provides a quick reference, takes up much less space, and saves you time you would have wasted typing up all those notes.

If you wanted to add a link to a file instead of a web address, you would do it very much the same way as you added hyperlinks. Just follow these easy steps:

1. Right-click on the selected text in the Excel 2007 worksheet cell and a pop-up window will come up much like in Figure 14-3 from which you can choose the Hyperlink option.

2. One you click on the Hyperlink option, a window much like in Figure 14-4 will come up titled Insert Hyperlink.

3. In the Insert Hyperlink window, click Place in This Document on the far left side, which will look similar to Figure 14-8.

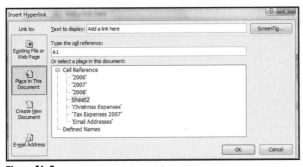

Figure 14-8

4. Make sure the Text to Display box has the correct text you want to show up in the Excel 2007 worksheet cell.

5. Select the worksheet you want to link to in this workbook, and you are done!

Create New Document

Once in a while you might need to create an extra document to supplement your work. You can do that easily right from the worksheet using the same technique as with setting up a web address link.

Just type what you want the title of the link to be in the cell you've chosen, hit Enter to accept the text, and then follow these easy steps:

1. Right-click on the selected text in the Excel 2007 worksheet cell and a pop-up window will come up from which you can choose the Hyperlink option.

2. One you click on the Hyperlink option the Insert Hyperlink window appears.

3. In the Insert Hyperlink window, click Create New Document on the far left side, which will look similar to Figure 14-9.

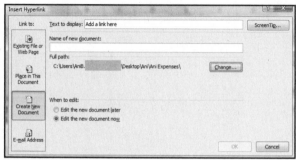

Figure 14-9

4. Make sure the Text to Display box has the correct text (probably the title of your new document) you want to show up in the Excel 2007 worksheet cell.

5. Add a name in the Name of New Document section.

6. Then select which folder you want the new document to be saved to (assuming the correct one isn't pre-selected by default) by clicking on the Change button and selecting a folder.

7. Select if you want to edit this new document now or later in the When to Edit section and you are done. Click the OK button.

E-mail Address

This is a great little trick to use to add email addresses to worksheets, especially if you know others will view this worksheet in electronic copy on their computers. On my worksheet, I can add a short sentence at the bottom that says, "If you have further questions please contact me at: Ani Babaian." where my name will become a link that someone can click on to open up an email with my email address already in the To line and send me an email.

Right now Ani Babaian is not a link, but I can set it up so when someone clicks on it, Excel automatically opens an email addressed to me by following these easy steps:

1. Right-click on the selected text (which in this case is my name) in the Excel 2007 worksheet cell and a pop-up window will come up, from which you can choose the Hyperlink option.

2. Once you click on the Hyperlink option, the Insert Hyperlink window appears.

3. In the Insert Hyperlink window, click E-mail Address on the far left side, which will look similar to Figure 14-10.

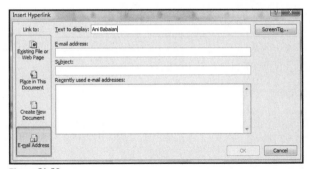

Figure 14-10

4. Make sure the Text to Display box has the correct text you want to show up in the Excel 2007 worksheet cell. In this case it should be your name; just double-check to make sure.

5. In the E-mail Address field just add the email address, as you would when you send an email. (Note that the Recently Used E-mail Addresses box will show other email addresses you have recently used.)

6. Fill in the Subject, if you want all emails about this worksheet to have a specific title, or number in the subject line, so you can find them easier later. A common choice is to put the document name in the subject line.

7. Click OK and you are done!

Share with Care

What if you wanted to email your work of art to a friend or boss? You can send it as an attachment, no matter what email client you are using (Hotmail, Yahoo, Gmail, Outlook, and others). Whatever you use the process is pretty similar. I spend a lot of time in Outlook since I work at Microsoft, so I will walk you through the process in Outlook. You can then use the same process with whatever email client you choose.

Outlook

Once you open Outlook, click on the New button on the toolbar at the top of the page (Figure 14-11). A blank window will come up where you can begin typing your email (Figure 14-12).

Click on the New button to begin typing a new email.

Figure 14-11

To attaching an Excel workbook to an Outlook email, address your mail and type the message. When you're ready to attach the file, follow these steps:

1. Go to the top of the Email box and click on the paper clip that appears on the Include section of the Message tab as shown in Figure 14-12.

Click on the paper clip to begin adding attachments.

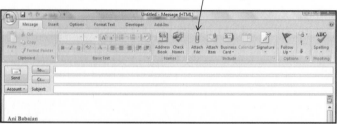

Figure 14-12

2. Once you click on the paper clip, a window much like Figure 14-13 comes up from which you can select the file you want to attach.

Select the workbook from the appropriate location and then click on the Insert button.

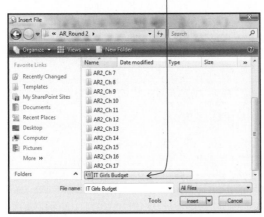

Figure 14-13

3. Once you click on the Insert button, the workbook is connected to your email. Click the Send button! Soon your friends will view it. Just make sure to look in the Attached section and see your file, much like shown in Figure 14-14.

Make sure the attached file appears in the Attached section.

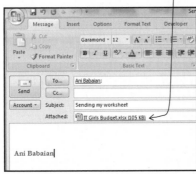

Figure 14-14

This is a great way to save paper, submit your homework or project, and work with technology to cut down on the amount of time and money you would otherwise spend on printing and delivering your work. Also, this way everyone can give you almost instantaneous feedback. Since they have the electronic copy in front of them, they can also make changes to the worksheet and email them back to you.

Other Email Clients

For most other email clients such as Hotmail, Yahoo, Gmail, or others you will use a similar approach to the one you learned in the Outlook section. You might have to work through different screens since most of the windows are on the web but just look for the attach option, usually a paper clip, to attach your workbook to an email. Once you attach the workbook, make sure you can see that attachment, and then click Send.

Backsave for Universal Access

When you're sending attachments to people, try to be considerate and remember that not everyone has the newest, coolest version of what you're sending. If you are working with friends who do not have Excel 2007, this is a good time to make sure you go back and save your work to be compatible with older versions of Excel, like Excel 97, 2000, or 2003. While in your workbook, use the Save As option from the Office Pearl as shown in Figure 14-15.

Make sure the Save as Type section has Excel 97-2001 workbook selected.

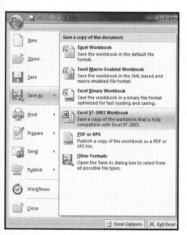

Figure 14-15

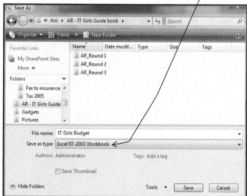

Figure 14-16

From the Save As section go to the right side and select Excel 97-2003 Workbook and a window much like Figure 14-16 will appear.

Make sure the Save as Type box says Excel 97-2003 Workbook. Then click the Save button and you are done! Now your friends who do not have Excel 2007 can open and view your work of art.

Relax, Refresh, Reward

This chapter was all about sharing what you've learned to create with others. The best kinds of workplaces offer this option in the form of mentoring. A mentor is someone you trust to guide you and support you as you make career and life decisions. For this chapter's reward, I'd like you to spend time with a mentor (or choose one if you haven't yet).

There are many reasons I love working at Microsoft. One such reason is the great mentoring program they have. Anyone I approached at Microsoft to be my mentor has always taken the role as an honor and tried their best to help me.

I learned early that if I don't take an interest and initiative in my future, no one will. You, too, need to plan, pursue, and use diligence. Find someone in your career field that you want to be like, model yourself after that person, and keep asking for help or guidance as you work through your projects.

One year at TechEd's lunch for women in technology, the General Manager for Vista was speaking and I was so taken by what she said that I walked up to her and asked her to mentor me. After looking over what I was asking for, she put me in touch with someone she thought would be the perfect mentor for me. I have now known my mentor for about a year and she has been great. We meet once a month and discuss a variety of things, from books and classes to take, to how to present, and what maneuvers and techniques to use as I advance in my career. I always feel like I can do and be anything when I leave her office. This woman has the unique ability to make me feel amazing and help guide me along. Because of her I have overcome some challenging situations in the work environment very gracefully.

I love my job because I have mentors such as her helping me. Most people say one or two mentors are enough, but I say if you are a woman you need six, especially if you are in a male-dominated industry such as technology. I select one male and one female mentor who are on the same level I am in to help me with my current role. Then I select another set of male and female mentors who are five years ahead of me on the career track, and two more who are ten years ahead of me. You don't have to pick someone ahead of you just in terms of your career either. They could also be ahead of you in life, spirit, or anything else you want to learn. I think of mentors as coaches; some are good for a while and others for a lifetime, depending on how fast you can learn their lessons and how much time and commitment they have for you.

I am always grateful for all the mentors I have had. One mentor has ended up as my manager and that is another reason I enjoy what I do so much. I always try to surround myself with people I like and who I know are there to help me become successful, and I do my best to return the favor. Mentors are an integral part of my life and I could not imagine where I would be without their tireless efforts and hard work.

Show Off: Importing Excel

To Do List

- Plug Excel tables into Word
- Plug Excel charts into Word
- Plug Excel tables and charts into PowerPoint
- Present your creation
- Rest your mind by working with your hands

The best way to do this is to have Microsoft Word 2007 and Microsoft Excel 2007 open at the same time. Once Word 2007 opens, here are the steps you follow to insert Excel data into your document:

1. Simply go back to your Excel 2007 worksheet, select the portion of your data with your mouse, and press down the right mouse button as you drag over the area you want to select.

2. Click and choose Copy from the drop-down menu, which comes up if you right-click after you are done selecting a section of Excel 2007 as shown in Figure 15-2.

Figure 15-2

3. Alternatively, you can use the Copy button on the Home tab of the Clipboard section on the Office 2007 Ribbon in Excel 2007, as shown in Figure 15-3.

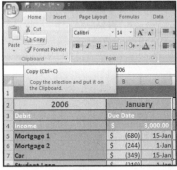

Figure 15-3

Vista Tip

As a side note, if you are running the Microsoft Vista operating system, you can hold down the Window key and hit the Tab key to put yourself in the Flip 3-D mode and select the Microsoft Word 2007 program when it comes forward. This works for PowerPoint 2007 in Vista, too.

4. Once you have selected and copied the data you want, go back to your Word 2007 document and go to the location you want to copy the Excel 2007 data to. Right-click to bring up the pop-up menu and choose Paste as shown in Figure 15-4. You can also press Ctrl+V. The table will automatically paste into Word 2007. Yes, it's that easy!

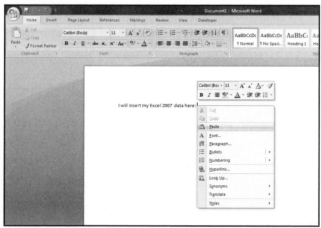

Figure 15-4

Once you paste the Excel 2007 table into Word 2007, a little clipboard with a few options (discussed in the following sections) will pop up on the bottom-right corner of the table you pasted as shown in Figure 15-5.

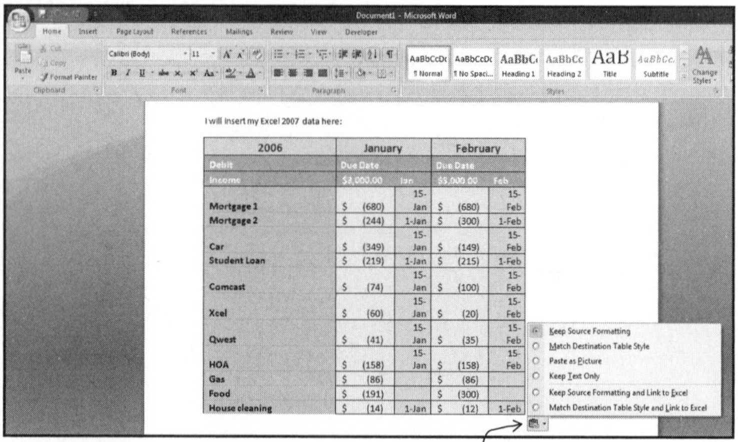

After you paste the Excel 2007 table, a little clipboard comes up on the bottom-right corner with further options.

Figure 15-5

The options that come up in the little pop-up box are as follows:

- Keep Source Formatting
- Match Destination Table Style
- Paste as Picture
- Keep Text Only
- Keep Source Formatting and Link to Excel
- Match Destination Table Style and Link to Excel

Keep Source Formatting

When you make this selection Word 2007 will save the Excel 2007 table the way it was without any changes. Therefore you keep all the formatting work you have already done to the data in the Excel 2007 worksheet. This will also allow you to make edits in Word.

Match Destination Table Style

When you make this selection Word 2007 will save the Excel 2007 table you pasted as if the table was created in Word 2007. Therefore you might lose the pretty colors and the nice formatting you may have had in Excel 2007. This will also allow you to make edits in Word.

Paste as Picture

When you make this selection Word 2007 will save the Excel 2007 table you pasted in as a picture and make the picture formatting functions available for you to further enhance your table. This means you cannot edit any table data via Word, but you can add shadowing and a 3-D (3-dimensional) look to the Excel 2007 table you just pasted into Word 2007.

In practice . . .

the best place I have found to use the Paste as Picture option is when you have a simple one- or two-column list of names or numbers that you want to paste into Word 2007.

Keep Text Only

When you make this selection Word 2007 will only save what is inside of the table and remove the lines of the table. Instead of the lines you will see tabs between each item. Keep in mind if you have multiple columns this might not look very pretty and you might have to make some adjustments to your data in Word 2007.

Keep Source Formatting and Link to Excel

When you make this selection Word 2007 will save the Excel 2007 table the way it was without any changes. The best part about this option is that you not only keep all the formatting work you have already done to the data in Excel 2007, but you also link the table to the Excel 2007 worksheet you copied from. So if you make

Office 2007 Factoid . . .

When you use the paste option of Chart (Linked to Excel Data), the chart is copied into the Word document but creates a link to the data in the original Excel workbook. Any changes you make to the data in the original Excel workbook are reflected in the chart (and vice versa). This is also true for PowerPoint.

any changes to your data in Excel 2007 it will magically be updated in this Word 2007 document. This is fantastic for documents you constantly have to update with current data. Once you make the changes in Excel 2007, the data and charts will update inside Excel 2007 and in this Word 2007 document when you select this option. Keep in mind if you change the file names, or move the files around the data will no longer transfer seamlessly and you will need to set this up again.

Therefore any changes to the Excel 2007 table will result in your data being changed in Word 2007. I love this option for documents in Word 2007 that always have to be updated because the data changes in Excel 2007. This option buys me back so much time, since I only need to make the change in Excel 2007 and it automatically takes place in Word 2007.

Match Destination Table Style and Link to Excel

When you make this selection Word 2007 will save the Excel 2007 table you pasted as if the table was created in Word 2007, but the content is still linked to the original Excel worksheet from which you pasted. Of course, you might lose the pretty colors and the nice formatting you may have had in Excel 2007.

So just like the prior option (Keep Source Formatting and Link to Excel), any changes to the Excel 2007 table will result in your data being changed in Word 2007. I love this option for the same reasons I love the other option: it buys me back so much time.

Insert an Excel 2007 Chart into Word 2007

Now that you have pasted in your tabular data, how about the wonderful charts you created in Excel 2007—can you transfer those to Word 2007 also? Yes you can.

You start very much the same way, by making sure the Word 2007 document you want to insert into is open. Then, execute these steps:

1. Select the chart you want to copy from Excel 2007. Right-click on it and select the Copy option from the drop-down menu (Figure 15-6).

2. Once you locate where you want to paste the chart in Word 2007, right-click again and select the Paste option from the drop-down menu.

Right-click on the chart to see the Copy option in the menu and select to copy the chart.

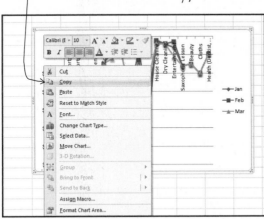

Figure 15-6

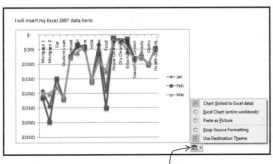

Once you paste the chart you will see the little clipboard on the bottom-right corner of the chart you copied into Word 2007 (Figure 15-7). These options are the basically the same as those explained previously when you copied an Excel table into Word.

After pasting the chart you will see the little clipboard on the bottom-right corner, where you can make further selections.

Figure 15-7

Now that you're finished inserting the chart into Word 2007 you might want to make a few modifications. Word 2007 offers a few more tabs to help you get the job done. Much like in Excel 2007 you will see the Chart Tools appear at the right end of the tabs on the Office 2007 Ribbon. There are also three new tabs to help with final touches: Design, Layout, and Format, as shown in Figure 15-8.

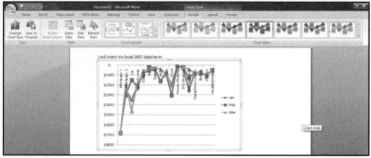

Figure 15-8

Inserting Excel into Microsoft Office PowerPoint 2007

There are many things that make a presentation outstanding; the first thing is having done the right analysis work to the data, which we have already done with Excel 2007. The second step is to find a presentation tool. Microsoft Office PowerPoint 2007 is there to the rescue!

Everything in Moderation

Having too many PowerPoint slides is not a good thing and causes PowerPoint fatigue, or as we say at Microsoft: "Death by PowerPoint."

It does make sense to have a few slides and comments to show off your beautiful work to help you present the idea you are trying to convey with your data.

Insert an Excel 2007 Chart into PowerPoint 2007

Inserting Excel 2007 charts into PowerPoint 2007 is just as easy as it was to insert an Excel 2007 chart into Word 2007. First, decide which worksheet you want to copy your data from, and then start PowerPoint 2007 (Figure 15-9). You must have both Excel 2007 and PowerPoint 2007 open at the same time for best results.

Start PowerPoint 2007 from Start, then All Programs, then Microsoft Office and select Microsoft Office PowerPoint 2007.

Figure 15-9

Once PowerPoint 2007 comes up, follow these steps:

1. Simply go back to your Excel 2007 worksheet, and select the portion of your data you wish to insert into PowerPoint 2007.

2. Now, right-click and choose Copy from the drop-down menu. If you'd rather, you can use the Copy button on the Home tab in the Clipboard section on the Office 2007 Ribbon in Excel 2007 as shown in Figure 15-10.

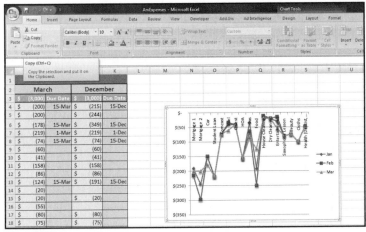

Figure 15-10

3. Once you copy the worksheet table, go to PowerPoint 2007, then to the part of the PowerPoint slide where you want to paste the chart, and right-click and choose the paste option you want from the clipboard pop-up menu as shown in Figure 15-11. You'll notice copying, cutting, and pasting is the same in all the products across Office 2007. This is true for most Microsoft products; it even works in Internet Explorer, which is the browser (the gateway) you use to surf the Internet.

Once you select the chart from Excel 2007 and paste it into PowerPoint 2007 you will see a small clipboard come up on the bottom-right corner of the chart. The clipboard only comes up when you first paste the chart into PowerPoint 2007 where you can make a couple of selections. Keep in mind you can pick two options from this menu; one from the top three and one from the bottom two. Let's look into what the options mean and where it is most appropriate to use them.

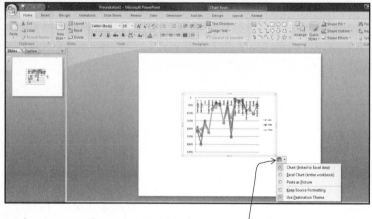

After you paste your chart into PowerPoint 2007, you can choose the paste option from the clipboard pop-up menu, which comes up on the bottom-right corner of the chart.

Figure 15-11

Chart (Linked to Excel Data)

When you make this selection PowerPoint 2007 will save the Excel 2007 chart the way it was without any changes. The best part about this option is that you not only keep all the formatting work you have already done to the data in Excel 2007, but you also link the table to the Excel 2007 worksheet you copied from.

Therefore any changes you make to Excel 2007 table data the graph is based upon will result in your chart being changed in PowerPoint 2007. I love this time-saving option because I only need to make the change in Excel 2007 and it automatically takes place in my PowerPoint 2007 slide. Excel 2007 and PowerPoint 2007 do not have to be open at the same time. Once you make any changes to Excel 2007, the next time you open PowerPoint 2007 the updates will be in the slides, since PowerPoint 2007 will have a reminder set to check Excel 2007 for updates, which will all happen without you noticing.

Excel Chart (Entire Workbook)

When you make this selection PowerPoint 2007 will save the Excel 2007 chart the way it was without any changes. In this case the chart you paste into PowerPoint 2007 will not be connected to Excel 2007, therefore any changes you make to the Excel data, and thus the chart, will not be reflected in your PowerPoint 2007 slide.

Paste as Picture

When you make this selection PowerPoint 2007 will save the Excel 2007 chart you pasted in as a picture and make the picture formatting functions available for you to further enhance your chart. This means you cannot change anything inside the chart but you can add shadowing and a 3-D (3-dimensional) look to the Excel 2007 table you just pasted into your PowerPoint 2007 slide.

Keep Source Formatting

When you make this selection PowerPoint 2007 will save the Excel 2007 chart the way it was without any changes. Therefore you keep all the formatting work you have already done to the chart in the Excel 2007 worksheet.

Use Destination Theme

When you make this selection PowerPoint 2007 will save the Excel 2007 chart you pasted as if the chart was created in PowerPoint 2007. Therefore you might lose the pretty colors and the nice formatting you may have had in Excel 2007; in most cases, though, you will not see a difference. However, if you do have a certain theme you are using in PowerPoint 2007 this is a great way to match your chart to that theme so your Excel 2007 chart will look its best.

Insert an Excel 2007 Table into PowerPoint 2007

Now that you have pasted in your chart into PowerPoint 2007, how about the wonderful tables you created in Excel 2007—can you transfer those to PowerPoint 2007 also? Yes you can.

You start very much the same way as when copying a chart. Follow these steps:

1. Choose the table you want to copy from Excel 2007. Right-click on it and select the Copy option from the drop-down menu (refer back to Figure 15-2).

2. Start PowerPoint 2007 (Figure 15-9).

3. Go to the slide you want to paste the Excel 2007 table to and use the Ctrl+V key combination to paste the table into PowerPoint 2007.

You should notice something different this time in the figure (Figure 15-12). No clipboard of special paste options! If you want special paste options you can always use the Paste button located on the Home tab on the Office 2007 Ribbon on top of PowerPoint 2007, where you can click the down arrow on the bottom of the Paste button to see further paste options (Figure 15-13). There you can make the selection that you need.

If you decide to use the Paste Special option, once you click on it a new window (Figure 15-14) will come up where you can make further selections. On this window you can select to paste the full table or just a link to the table data in Excel 2007. You can also select to paste your Excel 2007 table as a picture, or just unformatted text.

Unformatted text would just be a jumble of all the data in one area on PowerPoint 2007. If you try to paste a table of Excel 2007 data in the boxes that appear on PowerPoint 2007 slides, you will just see a bunch of numbers and letters. This means you did not delete the boxes before you pasted your table and PowerPoint 2007 recognizes your table of data as a bunch of text. This is the same thing that will happen if you paste the table of data as unformatted text. If you want the table from Excel 2007 to look like a table of data in PowerPoint 2007, you will have to delete the boxes that appear by default in PowerPoint 2007, by clicking on them and hitting the Delete button before you paste your table of data into PowerPoint 2007.

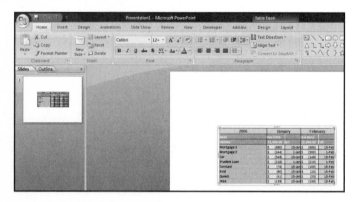

No clipboard this time. Once you copy a table from Excel 2007 to PowerPoint 2007, you will not see the little clipboard on the bottom-right corner.

Figure 15-12

Further paste options in PowerPoint 2007 can be found on the Home tab of Office 2007 Ribbon.

Figure 15-13

Once you click on the Paste Special option on the Paste button of the Home tab on the Office 2007 Ribbon, you can further customize how you paste the Excel 2007 table into PowerPoint 2007.

Figure 15-14

Relax, Refresh, Reward

After all this technology talk and work, sometimes it's just nice to do something that is not technology related at all. For this chapter's reward, it's time to find and do something unrelated to your technology. I don't know what inspires you, or what makes you feel connected with the earth. For some it's gardening, for others it's taking walks in nature, for me it's working with my hands. Whatever it is, find it and do it.

I love to work on small projects around the house. When I was little I saw my parents work so very hard with their hands to build the perfect home for my brother and me. If you like projects around the house, Home Depot in the U.S. is a fantastic place to learn anything from painting and tiling to basic electrical. Most of the courses are free; of course they want to educate you so you can purchase the products from them, and rightfully so. For others, there are community schools or stores that offer courses too.

This is also a great place to use your Excel 2007 Diva habits of tables and charts. As you learn what it will take to paint that room, or lay tile for that bathroom, you can use Excel 2007 to budget and save for the project and then go out buy the parts, and enjoy working with your hands and creating an exquisite part of your house. This is also a great way to feel a sense of accomplishment, since you will have something to show off to your friends. Who knows, this might just be another hobby or part-time source of income. You can always include your friends and have them help you. What a great way to connect with friends—spending time with them while you accomplish something great together.

To Do List

- Protect your personal information
- Guard your worksheets and workbooks
- Use passwords where you can
- Take small vacations

You have probably heard the old saying "You have to kiss a lot of toads before you find your prince." Well, I've been living on my own for more than a decade now; some of that time I've been in relationships, some of it I have been single. I've developed a bit of a test for the people I allow in my life. I noticed that sometimes, when people leave my space, they leave it in a mess! A *friend* cleans up after him- or herself. A *toad*, however, purposefully disregards my space and my things and takes better care of their own items. They just don't show respect for my things, which doesn't usually mean good things in regards to them respecting me. Well, I came up with a name for the habit of leaving my place chipped, burnt, or broken: Toad Syndrome, or TS.

Thank God when it comes to Excel 2007 there is a way to protect your data, worksheets, and workbooks from those infected by TS. I wish there was a way to protect your favorite things, whether they are dishes, soaps, candles, or shoes, from the toads, but at least with your data and worksheets, you can protect them from TS. Let's step into Excel 2007 and see how we can protect our data, worksheets, and workbooks from people with TS.

Inspect Worksheets for Personal Information

As the information age has improved, so has the ability to steal personal information. By using technology we can accomplish and do far more than we ever have before, but it means that malicious people can also access our personal information much easier because there are not as many rules to protect us in the digital world. Technology moves faster than lawmakers. Also, even if there were laws, some commonsense things need to be kept in mind. Let's begin by looking at a tool built into Excel 2007 that helps identify personal information contained inside your worksheet. It is the Excel 2007 Inspector tool, and you can access it by clicking on the Microsoft Office Pearl, then clicking on Prepare, and then clicking Inspect Document to display the window where you can see the Document Inspector options (Figure 16-1).

Click the Microsoft Office Pearl, click Prepare, and select Inspect Document.

Figure 16-1

Once you click on the Inspect Document option from Figure 16-1 the Document Inspector window (Figure 16-2) comes up where you can make a further selection, such as where you want to search for personal information that isn't visible to you at first glance of your workbook. The following list describes where the Excel 2007 Document Inspector will search for personal information.

Document Inspector window: select
where to search for personal information.

Figure 16-2

- **Comments and Annotations**—Searches the Excel 2007 comments and ink annotations for personal or hidden data. Search here if you have added any comments to specific sections of Excel 2007; in your case, you have not done this so far, so don't worry.

- **Document Properties and Personal Information**—Inspects for hidden metadata or personal information saved with the document. This is not something you have done so far, so you don't have to worry.

- **Custom XML Data**—Inspects custom XML data stored with this document. Again, you have not done this so far, so you don't have to worry.

- **Headers and Footers**—Searches in the headers and footers for personal data or hidden text. You have added headers and footers to your work so far, so if any warning arises in the Document Inspection report about this section, go to the Insert tab on the Office 2007 Ribbon, go to the Header & Footer section, and remove any information that is hidden or personal.

- **Hidden Rows and Columns**—Searches the document's hidden rows or columns for personal data or hidden text and shows it in the Document Inspection report (Figure 16-3). In this case you can go to rows or columns and select a column or row and right-click to get the pop-up menu and select Unhide Rows or Columns.

- **Hidden Worksheets**—Inspects the workbook for any hidden worksheets that you have open. You do not have any so far, so you don't have to worry.

- **Invisible Content**—Searches invisible content for personal or hidden data. Search here if you have added any invisible content to your workbook; in your case, you have not done this so far, so you don't have to worry.

Be aware that if you are working on a workbook that was created by someone else, when you run the Document Inspector you might see warnings in the Document Inspection report (Figure 16-3); in that case you might want to tell the creator of the worksheet.

Once you have selected where you want the Excel 2007 Document Inspector to search for personal information, click the Inspect button on the bottom of the window, as shown in Figure 16-2.

Once the button is clicked it will take a few minutes, and then a window (Figure 16-3) will display the results of what was found, and where the personal information is displayed. You will also see a Remove All button next to each vulnerable section (that is, where your personal information is contained). Click this button to remove all personal data from that section.

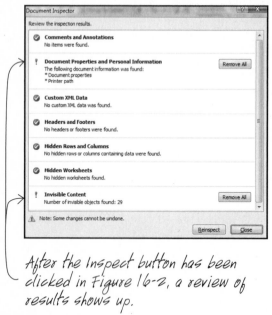

After the Inspect button has been clicked in Figure 16-2, a review of results shows up.

Figure 16-3

Protection from TS ("Toad Syndrome")

In addition to inspecting a workbook for personal data and removing traces of personal data where possible, it is also important to at times protect your work. Perhaps you are passing your work to coworkers for review or viewing, and you do not want them to make any changes or accidentally delete parts of your worksheet that took you forever to build. Well, there is a way. You can "protect" your worksheet and workbook. The following sections walk you through how to do it.

Protecting Worksheets

Protecting your worksheet is fairly easy.

Follow these steps to protect your worksheet:

I. Go to the Review tab on the Office 2007 Ribbon in Excel 2007 and find the Changes section (Figure 16-4).

Select the Review tab on the Office 2007 Ribbon and go to the Changes section where you can click on the Protect Sheet button.

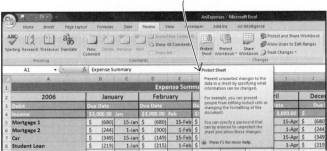

Figure 16-4

2. From there, click on the Protect Sheet button to see the Protect Sheet window (Figure 16-5).

Change Your Mind?

Note you can just cancel out of the window in Figure 16-5 by clicking on the Cancel button.

Select which actions the users can take when viewing this worksheet, and whether you want to add a password for extra protection.

Figure 16-5

3. Once you see the Protect Sheet window you can then add a password to the worksheet. The password can be anything—it can be one character or more, numbers, letters, anything you want. The password is case sensitive, though, so do keep that in mind. Make sure to remember the password, otherwise you cannot get back in!

4. Determine which privileges you want to grant users who view this worksheet by checking the box next to each privilege. If you want the users to have no privileges at all, leave everything blank. It is possible to grant the following privileges:

- Select locked cells
- Select unlocked cells
- Format cells
- Format columns
- Format rows
- Insert columns

- Insert rows

- Insert hyperlinks

- Delete columns

- Delete rows

- Sort

- Use AutoFilter

- Use PivotTable reports

- Edit objects

- Edit scenarios

Once you click the OK button, the Protect Sheet button on the Review tab turns into an Unprotect Sheet button (Figure 16-6).

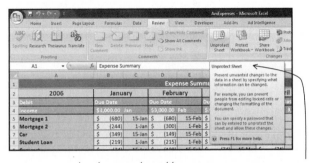

The Unprotect Sheet button only becomes available once you have protected the worksheet.

Figure 16-6

Protecting Workbooks

A workbook is made up of many worksheets, and each worksheet has many columns and rows. You can either protect the full workbook or a specific worksheet in that workbook, depending on what you need. In most cases it makes sense to protect a single worksheet and not the entire workbook. Look at the Office 2007 Ribbon in Figure 16-4 and select the Protect Workbook button to select options to protect your workbook. You can also Protect and Share Workbooks and just Share Workbooks. Each of them has buttons located on the Office 2007 Ribbon on the Review tab. Let's quickly cover what each of these sections do:

Figure 16-7

- **Protect Sheet**—Prevent unwanted changes to the data in a sheet by specifying which information can be changed as shown in Figure 16-7.

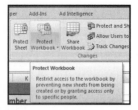
Figure 16-8

- **Protect Workbook**—Restrict access to the workbook by preventing new sheets from being created or by granting access only to specific people, as shown in Figure 16-8.

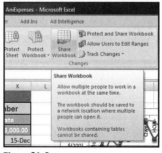
Figure 16-9

- **Share Workbook**—Allow multiple people to work in a workbook at the same time, as shown in Figure 16-9.

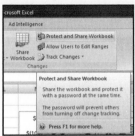

Figure 16-10

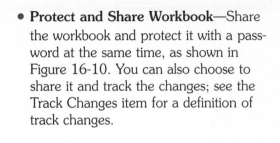

- **Protect and Share Workbook**—Share the workbook and protect it with a password at the same time, as shown in Figure 16-10. You can also choose to share it and track the changes; see the Track Changes item for a definition of track changes.

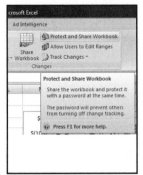

Figure 16-11

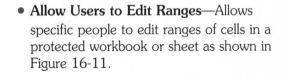

- **Allow Users to Edit Ranges**—Allows specific people to edit ranges of cells in a protected workbook or sheet as shown in Figure 16-11.

Figure 16-12

- **Track Changes**—Track all changes made to the document, including insertions, deletions, and formatting changes as shown in Figure 16-12.

When you select the Protect Workbook button from the Review tab on the Office 2007 Ribbon, you will see a menu like that in Figure 16-13, from which you can select Protect Structure and Windows (Figure 16-14). From there you will see the window shown in Figure 16-15, where you can make a selection of either protecting the Structure or the Windows.

Click the Protect
Workbook button and...

...select Protect Structure
and Windows.

Figure 16-13

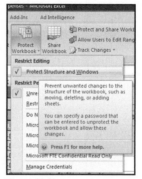

Figure 16-14

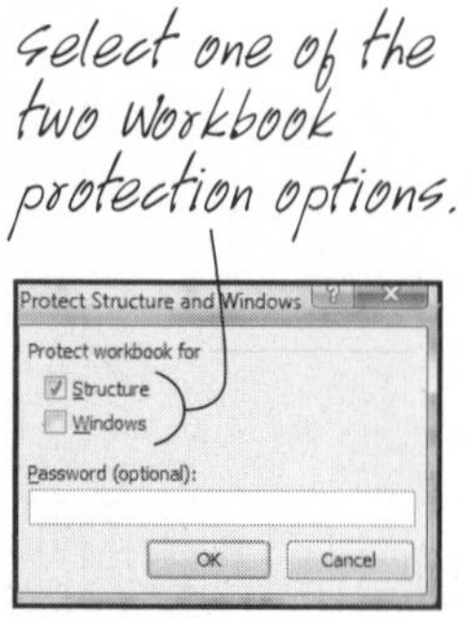

Select one of the
two Workbook
protection options.

Figure 16-15

By selecting the Structure option (by clicking on the check box until a check appears) you will prevent others who view the workbook from making changes to the position, the name, and the hidden or unhidden status of the worksheets in the active workbook.

When you select the Windows option (by clicking on the check box until a check appears) you will prevent others who view the workbook from making changes to the window, meaning the workbook's window cannot be closed, hidden, unhidden, resized, or moved and therefore the Minimize, Maximize, and Close buttons (Figure 16-16) disappear. Keep in mind you can always close the workbook by clicking on the Office 2007 Pearl and selecting the Close option (Figure 16-17).

Both of these options are great for when there are multiple people working on your PC, and you walk away, or if you are working together, and you don't want that person to add certain sections or close that worksheet.

*All of these buttons
(Minimize, Maximize,
and Close) disappear
when the Windows
option is selected
from Figure 16-15.*

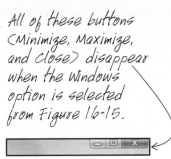

Figure 16-16

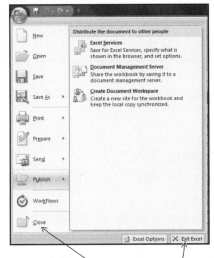

*Select the Close option or Exit
Excel to exit if/when a workbook
is Windows-protected (that is,
the Windows option is selected
in Figure 16-15).*

Figure 16-17

Keep in mind that all settings take effect immediately when you click the OK button. You will also see a checkmark next to the Protect Structure and Windows option in Figure 16-13 if the workbook is protected much like in Figure 16-18. To undo you can simply right-click once on the Protect Structure and Windows option in Figure 16-18 to undo the protection.

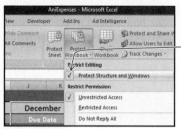

By clicking on the check box next to the Protect Structure and Windows option, you can undo the protection.

Figure 16-18

Must Have the Magic Password to Gain Access

What if you have your prized possession on a few cells where you do not want anyone to touch or change them? Well Excel 2007 has an answer for that too. There's a nifty feature that allows you to password-protect specific cells of your data. If that was not enough you can also specify who can access your data. By going to the Review tab on the Office 2007 Ribbon, you will see the Changes section where you can click the button Allow Users to Edit Ranges, which brings up the dialog box titled Allow Users to Edit Ranges as shown in Figure 16-19. In the Allow Users to Edit Ranges dialog box you can begin to select the users you want to give access to edit the full workbook, parts of the workbook or not edit the workbook at all.

This is a great way to protect against TS's (people with Toad Syndrome). These are the people who love to look at your great work, then try to figure out what you did by pressing incorrect keys and end up ruining what took you forever to build. So if you are unsure of who might see your work and who might touch it, then use the Allow Users to Edit Ranges option. However, if you cannot protect your work, then save a backup somewhere other than on your computer, such as an external hard drive, a flash drive, or send it to yourself in an email (although this option might not be feasible for those of you working with large workbooks).

Select Allow Users to Edit Ranges to define which range of cells the users can have access to edit as well as who can edit these specific sections.

Figure 16-19

Follow these steps to protect your worksheet:

1. Select an area in your worksheet (a set of columns, or rows, or both).

2. Go to the Review tab on the Office 2007 Ribbon in Excel 2007. Find the Changes section and click on Allows Users to Edit Ranges, as was shown in Figure 16-11.

3. A window like Figure 16-19 comes up; click on New.

4. The New Range window comes up. Enter the range of cells either by typing them in or by clicking on the button indicated in Figure 16-20 and selecting them.

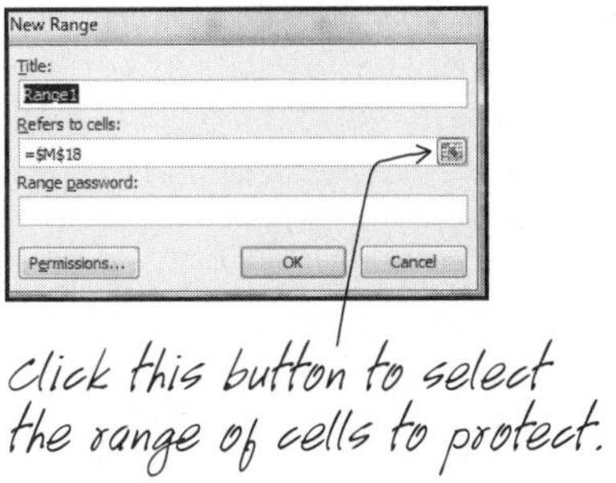

Click this button to select the range of cells to protect.

Figure 16-20

5. Click the Permissions button for the Permissions menu (Figure 16-21) where you can add users or groups and change their edit rights.

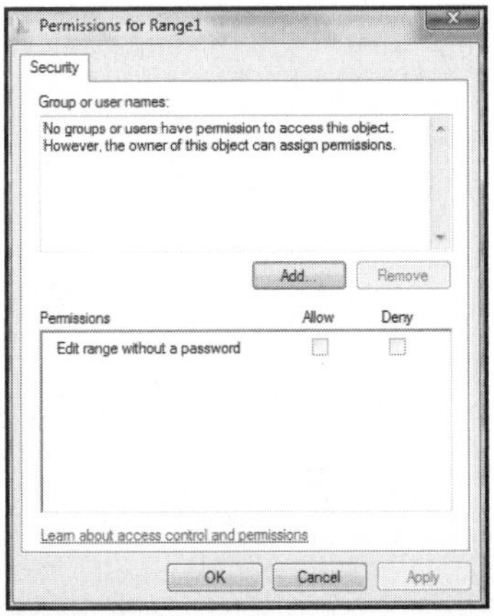

Figure 16-21

6. In the Permissions for Range1 window (Range1 is the name of your range), you will see the Group or User Names section under which is an Add button. Click the Add button to bring up the Select Users or Groups window (Figure 16-22). You can make modifications here.

7. In the Select Users or Groups window, click on the Locations button. This button will help you select a new location (such as your company's set of computers) or you can stay with the default, your PC.

8. Begin adding names to the Enter the Object Names to Select section, if there are other users on your computer. Once you are done with this section, click OK, and you will go back to the Permissions for Range1 window. You can now begin giving the person that you have added access to your selected range of cells.

Once you are done, click OK, which returns you to the Allow Users to Edit Ranges window. This time it shows you the title and refers to cells with the cells you select and the name (much like in Figure 16-22) and you are done! Click on the OK button to exit.

Figure 16-22

Relax, Refresh, Reward

I think if you are going to work hard, then the only way to feel good about it is to play hard. If you are going to perform at 100% all the time, the only way to keep yourself creative and thinking clearly and doing your best work is to give your mind a variety of activities. For this chapter's reward, start investigating a little getaway.

Think of how much work you get done when you are thinking about that airplane you are about to get on that will take you to that cool beach vacation you have been anticipating for the last 6 months. It's amazing—you can get three days of work done in a matter of hours.

Well if you had more of those vacations to look forward to, then you would most likely perform far better too. The reason I say that is because you would constantly feel: "I've really got to get this done so I can catch that flight, drive, or train to my vacation." That's why it is critical to plan small vacations in between your big ones, to get a quick rest and come back to work with new ideas and fun memories and have things to look forward to.

These little vacations can be once a month, or every other month or two, it's all up to you and how well you budgeted in Chapter 12. But either way they can be very inexpensive. You can always do a day-long hiking trip, which will cost you half the gas if you carpool, and you can pack the sandwiches and water at home and look forward to a great day outdoors. If you think "Oh man, that will be cold and wet, full of bugs or dirt," then find a new museum or attraction in your area that you've been curious about, and make it a mini-vacation. No matter what it is you end up deciding to do, be sure it's something that allows your brain to rest from your daily grind.

To Do List

Find out where to look for help

Meet the online community and read the blogs

Discover special additions to Excel 2007

Enjoy a dinner out

Ask the Guide Next Door

After moving from Denver to Seattle, I found myself having to approach people about the best restaurants, service providers, bank, dentist, etc. I've determined that sometimes, I don't really get the best information from others; they may not share my experiences or my tastes. In fact, sometimes the best way to find a restaurant is to get lost (something I do often in my new city) and end up eating at one of those hole-in-the-wall places that always seem to have the best food.

Well the same is true about learning a new program such as Excel 2007. If you are surrounded by people who know a lot about Excel 2007 then you are more likely to learn from them and become more excited about Excel 2007. However if you are surrounded by people who know very little about Excel 2007 they might feel the program is too hard. For those times there are other ways to get the help you want.

It's not always the best to have an expert tell you the answer. Many people learn best when they have to search for the answer to a question themselves. However, if you do not have an expert for those days when you have tried everything and you just don't know where to turn, a good network of people and websites comes in handy. This appendix offers a few places to look in the event you find yourself with a question and no answer.

Where to Look

The best way to begin your search is to make sure you are online and connected to the Internet. Open Excel 2007. Then, just use the F1 key and begin typing. By pressing the F1 key, a window (Figure A-1) will open where you can type what you are searching for.

If you are not connected to the Internet you will only have access to help on your local computer which in most cases may be out of date, and when you do press the F1 key a window much like Figure A-2 will appear, letting you know you are offline.

By pressing the F1 key, notice you are connected to the online help at Office Online.

Figure A-1

Notice you are not connected to the online help and you are offline.

Figure A-2

Just Get Online

It is far better to be online, because the online help is the most up to date and any changes, fixes and additions to help occur online first and may not be updated to your computer.

Notice the help window still comes up and will let you search for items, but on the bottom of the window you see the word "offline." This indicates you will only be able to search on your computer for help.

If you are offline, pressing the F1 key results in the Offline message on the help window. If your Excel Help window says you're offline and you know for sure you are connected to the web, you can click on the Offline area and a menu will come up from which you can select "Show content from Office Online" as shown in Figure A-3.

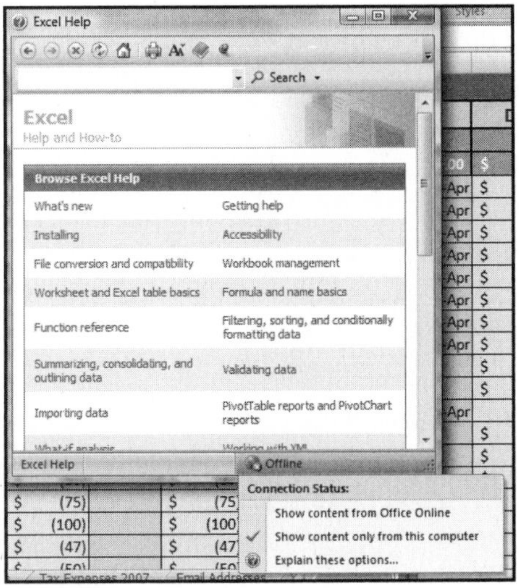

Figure A-3

There are a few key things to keep in mind when you type key terms. First, keep the search words as close to 2–3 words as possible. So if you want to type **How do I find Mail Merge,** just type **Mail Merge**. (Computers search for word patterns that occur in a text body, so if you type "How do I" most of the results will have "How do I" inside them.) Second, you can click on the push pin as shown in Figure A-4 to keep the help window on top and be able to do your work while having the help screen right there.

For future reference . . .

If you find something great in a help window, you can print by clicking on the print button on the Search window. Make sure you're connected to a printer, of course.

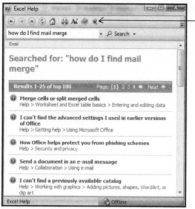

Press on the push pin to keep the Help window on top so you can see it as you do your work in Excel 2007.

Figure A-4

Online Help

If you find that you are not having luck finding what you need in this window another option is to search online. A great place to start is by going to http://www.Live.com, which is Microsoft's latest search engine where you can then type "Excel 2007." (Figure A-5) Once you hit the Enter key you will see a list of items come up (Figure A-5) where you can select the first link under the gray box which comes up in the search results page titled: "Excel Home Page – Microsoft Office Online" to go to Office online.

Office online can also be seen if you go to: http://office.microsoft.com. This option provides you with the same layout as Excel 2007 with the Office 2007 Ribbon on top (Figure A-6). Immediately you can see a few great options on top such as: Home, Products, Help and How-to, Downloads, Clip Art, Templates and Microsoft Office Live. In the Products section where you are you can also see the Microsoft Office Excel Search area where you can try your search item again as well as Highlights, Chart of the month and Office downloads to get any new updates.

This is a great website to visit when you are searching for help as well as how to get certain things done with Excel 2007. Plus there is some great clip art you can use to enhance your spreadsheet and templates.

Search on Live.com for Keywords "Excel 2007"

While on the Excel 2007 Products page (Figure A-6), you will also find Excel 2007 basics section that includes an Excel 2007 demo, help with creating charts and learning what's new with Excel 2007. If you do not have Excel 2007 already, this is also a fantastic place to download a 60-day free copy of Excel 2007 just to try out all the new things you are learning in this book. You can also find system requirements and information about older versions of Excel.

Figure A-5

Check for free updates for Excel 2007 here. These updates are specific to Office 2007 as shown in Figure A-6 and are fixes to bugs that might come up after the product is shipped. Keep in mind there are multiple pages that rotate through, so the next time you go to this page it might have different content. But you should be able to find what you need by looking around a little bit.

Click on the "Check for free updates" section to check for free updates.

Figure A-6

The page about Excel 2007 shown in Figure A-6 is not just about Excel 2007 rather about older Excel versions as well. Microsoft thought about those who may not have yet upgraded to Excel 2007 and has help for other versions as well. There is a variety of other items as well, such as: product details and articles by the Crabby Office Lady related to Excel 2007.

You can find a section called Crabby Office Lady where you can find out helpful tips and solid advice (with a little attitude, but good advice for sure), look for her under the Help and How-to tab as shown in Figure A-7.

Chat with Experts

For those of you who are still not able to find what you are looking for there are the office.microsoft.com discussion groups where you can post your questions to experts. Go to: http://www.microsoft.com/office/community/en-us/default.mspx, as shown in Figure A-8. From the left navigation you can hover over Excel, then New Users to get started.

Check out the Crabby Office Lady for helpful advice and sign up for the RSS to get tips and tricks about Excel 2007.

Figure A-7

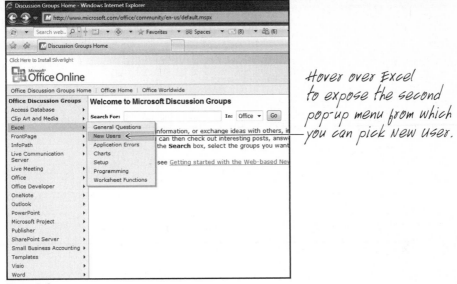

Hover over Excel to expose the second pop-up menu from which you can pick New user.

Figure A-8

Once you select New User, you will read a lot of posts by people who are also new to Excel 2007 and have most likely asked similar questions you may ask. This is a great place to read about topics. As you read you might not find the question to your exact question, at that time you can post your question to this list. To add your questions you will need a Windows Live ID login. So you can go to the New button click on it and choose to add a question as shown in Figure A-9.

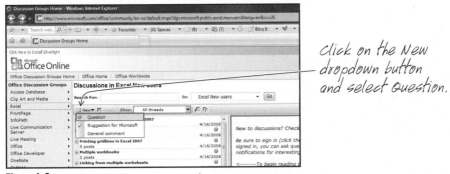

Click on the New dropdown button and select Question.

Figure A-9

Once you click on the Question button you'll be routed to a page where you need to type in your login and password for MSN Hotmail, MSN Messenger, Passport or Windows Live ID as shown in Figure A-10. If you do not have one, you can create one.

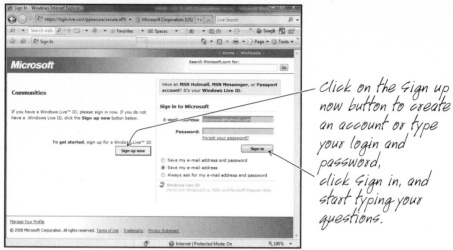

Click on the Sign up now button to create an account or type your login and password, click Sign in, and start typing your questions.

Figure A-10

Figure A-11

After you're done logging in, you will be routed back to the page that looks much like Figure A-9 only this time you will notice on the top right corner of the web page there is a link that says 'sign out,' indicating that you are signed in. Now you can click on the New button much like in Figure A-9. Next, click on the Question link and this time a window much like in Figure A-11 comes up where you can begin typing your question.

The discussion group is monitored by both Microsoft employees as well as Microsoft Valuable Professionals (also known as MVPs). These professionals are identified by Microsoft for the outstanding amount of effort and hard work they have put into learning the Microsoft Office Products and they are there to help with questions. They are also the professionals who not only use Office 2007 but also write programs, macros and create charts everyday for their own work.

Befriend the Bloggers

Wikipedia defines a Blog as:

"A blog (short for web log) is a website where entries are made and displayed in a reverse chronological order. Blogs provide commentary or news on a particular subject, such as food, politics, or local news; some function as more personal online diaries. A typical blog combines text, images, and links to other blogs, web pages, and other media related to its topic. The ability for readers to leave comments in an interactive format is an important part of most early blogs. . . ."

This type of diary has become a very popular way to professionals and novices to share what they learn about technology and share it with everyone who reads their blog. It is also a great way to learn from other people's mistakes.

By blogging you not only learn and share but also belong to an online community of Excel 2007 users who are there to help you and you will feel like a Diva when you begin answering their questions. This is a great way to build a network of Excel 2007 users and stay connected to other interests you may have. As you can see from the Wikipedia definition above blogging is not just about technology, it can be about anything since it is a web diary.

One of the most common blogs for Excel 2007 is at: http://blogs.msdn.com/Excel (see Figure A-12).

A Shout Out

Also, if you do feel like putting together your own blog as you learn Excel 2007 and share what you are learning look up *IT Girl's Guide to Blogging with Moxie* by Joelle Reeder and Kathy Scoleri (ISBN: 0-978-0-470-16800-4) where you can learn all about blogging and starting your own blog to share your knowledge about Excel 2007 and all other things Diva.

You can sign up for the RSS feed, which will send you updates anytime a new blog post is written so you can stay current.

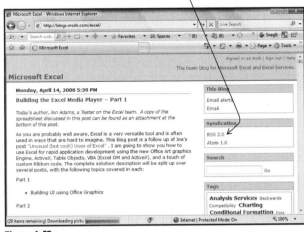

Figure A-12

If you ever feel you know all there is to know about Excel 2007, guess what, there's always a surprise waiting for you. Check out the cool 3-D Game engine which can be built using Excel 2007. Yes it does take some programming skills, check out Peter Rakos 5 page blog post explaining how it's done at: http://www.gamasutra.com/view/feature/3563/microsoft_excel_revolutionary_3d_.php.

Another blog to keep in mind when you are looking for bloggers is: https://blogs.msdn.com/inside_office_online/default.aspx.

Watch Free Videos for Tips

Videos are a great way to learn quickly with a visual overview and virtual teacher. Start by looking on http://office.Microsoft.com and searching for videos for Excel 2007. As a matter of fact, videos are so wide spread that you can go to http://www.Youtube.com and search for Excel 2007 videos, where you can find a lot of videos showing different tips and tricks about Excel 2007, as shown in Figure A-13. You can send the links you find valuable to your friends. I would love to see you make your own Excel 2007 videos and share it with everyone on YouTube. Just be sure to tell them you learned it here first!

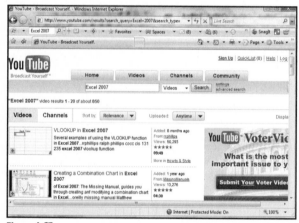

Figure A-13

Excel 2007 Additions

So what happens when you are looking thru all the help but there is something more you want to do with Excel 2007 that just is not part of Excel 2007? Well don't give up before trying some of the add-on applications that are written by people or companies that have found something Excel can't do, and they find a way to make it happen, then share it either for free or for purchase. The add-ons are often referred to as plugins. In some cases they are also written by Microsoft to help Excel 2007 users get the best experience from Excel.

Two places to look for Excel add-ons are Able Bits as shown in Figure A-14 as well as Office-Excel.com shown in Figure A-15. The quality of the Able Bits products may vary. I have had great experience with their add-ins. Also, the http://www.Office-Excel.com site is a Microsoft-owned site.

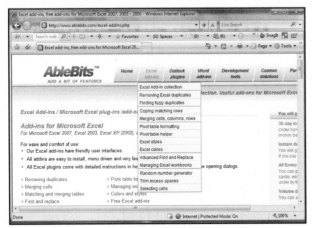

Figure A-14

Figure A-15

Microsoft's Place for Excel 2007 Plugins

In Office-Excel.com you can not only find information about the new tool but also samples of how it works and you can download it to add to your current Office Excel 2007. One of my favorite add-ins is made by the adCenter team and can be found at: http://advertising.microsoft.com/advertising/adcenter_addin. This is a fantastic add-in into Excel 2007 to help find out what popular keywords are and how to better rank with your blog. In the *IT Girl's Guide to Blogging with Moxie* by Joelle Reeder and Kathy Scoleri (Wiley Publishing, Inc.) you learned all about blogging. With this Excel 2007 add-in you can learn how to use the right keywords to be more educated about how to attract more visitors to your site. It takes $5 to sign up for an adCenter account and you will be well on your way.

The add-in also helps you learn more about the traffic to your blog site, which geographic locations uses which type of keywords, what monthly and daily traffic looks like for each keyword, and which category the keywords fit into. Figure A.16 shows a little glimpse of what you can accomplish with the Excel 2007 adCenter add-in.

In a quick minute I have been able to pull back my top 15 keywords, find out where geographically most of the traffic that searched for those keywords comes from, and the gender of the searchers.

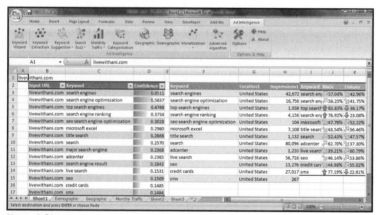

Figure A-16

Other Books

Once you have reached a level of Diva-ness, you might want to take it up a notch. Here are some other great books about Excel:

- *Excel 2007 Bible,* by John Walkenbach (Wiley Publishing, Inc.)
- *Microsoft Office Excel 2007 Inside Out,* by Mark Dodge, Craig Stinson (Microsoft Press)

Relax, Refresh, Reward

I love eating out with friends, it's such a fun time plus I get to experience some new places I would never know to look for by myself. This is a great way to treat yourself at the end of a hard week or a long month.

Since you now know where to look for answers and you have a way to make Excel 2007 more than help you with work but also help with your expenses and life in general, you can definitely enjoy a great meal for fun and having a great time with your friends celebrating your knowledge of Excel 2007. Plus you might just get inspired about how to spice up your next Excel 2007 project.

Wow! You're still reading! I was hoping it would come to this, where you have learned and enjoyed this book so much that you would keep looking to see if there is more. But all good things come to a temporary end while we look for ways to better it and move forward. I also look forward to hearing from you and your experiences of how much this book has helped you.

If in high school someone had told me I would be an author one day, I would have laughed out loud. My English teacher was happy to give me a D– if I would just not show up for the class. But I didn't give up. I was an immigrant student who stuttered and didn't know English very well in a class full of students who not only spoke English very well, but also came from private school backgrounds. Along the way I found many others like me who have looked to improve themselves and found help, so I thought "if I only keep trying . . ." Needless to say that was the biggest fear for me to overcome when I heard from Wiley in August of 2006. I remember telling them, "But my written English is not very good." They said they would work with me and help me and that all I had to do was to concentrate on the ideas and ways I communicate with women in my everyday life. I can say that by holding up their end of the bargain they helped me hold up mine and complete this book.

I was looking for three things from this book:

- To give you a taste of how easy technology really is.
- To show you the Diva qualities you already have and enable you to use Excel 2007.
- To encourage and motivate you to live up to your fullest potential.

Nearly a year ago, writing a book like this was a dream, a wish I would share with my friends and family. I didn't know that one of my friends would one day introduce me to someone at Wiley and say okay, now explain to them what you told me. This is what caused me to share my idea with Wiley about how much I wanted to reach all of you and help you learn and excel in technology. I have been in technology for most of my life and all of my adult life, and was always the only woman. Yes, it's great that the lines in the restrooms are not long and I never have to open my own door (well, in most cases), but the reality is, it does feel lonely at times. I was hoping if I had a chance to explain technology to other women, like I do in my life with my friends, surely women everywhere would fall in love with technology just as I have and I would no longer be alone.

I also hope to have motivated you to realize you are not alone in the ups and downs you feel in life. I have had a great challenge to come home every day, day after day, and at times while flying in early hours of the morning and late hours of the night, to finish this book, but I still kept typing because I had a goal and a wish. My goal is to help you and my wish is to help you live out your fullest potential. Thank you very much for the opportunity to help you become better with Excel 2007.

Index

cell address
  defined, 29
  inserting into functions, 120, 123
cell referencing, 97
cell series
  colons and, 105, 117
  typing in SUM function, 117–118
Change Colors button, 187–188
chart
  Axes section, 207
  axis names and labels, 201–203
  beautifying, 204
  budget worksheet, 228
  creating, 195–198
  Data Labels section, 206–207
  Format window, 205–206
  Gridlines area, 207
  importing into PowerPoint, 272–275
  importing into Word, 270–272
  Insert section, 206
  moving, 198–200
  overview, 194
  PivotChart and PivotTable, 208–212
  types of, 196
Chart (Linked to Excel Data)
  option, 274
Chart Layouts section, 211
Chart Title button, 206
Chart Tools tab, 39
Chart Wizard, 195
chatting with expert, 300–302
"Check for free updates" section, 299
Check for Updates button, 19
Choose a SmartArt Graphic
  window, 185
clip art, 170–172
Clipboard feature, 50–51, 273–274
closing
  workbooks, 288–289
  worksheets, 31
colon (:), 105, 117
color
  SmartArt, 187–188
  tab, 85
  theme, 8
  worksheet, 226–227
color scale, 140
column
  defined, 25
  deleting, 59
  inserting, 58

Column category, 194
column chart, 196
Concourse theme, 146
Conditional Formatting feature
  color scales, 140
  data bars, 139
  icon sets, 140–141
  overview, 6, 138
conditional statement, 138
Contact Us button, 21–22
Copy All button, 51
Copy command
  formulas and, 102–105
  location of, 5
  Paste command and, 50–52
copying worksheet, 86–87
Copyright symbol (©), 80
COUNT (Count Numbers) function,
  127–128
Crabby Office Lady section, 300
Create New Document option,
  257–258
Create new worksheet button, 24
cross referencing cell, 105–107
Currency format, 149
Current Folder section, 255
Current worksheet tab, 24
Custom Date format, 150
Custom Margins option, 158–159
Cut command
  location of, 5
  Paste command and, 53
  Undo and Redo buttons, 55–56

D

Data and Model section, 143
data bar, 6–7, 139
data entry
  Copy command, 50–52, 102–105
  Cut command, 53
  inserting rows and columns, 57–58
  overview, 48–49, 71–72
  Paste command, 53–54, 102–105
  Paste Special option, 54–55
  symbols, 79–81
Data Labels section, 206–207
defined name, 10
defining macro, 232–236
Delete All button, 51

Inspector tool, 280–282
Installation Wizard, 19
Installed Templates group, 43
italic text, 135

K

Keep Source Formatting options,
269–270, 275
Keep Text Only option, 269
keyboard shortcut. *See* shortcut
Kiyosaki, Robert, 229

L

label
  axis, 201–203
  chart, 206–207
Labels option, 245
Landscape layout, 156–157
launching Excel, 18
Layout tab, 205–206
left mouse click, 57
Legend button, 206
Lemen, Jen, 153
Letters option, 245
line, adding, 174–175
line chart, 196
lingo, Excel
  cell, 29–30
  common terms, 25–29
  shortcuts, 31–33
  workbook, 23–24
  worksheet, 23–24
linking to worksheets, 252–259
Live.com search, 298–300
locking data into cells, 71
Look In section, 255
Lotus 1-2-3 program, 3

M

macro
  advanced tips, 243
  defining, 232–236
  deleting, 242–243
  enabling, 233–236

recording, 238–240
  using, 236–243
  viewing recorded, 240–242
Macro Settings screen, 236
Mail Merge feature, 243–248
margin, 158–160
Match Destination Table Style option,
  269–270
MAX function, 128
Maximize button, 31
MEDIAN function, 122–123
mentoring, 263
merging cell, 62–63, 76–78
Microsoft Office Online website, 43
Microsoft Office PowerPoint 2007.
  See PowerPoint 2007
Microsoft Office Ribbon. *See* Ribbon
Microsoft Office Word 2007. *See*
  Word 2007
Microsoft Valuable Professional
  (MVP), 302
MIN function, 128
Minimize button, 31
monetary denomination, 125
monetary display format. *See*
  DOLLAR function
More Accounting Formats option, 125
More Number Formats option, 148, 222
More Paper Sizes option, 157
mother cell, 30
moving
  charts, 198–200
  worksheets, 87
MVP (Microsoft Valuable
  Professional), 302
My Templates option, 43

N

nail care, 191
name
  axis, 201–203
  defined, 10
  worksheet, 28, 85–86
Name box, 30
navigating worksheet, 70–71
negative number, 201

New button, 260
New Cell Style option, 142
New from Existing option, 43
New Table Style option, 142
Normal view button, 162
number format, 143, 148–152
Number group, 59
Number section, 72, 127, 148

O

Object In option, 200
Office Online website, 43
Office Pearl button, 5
Office PowerPoint 2007. *See*
    PowerPoint 2007
Office Ribbon. *See* Ribbon
Office theme, 146
Office Word 2007. *See* Word 2007
online help, 13–15, 20–23, 109,
    297–298
online resource
  blogs, 302–304
  chatting with experts, 300–302
  Live.com search, 298–300
  overview, 296–298
  plugins, 304–306
  videos, 304–306
operation, order of, 97
Options option, 242
orientation, print, 156–157
Orientation section, 62–63
Other Charts option, 194
outcome cell, 101
Outlook program, 248, 260–262

P

page break, 160
Page Break Preview view, 12, 162–163
Page Layout view, 6, 12–13
Page Setup section, 156–162
pane
  freezing, 90–91
  splitting worksheets into, 88–90
paper size, 157–158
parentheses, 96, 101
password, 284, 290–292

Paste as Picture option, 269, 274
Paste command
  Copy command and, 50–52
  Cut command and, 53
  formulas and, 102–105
  location of, 5
  overview, 53–54
Paste Special option, 54–55, 275–276
Pearl button, 5
percentage, calculating, 220
Percentage format, 149
Permissions menu, 291
picture
  clip art, 170–172
  inserting, 189–190
  shapes, 172–178
Picture button, 189
pie chart, 196
PivotChart, 27, 208–212
PivotTable, 27, 208–212
Place in This Document option,
    256–257
plugin, 304–306
plus sign (+), 117
Portrait layout, 156–157
PowerPoint 2007
  importing charts into, 272–275
  importing tables into, 275–276
  overview, 9
Pradipika, Hatha Yoga, 44
Pranayama breathing, 44
previewing work, 12–13, 48, 162–164
Print Layout view, 12–13, 48
Print Preview feature, 162–164
Print Range section, 165
Print What section, 165
printing
  finding printers, 166
  headers and footers, 160–162
  margins, 158–160
  orientation, 156–157
  overview, 155
  page break, 160
  paper size, 157–158
  Print Layout view, 12–13, 48
  Print Preview feature, 162–164
  selecting properties, 165
  sending data to printer, 166

updating Excel, 14
Use Destination Theme option, 275
Use Relative References option, 237–238
"Use the current document" option, 246
user-defined function, 10

V

vacation, 293
VBA (Visual Basic for Applications) code, 233
vertical Split bar, 89
video, online, 304–306
View Macros option, 237, 240
View tab, 237
viewing recorded macro, 240–242
Visual Basic for Applications (VBA) code, 233
Visual Studio Tools for Office (VSTO) code, 114, 233

W

Walkenbach, John, 306
When to Edit section, 258
Windows option, 288
word, adding to formula, 99
Word 2007
  importing charts into, 270–272
  importing tables into, 266–270
  overview, 8–9
WordArt, 174, 182–184
workbook
  creating, 41–43
  defined, 23–24
  protecting, 285–290

worksheet. *See also* budget worksheet; data entry; editing data; printing
  copying, 86–87
  defined, 23–24
  deleting, 83–84
  emailing, 260–262
  freezing panes, 90–91
  inserting, 83–84
  inserting formulas into, 98–102
  linking to, 252–259
  moving, 87
  navigating, 70–71
  overview, 69–70
  protecting, 283–285
  rearranging, 83–85
  renaming, 28, 85–86
  sizing cells, 73–79, 225–226
  splitting into panes, 88–90
  symbols, 79–81
  zooming, 26, 28, 92
Wrap text check box, 75

X

X-axis, 194
XLSX format, 11

Y

Y-axis, 194
yellow diamond device, 175–178
"Your Text Here" box, 182–183

Z

zooming, 26, 28, 92